LATE MODERNITY
AND SOCIAL CHANGE

In this book Brian Heaphy unravels debates about modernity in contemporary social theory and examines key sociological ideas about the nature and implications of social change from modernist, post-structuralist, postmodernist and late modernist perspectives.

Late Modernity and Social Change begins by outlining founding sociological ideas about modernity and social change and considers different definitions of what some refer to as 'postmodernity' and others term 'late modernity'. In doing so, it introduces the ideas of founding social thinkers including Marx, Durkheim, Weber, Simmel and Freud, and the work of key contemporary theorists, among them Lacan, Foucault, Lyotard, Baudrillard, Bauman, Giddens and Beck. It also discusses feminist, queer and postcolonial ideas about studying modern and postmodern experience. A special feature of the book is that it brings contemporary theories of modernity and social change to life through extended examples from personal life (including self and identity, relational and intimate life, death, dying and life-politics).

Wide-ranging, accessible and comprehensive, *Late Modernity and Social Change* will be invaluable for students of social and cultural theory, and sociology more generally. The book will also be essential reading for those who want to understand whose experience is included or excluded in contemporary debates about modernity, and who seek an original and powerful evaluation of the relevance of these ideas for 'thinking' and 'doing' sociology.

Brian Heaphy is Lecturer in Sociology at Manchester University. His sociological interests include theories of social and cultural change and changing patterns of personal life.

LATE MODERNITY AND SOCIAL CHANGE

Reconstructing social and personal life

Brian Heaphy

Routledge
Taylor & Francis Group

LONDON AND NEW YORK

First published 2007
by Routledge
2 Park Square, Milton Park, Abingdon, Oxon OX14 5RN

Simultaneously published in the USA and Canada
by Routledge
270 Madison Ave, New York, NY 10016

Routledge is an imprint of the Taylor & Francis Group, an informa business

© 2007 Brian Heaphy

Typeset in 10½/13pt Sabon by
Book Now Ltd, London
Printed and bound in Great Britain by
TJ International Ltd, Padstow, Cornwall

British Library Cataloguing in Publication Data
A catalogue record for this book is available from the British Library

Library of Congress Cataloging in Publication Data
Heaphy, Brian, 1961–
Late modernity and social change: reconstructing social and personal
life / Brian Heaphy.
p. cm.
1. Social change. 2. Civilization, Modern–21st century. I. Title.
HM831.H43 2007
303.409′051–dc22

ISBN10: 0–415–28176–8 (hbk)
ISBN10: 0–415–28177–6 (pbk)
ISBN10: 0–203–50568–9 (ebk)

ISBN13: 978–0–415–28176–8 (hbk)
ISBN13: 978–0–415–28177–5 (pbk)
ISBN13: 978–0–203–50568–7 (ebk)

CONTENTS

ACKNOWLEDGEMENTS

This writing of this book has its own history, with many twists and turns. Many colleagues and friends, as well as my family, helped me to negotiate these and to write the book. The original idea for the book came from a collaborative project with Jane Franklin. I am indebted to Jane for our conversations and her insights which have in many ways made the book what it is. I am even more indebted to her for our friendship. Thanks to Marie Shullow who originally took up the idea at Routledge, and to Gerhard Bloomgarden for continuing to support it and for his incredible patience. Jeffrey Weeks gave me the confidence to write in the first place, and I am grateful to him for his guidance and friendship over the years. Thanks to Catherine Donovan, Rachel Thomson and Matthew Waites who as colleagues and friends helped me, as always, with their support and ideas. Thanks also to my sociology colleagues at Nottingham Trent University – and especially to Tony Fitzgerald for his sociological insights. I was only at Leeds University for a short time, but many thanks to the colleagues I briefly worked with there. At Manchester, I am very grateful to Lisa Adkins (now at Goldsmiths), Wendy Bottero, Vanessa May, Carol Smart and to my Morgan Centre colleagues for making work such a pleasure, and to Fiona Devine who helped take pressure off when it counted. Many thanks to my family for supporting me. Finally thanks to my partner Al-noor for putting up with me and for so much more. Jane helped me to start the book, and Al-noor helped me to finish it. I dedicate the book to them.

1

INTRODUCTION

The idea of modernity is an important one in contemporary social theory, and has been influential in debates about the direction sociology should take in the twenty-first century. The history of sociology itself is closely bound up with that of the modern, and some argue that sociology's destiny is intrinsically intertwined with that of modern society. These interconnections have been articulated and debated since sociology's inception in the nineteenth century, but with heightened intensity more recently. Since the latter quarter of the twentieth century the inter-related fate of modernity and sociology has been the subject of social theoretical debates about 'post' and 'late' modernity. These debates, in turn, have profoundly impacted on all areas of sociological study, and influence the 'thinking' and 'doing' of sociology at all levels.

This book examines social theoretical debates about modernity to explicate the insights they generate for the sociological project as it concerns social change – especially with reference to personal life. In doing so, it has a number of aims. First, to theoretically situate recent claims about late (or reflexive) modernity and contemporary social change, and arguments about emergent universalizing tendencies that are said to be reshaping social, cultural and political life. Second, to explore how these theories bring modernity down to earth by incorporating issues of personal life (for example, self-identity, intimate relationships, emotional life and the like). On the one hand, the focus on personal life facilitates more grounded exploration of modernity than theoretical 'grand' narratives usually allow. On the other hand, it illuminates arguments about the radical nature and depth of interconnected global and local developments in late modernity. This book takes up arguments about the implications that social change in late modernity is said to have for personal life to ask how contemporary experience might

1

be interpreted differently by diverse frames for understanding modernity. In doing so, it asks *whose* experience is the subject of theories of late – or reflexive – modernity, and whose fails to register or feature. These questions can help us to evaluate the relevance of theories of modernity for (re)imagining and reconstructing the sociological project.

The concern with differing conceptualizations of modernity and their implications for understanding social change and personal life shapes this book in a number of ways. First, it provides the organizational structure and themes that make up the book. Second, it provides the basis for a number of arguments I put forward in the book, that are introduced in the following section. In terms of structure, Chapters 2 to 5 outline one story (my own) of sociology's relationship to modernity by considering key constructive, deconstructive and reconstructive movements in social theory and sociology with respect to modernity. These chapters follow a 'chronological' order, considering founding ideas about the logics of modernity and social change, radical deconstructive ideas about postmodernity, and recent reconstructive ideas about late or reflexive modernity. To be sure, this ordering represents a subjective reading of theories and debates about modernity, and of sociology's relationship to the latter. Indeed, it reflects my own experience of studying sociology in the mid-1980s and cultural studies between the late 1980s and the early 1990s, before returning to sociology from the mid-1990s onwards. This has influenced my view of debates about modernity, and what they imply for sociology. The sociological story of modernity presented here may be, in some ways, familiar to some readers. But readers are unlikely to have come across the combined deconstructive influences on 'post' modern thinking as they are conceptualized here, or the arguments that are made about reconstructivist theories of late or reflexive modernity and their implications for sociology. There are several texts about sociology's constructive and deconstructive movements, although texts about the deconstructive 'turn' tend to be limited in the range of influences they include. But there are few about its reconstructive ones, and none that explicitly explore the theory of reflexive modernity *as* a reconstructive shift in thinking about modernity and sociology.

Chapters 6 to 9 examine the implications that contemporary social change has for personal life, as understood by the reconstructive theory of reflexive modernity. They critically compare these to competing ones generated via different constructionist and deconstructionist frames for conceptualizing modernity and modern experience. These chapters follow a 'thematic' order, centred on the themes of self and identity; relating and intimacies; and mortality and life-politics. Chapter 9 draws together the analyses presented in both 'halves' of the book, to evaluate the contribution of theories of late modernity for understandings of the sociological project. It pays especial attention to evaluating the potential contribution of the theory of reflexive modernity, and the sociology of reflexive life (social and personal) that it promotes, to a reconstructed sociological project.

The argument

A number of interlinking arguments are forwarded in this book. In the first part of the book (Chapters 2 to 5) it is argued that sociological concerns with the modern have been influenced by a number of critical shifts or 'movements' in theoretical conceptions of modernity. Three major or overarching movements correspond to the construction, deconstruction and reflexive reconstruction of modernity. These three movements are not the only notable ones, and some might argue that they are not the most important ones. These movements are made up of diverse theories, ideas and understandings of modernity, and of diverse approaches to analysing its directions and implications, and are themselves comprised of diverse critical 'sub-movements'. The differences between these sub-movements are important as they characterize modernity and the sociological problems it raises in distinctive ways. But when they are grouped together they gain a significance that is greater than the sum of their parts for a general view – or diagnosis – of the nature, orientation and direction of modernity, and for envisioning the sociological project.

Chapters 2 to 5 argue that each of the three overarching movements towards constructing, deconstructing and reconstructing modernity have profound implications for conceiving social order and social change, which are further illuminated in the second part of the book (Chapters 6–8) by focusing on issues to do with personal life. Reconstructivist theories of late or reflexive modernity claim to generate especially profound insights into social change and its implications for social and personal life through their emphasis on the mediation of the global and the local, institutional and subjective, and structure and agency. However, by comparing the insights into social change and personal life that theorists of reflexive modernity claim to have generated with those derived via other frames for conceptualizing modernity and postmodernity, it becomes clear how problematic and contestable recon-structivist interpretations are. The reconstructivist theory of reflexive modernity proposed by Giddens and Beck, for example, has argued the emergence of new universalities and commonalities in global and indi-vidualized experience where there are no 'others'. This argument may be (relatively) convincing when it is focused on the abstract theoretical working out of the 'reflexivity' of modernity, but it fails to be convincing when the theory is brought down to earth and compared to other argu-ments about how otherness and difference are centrally important – locally and on a global scale – to shaping personal life and day-to-day experience, and to strategies of power.

The main argument of the book concerns the different envisioning of the sociological project that emerges from diverse conceptions of moder-nity, but especially the reconstructivist envisioning of sociology that emerges from the theory of reflexive modernity. The relationship between different visions of modernity and sociology is an issue that is touched on throughout the book, and it is reconstructivist envisioning that is mostly focused in the concluding chapter. Early approaches to constructing modernity and later approaches to deconstructing it implied a corresponding orientation to the sociological project. In constructing modernity, early social thinkers were also constructing the modernist sociological project. In deconstructing modernity, later thinkers were deconstructing the modernist sociological project. The same is true of the reconstructivist approach to late or reflexive moder-nity: it is not only reconstructed understandings of modernity that are at stake but also of sociology itself. It is on this basis that we can under-stand the notable influence of reconstructive theories (such as those of Giddens and Beck) in such a relatively short time – because they hold out the promise of sociological renewal. But while these theories appear to open up renewed possibilities for sociology, they have their own prob-lems. These become evident when they are compared to the insights generated by the movements in constructing and deconstructing moder-nity they claim to have surpassed. This is especially the case in how they inadequately address questions of difference and power. In this respect, despite the understandings they promote of reflexive modernity and the sociology of reflexive (social and personal) life, they fail to provide a convincing basis for reflexive sociology.

In conceptualizing a reconstructed sociological project, the issue of reflexivity is important. Indeed, the deconstructive turn in sociology itself (that the theory of reflexive modernity defines itself against) can be viewed as part of the reflexivity of modernity – and as a prompt to and expression of sociology's own reflexivity. On the one hand, the deconstructive turn represented a crisis for sociology by undermining the philosophical meta-discourses and theories of knowledge that sociological grand narratives were founded on, and by emphasizing the cultural over the social. On the other hand, it represented the demand and opportunity for sociology to reflect on itself and to rethink its project anew. Reconstructivist theories of late or reflexive modernity should be understood as a response to and rejection of the deconstructive turn. Despite the attraction of their claims, especially in terms of retrieving the social and reintroducing political and personal agency, there are reasons to be cautious about the re-envisioning of modernity and sociology they promote. Chief among these is the erasure or putting aside of the significance difference that goes hand in hand with their promotion of new universalities, and the lack of reflexivity with respect to how sociological narration is involved in the flow of power.

Directions

Chapters 2 to 5

There is little dispute about the influence of founding social thinkers for the models of modernity that subsequent generations of social theorists have worked with, and for shaping the concerns of modernist sociology. Chapter 2 discusses how modernity as a sociological construct has its foundations in the grand, overarching or universalizing frames for understanding social, cultural, political and personal life that first emerged in the nineteenth and early twentieth centuries. The historical backdrop to sociology's inception is one that is often characterized as a critical period of social upheaval and political crises. These crises shaped and influenced the work of Marx, Durkheim, Weber and Freud, which taken together is symbolic of a founding critical movement in social theoretical constructions of modernity and of modernist sociology. In talking about the dynamics of social and cultural change, the processes that underpinned and shaped them, and their consequences, these theorists imbued modernity with certain orientations, logics and order. While each conceptualized the energizing impulses that shaped modernity in different ways, they each envisioned modernity as a movement towards something or somewhere, whether it was some utopian vision of harmony and equality, rational-bureaucratic entrapment, disenchantment or civilized order. In each case there was a concern with the shifting social order or transition towards some final or ultimate balance of order. Coupled with this, each theorist constructed a vision of modernity in ways that had crucial implications for understanding how the modern should be studied, emphasizing differently the interconnections between the social and the economic, cultural and subjective. They, in turn, influenced different ideas about what the sociological project could and should be.

Many theorists nowadays acknowledge that despite being historically overshadowed by the four thinkers mentioned, it was probably Simmel, above all, who best expressed the dynamism of modernity. Simmel's work is nowadays appreciated for its analysis of fragments and psychology of early modern urban experience, and its insights into the implications of modernity for depleted subjective culture. The concern with fragments explains why he is sometimes deemed to be more properly the first 'postmodern' theorist. This, in turn, explains why it is only relatively recently that his ideas have been fully acknowledged for the sociological insights they provide. It further explains why his understandings of modernity were not so systematically taken up or deconstructed as those of other founding social thinkers by the 'critical' and poststructuralist theorists considered in Chapter 3.

Chapters 3 and 4 discuss the deconstructive movement in theorizing about modernity, along with corresponding deconstructive approaches to modernist sociology. Chapter 3 begins by considering some of the insights that the Frankfurt School critical theorists generated into the nature and orientations of modernity by combining Marxian, Weberian and Freudian ideas, amongst others. Despite the critique of modern culture's ideological functions, critical theory held out some hope with respect to modern progress, and aimed to provide 'enlightened' insights into conditions of domination and strategies for emancipation. Habermas, the influential heir to Frankfurt School critical theory, is the contemporary theorist most identified with the idea that modernity is an unfinished project. Through his ideas about communicative action and ideal speech situations he has outlined the theoretical basis for an emancipated order that is balanced in terms of instrumental reason and the life-world.

In contrast to Habermas, 'founding' poststructuralist thinkers, who are also considered in Chapter 3, questioned any basis for faith in the idea of modernity as an unfinished project, and demolished the possibility of the kind of enlightened, emancipated or democratic social order that critical theory promoted. Of the influential poststructuralist thinkers Derrida, Lacan and Foucault, it is the latter's work that has been most influential in sociology and most amenable to sociological analyses, and that is mostly discussed in this chapter. The poststructuralist position, through its emphasis on discourse, demands that we challenge and deconstruct the foundational philosophical beliefs and assumptions about social knowledge that underpin social theoretical understandings of modernity and that infuse modernist sociology. It argues the case for bringing discourse and difference into the centre of the analytical frame. This, in turn, problematizes ideas about reason, progress, agency, power and subjectivity that were at the heart of both founding and critical theories of modernity and modernist sociology's self-understanding.

The poststructuralist theoretical movement is a crucial element of a broader deconstructionist movement with respect to modernity and modernist sociology that emerged in the last quarter of the twentieth century. This broader movement is not reducible to poststructuralism – or even to theoretical postmodernism (considered in Chapter 4). Rather, other influential elements include feminist, queer and postcolonial theoretical and sociological movements that also challenge modernity and modernist sociology – with and without recourse to poststructuralism. These elements combined with poststructuralism to further influence movements in reflexive methodology. These challenge modernist sociology's claim to knowledge on the basis of its historical relationships to power and subordination. On the one hand, it is argued, the theory and sociology of modernity has historically privileged class relations to the detriment of other kinds of subordination. On the other hand, despite – and because of – its claims to truth and legitimate knowledge, the social theory of modernity and the modernist sociology have often been imbued with patriarchal, colonial and hetero-normative interests. Radical difference and reflexive methodological deconstructionist movements are often afforded limited regard in social theoretical responses to the deconstructive turn (and modernist sociology more generally), but they have been crucial in bringing radical political interests associated with social and cultural difference into debates about modernity and modernist sociology. Their challenging of phallo-, logo- and Euro-centric constructions of modernity and modernist sociology has been crucial to the overall 'spirit' of deconstruction. While there is no space in this book to discuss these latter influences in depth, Chapter 3 does consider their influence in deconstructive debates about radically reflexive methodologies. The emphasis in these debates is placed less on producing knowledge that would stand up to modernist sociological requirements of neutrality and objectivity, and more on narratives of the social, cultural, political and personal that are attuned to issues of difference and power in the production of sociological knowledge. They emphasize self-critical approaches to social analysis. These arguments are important in their own right, but they are included here because they have distinct implications for envisioning a 'post' modernist sociological project.

Chapter 4 considers what is probably the most contested and widely debated theoretical deconstructive sub-movement with respect to modernity and modernist sociology: the theory of postmodernity. The chapter considers different approaches to theorizing postmodernity and assessments of its implications for sociology. Via consideration of ideas about an emergent postmodern paradigm, the chapter considers arguments for distinguishing between deconstructivist and reconstructivist approaches to postmodernity, to identify 'extreme' and less extreme positions. This case is rejected on the basis that 'extremism' is not an analytically adequate basis on which to evaluate theoretical or sociological arguments. It is argued instead that a deconstructivist/reconstructivist frame is better suited to talking about the distinctions that exist between broadly postmodernist approaches that share a concern with deconstruction and are suspicious of theoretical unities, universalities and the like (and that aim for a deconstructed sociology), and those contemporary approaches to late modernity that self-consciously reject the deconstructivist orientation and argue the case for focusing on new unities, universalizing tendencies and the like (and that aim for a reconstructed sociology). The latter seek, in some way or another, to retrieve or reinvigorate aspects of the modern project and sociology of modernity – but without necessary recourse to the meta-discursive and epistemic claims for knowledge and truth that poststructuralists and postmodernists have critiqued.

In considering arguments about the distinction between the terms 'postmodernism' and 'postmodernity', this chapter also suggests the value of distinguishing between radical postmodernist, strategic postmodernist and radical modernist arguments as the basis for a more finely tuned evaluation of approaches to postmodernity. The radical and strategic categories are, I argue, a helpful way of loosely grouping different theories of postmodernity, while the radical modernist category is useful for thinking about reconstructivist theories of modernity and sociology. I illuminate these categories by considering Lyotard's and Baudrillard's ideas as radical postmodernist (whilst also pointing out the significant differences between their arguments), and by framing Bauman's arguments about postmodernity as 'strategic'. I also consider strategic arguments about the need to reincorporate the social within postmodern analyses, which articulate a reconstructive basis for thinking about a postmodern sociology. Such arguments raise a question that gets to the heart of the problem that poststructuralist and postmodernist deconstructive movements pose for sociology: what is sociology without the modernist emphasis on the social? Contrary to the fears of many sociological critics, however, some commentators argue that while theories of postmodernity have tended to be preoccupied by the cultural, this does not mean that they invariably do not – or cannot – also incorporate the social.

Chapter 5 develops the case for considering how some contemporary theories of modernity might be conceptualized as reconstructive ones that have important implications for reconstructed sociology. It does so by considering the arguments about what is variously termed late, second or reflexive modernity as put forward by Giddens and Beck. Giddens and Beck reject the deconstructive orientation to modernity and modernist sociology, and argue instead for a reconstructed understanding of modernity and reconstructing sociology. Giddens and Beck both acknowledge that modernity has changed, and they argue that developments on a global scale warrant rethinking modernity and, by implication, modernist sociology. They agree with postmodernists that uncertainty and ambiguity are defining aspects of the contemporary culture, and they also agree that the Enlightenment principles relating to reason, truth and progress can no longer be relied on to generate order and security. This leads to uncertainty that, they acknowledge, hits at the heart of sociology itself. There can be no scientific – including social scientific – claim that is beyond doubt and contestation. Rather, the current period of modernity, both argue, is marked by radical doubt as a consequence of reason's reflection on – or confrontation with – itself.

In such circumstances, one might suspect that these theorists would agree with their postmodernist counterparts' arguments about fragmentation and the demise of the modernist project. On the contrary, Beck and Giddens instead emphasize new universalizing tendencies that, they argue, are afoot in a global world. While they theorize these differently, both emphasize new commonalities emerging in societies being reconfigured by a heightened sense of 'man-made' risks that cut across old boundaries of class, generation, geographical location and the like. Late modernity, risk society or reflexive modernity – whatever we choose to name it – is, both theorists argue, an experimental society. It is experimental in that the social, cultural and political forms associated with simple or first modernity are fast becoming redundant, and there are no new forms to replace them yet. Modern social institutions such as class and the family are, Beck says, zombie institutions. This implies living without the certainty of tradition, and with the consequences of radical disembedding processes that lift forms of connectedness out of their old social settings, and undermine given sources of social and personal identity. For both Giddens and Beck, self-identity nowadays has to be reflexively made, and individualization means that we are in the era of do-it-yourself biographies. Further, it is not only ourselves and our lifestyles that must be constantly (re)made, but also our modes of relating to others. While these arguments share some common ground with radical and strategic postmodernism, Giddens and Beck emphasize the new forms of connectedness these developments give rise to – as everybody irrespective of social class, gender, 'race' and ethnicity, generation and geographical location comes under the influence of these developments. Also, in a global world, new opportunities arise for individuals and agencies to recognize new commonalities and shared interests.

Giddens places more emphasis on the new opportunities emerging in reflexive modernity than Beck, who talks more cautiously about conflicts and opportunities that arise. Both theorists agree, however, that sociology must rethink its established frames, and the dualisms that comprise them, to grasp the current situation, and to interpret the challenges and opportunities that come with it. Delanty's suggestion that we could see the concern with reflexivity as a concern with mediation is insightful in this respect, and it is the case that Giddens' work especially appears preoccupied with mediation. This points to one notable difference between Giddens and Beck: the extent to which the former is more preoccupied with theorizing the possibilities of mediated order than the latter. Beck talks instead about potential conflicts and opportunities whose outcomes are unknown and possibly unknowable. This difference is partly due the stronger normative thrust driving Giddens' analysis – the vision of how things *should* be. While the differences are important, the significance of Giddens' and Beck's theories lies partly in how their combined work articulates a reconstructive theory with respect to modernity. The implications of this for 'thinking' and 'doing' sociology become clear when we look at their specific arguments with respect to contemporary social change and personal life. These are considered along with competing arguments in the second part of the book.

Chapters 6 to 9

While the social theory of modernity and modernist sociology have always, in some way or another, been concerned with subjectivity, the issue came to the fore in theoretical and sociological debates as a consequence of deconstructionist arguments about the fragmentation and fluidity of self and identity. Chapter 6 begins by exploring how Giddens' reconstructivist approach to modernist sociology rearticulates the contemporary self as a reflexive project. In this way he confers on the contemporary self an empowered agency. He argues that instead of fragmenting, contemporary self-identities are constantly reworked and reordered by subjects themselves through their construction of lifestyles and the engagement with expert systems (through lifestyle, self-help, health, financial knowledge and the like) that this affords. Giddens' arguments are, in significant ways, similar to Beck's arguments about the consequences of individualization for 'do-it-yourself' biographies. Central to both arguments is the idea that self-identity and biography are for 'everybody' becoming open and malleable, and that individuals nowadays have little choice but to engage in self-making. Giddens' arguments especially emphasize the universalities and commonalities that exist with respect to self-identity through a number of interlinked arguments about the essential foundations of psychic trust; human beings' essential needs for ontological security; the threats to psychic coherence that risk presents; and the increased quanta of power that reflexive modernity makes available to individuals for their empowerment. This raises crucial questions about increased agency with respect to self-identity; new possibilities that are open for self-making; the coherence that the constructed self achieves; and the resources that count in self-making and who has access to them. It also raises questions about the overly optimistic view of social change that is implied. Through consideration of a range of other arguments about self, identity and power – derived via modernist and postmodernist frames – the chapter questions how convincing the arguments about reflexive self-identities are, and explicates the problems of the universalizing and essentialist assumptions that underpin them. Psychoanalytic frames, for example, highlight how 'difference' and 'conflict' are central to the human psyche and modernist and postmodernist developments in psychoanalysis alike have theorized operations of power with respect to self and subjectivity that Giddens ignores. Foucault, through his arguments about discourse, and knowledge-power focused on the body, argues for a more disciplinary understanding of modern and 'reflexive' subjectivities. Also, postmodern theories of various kinds suggest the contemporary self is a 'surface', 'fragmented' or consumer self that has only fleeting coherence. Further, modernist arguments about self and identity direct our attention to how economic, social and cultural resources combine to determine the possibilities and limits of self-constitution. Combined, these arguments provide some considerable basis for scepticism about the reflexive self and the significance and possibilities it is afforded in the reconstructive theory of reflexive modernity.

The emphasis in Chapter 7 shifts towards the insights that reconstructivist theories of modernity claim to generate for social change with respect to egalitarian relational and intimate life; the relationship between these and structural changes that promote new levels of gender equality with respect to paid work; and how modernity's 'emotional history' illuminates developments in the democratization of contemporary social life. The theory of late or reflexive modernity argues that there are profound changes afoot in intimate and relational life that link to global processes. These changes, it is argued by Giddens, include a new emphasis on intimacy that has profound implications for the democratization of personal life. This in turn, he suggests, could have a subversive influence on modern institutions as a whole. Giddens and Beck are in agreement that there is a new shift towards equality in personal relationships that stems from how, in late or second modernity, all aspects of social life are experiments. The dynamics underpinning intimate and relational experiments, they argue, stem partly from new gender equalities in the labour market. This combined with necessity for everyone – male and female – to continuously work at realizing an identity or biography means there is a contingency in intimate and relational life that compels participants to actively work at their commitments. While Giddens theorizes this in terms of historical reconfigurations of gender relations, and as opening up new demands for active negotiation within relationships, Beck (with Beck-Gernsheim) explores it as the consequence of demands on men and women to construct a flexible and mobile life that is defined by the needs of the labour market. This sets the grounds for intimate or relational conflicts. The upshot for 'everybody', however, is that intimate and personal life and gender relations entail new demands and possibilities for experimentation. This is indicative of the detraditionalizing orientations of modernity as a whole, but it also has potentially profound implications in terms of an ethos of equality that could permeate social life more broadly.

Again, these analyses emphasize emergent universalities and the radical social, political and personal implications of these. Personal life is becoming more individualized for everybody, and because of this individual agency has no choice but to be mobilized. Also, everybody nowadays – men and women alike – must learn to get along as equals. In Giddens' analysis especially, there is the sense that reflexive modernity has a democratizing impulse. Despite his explicit rejection of a teleogical understanding of history and modernity (a *certain* vision of how things will transpire), the normative thrust of theory again produces an optimistic interpretation of social change that many would disagree with. Indeed, consideration of different interpretations of intimate and gender relations derived from various modernist and postmodernist frames highlights a number of ways in which the thesis of reflexive intimacies and gender is problematic. A wide range of broadly modernist theoretical arguments suggest different positions from which it could be argued that the idea of individualized intimate life is unconvincing. There is also a range of modernist and postmodernist arguments that would suggest that the thesis of reflexive intimacy and gender inadequately comprehends the working of power. Foucauldian theories would, for example, argue that, viewed from the perspective of the historical centrality of monitored sexuality to modern forms of social order, self-monitored intimacies and gender relations are forms of governance. They would also argue that there is more to power than Giddens acknowledges, and that the discourse of dialogical or negotiated intimacy that he promotes is itself linked to strategies of governance. Modernist feminist frames also provide a strong basis for countering the arguments about reflexive intimacies, personal life and gender. Indeed, there is a long tradition of feminist theorizing and sociology that both Giddens and Beck *must* ignore to mobilize their arguments. Further, other critics have pointed out that the bases on which Giddens interprets that democratization of gender and the consequent democratizing of society could as easily support Marxian arguments about how male and female experience is homogenized as a part of the process of commodification, or Weberian arguments about rationalization. Combined with this, sociological research on the demands made on women in work and in personal relationships would suggest that reflexivity as Giddens sees it, could be argued to work *against* gender equality as much as it works for it – and that reflexivity itself is not neutral.

Chapter 8 considers how the issue of mortality has been taken up in the theory of reflexive modernity to talk about an emergent form of politics: life-politics. While the issue of death is often employed in modernist and postmodernist social theory to illustrate the loss of shared meaning in contemporary societies, in the theory and sociology of reflexive modernity it is used to talk about the 'return' of institutionally repressed life experiences. Death is important to the reconstructive theory of reflexive modernity because it talks to one of the few incontestable universalities in human life: that everybody dies. Modernity, the theory of reflexive modernity argues, puts aside or hides death because of the existential issues it raises, which are fundamentally troubling for the modern individual. Having demystified pre-modern and traditional frames for understanding death, modernity gives no answer to it – death has no meaning. Coupled with this, in late modernity increasing individualization means that death is an existentially troubling issue that people must increasingly face alone. This appears a damning indictment of modernity, but in the theory of reflexive modernity existential issues related to human mortality are drawn upon to articulate the potential for remoralizing social life. The return of institutionally 'repressed' moral and ethical issues provides the basis for movements in reflexive modernity to reincorporate them into life. Modernity made human mortality something that separates people because the tendency is to avoid contact with death and the dying due to the existential crises it threatens. In late modernity, however, people are potentially brought together by the growing recognition of a moral void. Such awareness promotes, Giddens argues, a post-emancipatory life-politics. It is in theorizing life-politics that the themes of self-identity, intimacies and mortality come together to form a coherent narrative about social change and reflexive personal life in late modernity. On the one hand, the dynamism of modernity makes personal life more insecure and vulnerable – to perceived risks, but even more so to ontological insecurity. On the other hand, 'universal' post-emancipatory concerns emerging in personal life feed back into public life through a reflexive loop – where they are mediated and negotiated as public issues. Unlike other modern and postmodernist arguments considered in the book, personal life and subjective culture are far from depleted in the theory of reflexive modernity; rather they are being vigorously renewed and are influencing changes 'out there'. However, the degree to which reflexivity is not neutral emerges again as a crucial matter, which is illuminated via a brief discussion of AIDS (often viewed as the life-political issue par excellence). This raises the question of whose lives and experience are imagined in the theory of reflexive modernity, and whose fail to feature.

In this respect, it raises the differences that still matter (not least between post-emancipatory and non-emancipated experience).

The concluding chapter, Chapter 9, brings together criticisms of the theory of reflexive modernity and the sociology of reflexive personal lives it promotes. Consideration of these raises important questions about the kind of sociological endeavour we want to reconstruct and be part of. While the allure or promise of sociological renewal is a powerful one, we should be cautious about embracing the reconstructivist theory and sociology of reflexivity, and question if it represents the kind of sociological renewal that we should subscribe to. We might also be cautious about arguments that suggest that the deconstructive moment in sociology is a spent force. Rather this moment – or movement – and the various sub-movements that constitute it offer various approaches for thinking about sociology in the twenty-first century. Ironically, it is the sub-movement that is least regarded in theoretical responses to the deconstructive turn in sociology that provides the most convincing counter-argument against the reconstructivist theory of late modernity and the sociology of reflexivity it promotes. This is the movement associated with deconstructing modernist sociological practice, and reconstructing reflexive sociological practice, which is closely associated with social and cultural difference. It advocates recognizing how the dynamics of power and difference shape the sociological narratives that we tell. This movement promotes reflexive sociology that, I argue, is very different from the sociology of reflexivity that reconstructivist theories of modernity promote. The distinction between these two loose kinds of sociology is important. Whereas one – reflexive sociology – emphasizes reflection on the dynamics of difference and power that shape the sociological narrative, the other – the sociology of reflexivity – is more concerned with constructing a powerful narrative and erases difference for the sake of coherence. These are not necessarily mutually exclusive approaches to conceptualizing modernity and sociology. But it is fair to say that the latter (in the form considered in this book) has so far failed to engage with the arguments of the former. The latter will remain an unconvincing account of the dynamics of modernity (global and local, institutional and personal), as well as an unconvincing basis for reconstructing sociology, to the extent that it fails to also become the former.

2

FOUNDING NARRATIVES OF MODERNITY AND THE LOGICS OF SOCIAL CHANGE

Introduction

Modernity, as a sociological construction, has its foundations in the overarching frames for conceptualizing the economic, social, cultural, political and subjective that emerged in the late nineteenth and early twentieth centuries. This chapter considers the models of modern society proposed by founding social thinkers, and their influences on the modernist sociological project. In doing so, it discusses the ideas underpinning core traditions of social thinking about the modern, and traces the roots of contemporary frames for conceptualizing modernity and social change. Viewed together, the ideas considered in this chapter constitute a constructive movement or 'moment' in theorizing about the modern that is crucial to understanding contemporary (reconstructive and deconstructive) approaches to modernity. By considering this constructive movement, the chapter aims to situate the recent heightened interest in modernity with respect to sociology's longstanding concerns. The chapter explores how the analyses of Marx, Durkheim and Weber envision modernity. It also considers the work of Simmel and Freud that has been influential in debates about modernity and postmodernity. It concludes by briefly discussing the implications of these thinkers' combined ideas for a general understanding of modernity and the modernist sociological project.

Narrating the modern, envisioning the social

Modernity, as a sociological concept, has from its inception been articulated in terms of dualisms that highlight the core processes, dynamics and relations that were thought to be central to it. The conceptual frames

16

that contribute to the constructive movement in theorizing modernity articulate these dualisms differently, as Delanty (1999:18) points out, as conflicts between capital and labour (Marx); anomie and disintegration (Durkheim); freedom from tradition and rationalization (Weber); and desire and repression (Freud). Delanty himself argues the case for a reconstructed understanding of the central conflict of modernity – which sociologists often discuss as structure and agency – as the tension between integration and differentiation. However, in thinking about the common themes in founding constructions of modernity, it is more insightful to focus on overlapping tensions between disintegration and order; domination and agency; emancipation and the impoverishment of personal culture. In considering these founding constructions in more detail, it is appropriate to begin with Marx, whose ideas about capitalist society amount to an especially influential analysis of the modern.

Capitalistic modernity

Marx's ideas about the origins and destiny of capitalist society provide a powerful founding narrative of modernity. A key feature of modernity, he suggested, was commodification – where capitalistic social relations penetrated and reconfigured all aspects of social life (Delanty 1999: 18). From the mid to late nineteenth century Marx (1818–83) generated a detailed analysis of capitalism as the motor of modern social change (see Calhoun *et al.* 2002b; Craib, 2004; Dodd 1999; Marx and Engels 2003; Morrison 1995; Rigby 1998; Turner 1999). He sought to explicate the logics of capitalist development and the social forms it gave rise to, but also to understand how its demise would be brought about. The world that Marx saw around him was one characterized by social upheaval and political turmoil that was being transformed by economic and technological developments. Through his historical-materialist conceptual frame, Marx conceptualized modern – capitalist – society as a phase in historical patterns of social order that was ultimately defined by the nature of the economic relations that underpinned it. His approach entailed a radical and sustained critique of the social conditions and endemic inequalities he associated with the capitalist relations of production, and the patterns of domination and subordination they promoted.

Marx conceptualized nineteenth-century social change in historical-evolutionary terms as part of the inevitable movement from feudalism to capitalism and towards a post-capitalist order. Adopting a dialectical logic, he conceptualized this movement as one of progress towards full emancipation. This approach emphasized how the contradictions inherent in capitalism would be overcome by a final stage in human history: one defined by egalitarian and harmonious order. Marx rejected Hegel's notion of the dialectic (where the emphasis was on how ideas produced society) and argued instead for an understanding of the dialectic that was focused on material conditions (see May 1996). From this perspective, society is the product of the material base – or, put another way, an economic foundation – and Marx proposed a frame for comprehending history as a dialectic resulting from changes in these foundations. In emphasizing the material and economic base, he brought the issue of human relations into the centre of his analysis of how historical change comes about, and put a social explanation 'on its feet' (Latour 2005: 64). Modern society, the state and social relations could thus be analysed in terms of how societies reflected their material or economic foundations, and how these gave rise to distinctive social, institutional, cultural and political forms, and determined personal experience. For Marx, capitalist society was a post-feudal and pre-communist one whose economic organization was grounded in the systematic exploitation of workers (the proletariat) by the dominating class, who owned the means of production (the bourgeoisie). While modern progress was something to be welcomed in itself, modernity would only be fully realized when capitalism was superseded by an egalitarian socialist order.

In contrast to liberal arguments that economic prosperity would lead to increased wealth for everyone and to a society integrated by liberal values (Delanty 1999; Dodd 1999), Marx emphasized instead the implications for social conflict, estrangement and alienation. The inevitability of conflict was partly rooted in how capitalism promoted dehumanization and alienation. Workers suffered dehumanization as a consequence of being unable to participate in meaningful and satisfying work under capitalism, and this would only intensify as capitalist competition heightened. Coupled with this, the capitalist system reduced the human needs of workers to basic requirements and living conditions that led to poverty, but also to social estrangement. However, the alienating effects of exploitation sowed the seed for workers' consciousness of their shared position and mutual interests. The dehumanizing and deskilling of labour went hand in hand with the concentration of workers in large urban working environments such as factories. This would ultimately lay the foundations necessary for workers' collective self-consciousness and their organization as an exploited class. The proletariat would become a class *for* itself, and through revolution would overthrow the hitherto dominant class (for discussions of this aspect of Marx's thought, see Callinicos 1989).

Freedom from domination was, for Marx, freedom from the social relations and inequalities that capitalism was grounded in and promoted. In an emancipated order, collective ownership of the means of production would undo the inequalities that existed under capitalism between the propertied and working classes. Despite the critique of capitalist modernity, Marx had faith in the emancipatory direction of modernity itself, as it was modernity's completion that would result in the post-capitalist order. Capitalist modernity indicated the possibilities that technological progress afforded, but the overthrowing of capitalism through class revolution was necessary to modernity's full realization. Marx therefore generated a theory of modernity as double-edged, but emphasized more its 'opportunity side' (Giddens 1990: 7). Ultimately, his analysis of capitalist society and social change invoked the promise of progress and the goal-orientated direction (teleology) of social change that modernist theories are drawn to under the influence of Enlightenment philosophical thought (see Turner 1999).

Industrial modernity

Durkheim's work is often viewed as a testament to modernist sociology's dual preoccupation with questions of social order and envisioning a clearly delineated field of scientific authority with respect to the social. Recently, there has been a renewed interest in his later work, which challenges the narrow view of him as a founding thinker of sociological positivism whose main concern was articulating the basis of order (Turner 1999). Despite this, Durkheim (1858–1917) famously adopted an organic analogy to talk about society, and envisioned it as a well-functioning organism that developed according to an evolutionary logic (see Calhoun *et al.* 2002b; Craib 2004; Dodd 1999; Durkheim and Hall 1984; Giddens 1997; Morrison 1995; Turner 1999). This evolutionary view was crucial in shaping his understanding of the advanced division of labour in modern societies. Durkheim argued that the collective conscience that had bound traditional societies together, that were socially integrated through a 'mechanical' form of social solidarity, was undermined by industrialization. This would, he thought, be replaced by forms of social integration achieved through an advanced division of labour. Durkheim termed this 'organic solidarity' – that which stemmed from the recognition of social interdependence in highly differentiated societies. In such contexts, autonomy and mutuality would be combined under a kind of moral individualism that differed from the egotistic individualism that liberalism promoted (see Dodd 1999; Giddens 1990; Turner 1995).

Modern society and its institutions were, from Durkheim's viewpoint, better understood from the perspective of industrialization than that of capitalism. Durkheim disagreed with the argument that capitalist competition and commodification were the defining features of modern society and motors of social change. The dynamic character and challenges of modern social life sprang instead from industrialization and 'the energising impulse of a complex division of labour' (Giddens 1990: 12). Despite their differing emphases on capitalism and industrialization, Durkheim shared with Marx the view that the modern era was a potentially troubled one, but like Marx ultimately emphasized the opportunities that modernity held out for harmonious social existence. While Durkheim recognized the problems associated with social integration in industrial modernity, he viewed these as temporary ones that could be remedied. Durkheim saw social and moral dislocation (anomie or normlessness) as temporary problems on the journey towards advanced forms of social integration. Whereas Marx viewed the question of solidarity in terms of the politics of class interests, and in terms of working-class solidarity bringing about capitalism's demise, Durkheim viewed solidarity in terms of the bases for social cohesiveness. Also, whereas Marx envisioned that capitalist societies would be superseded by a new and harmonious social order, Durkheim viewed the issue to be one of adjustments within the industrial social order to balance it as opposed to transcending it. For Durkheim, the troubles of modern societies were rooted in the speed of industrial expansion. This eroded mechanical forms of solidarity associated with pre-modern or simple societies without fully establishing the bases for organic solidarity. Modern social order would, however, emerge through the evolving social system that would meet mutual needs and integrate through the complex division of labour that was suited to industrial society.

Rationalistic modernity

Like Marx and Durkheim, Weber (1864–1920) viewed modernity as affording some degree of emancipation from traditional influences on social action (see Calhoun *et al.* 2002b; Craib 2004; Dodd 1999;

Morrison 1995; Turner 1999; Weber 1978, 2003). However, compared to Marx and Durkheim, Weber's analysis is often deemed the most pessimistic assessment of modernity. Marx's vision of capitalistic modernity emphasized the social estrangement and alienation it promoted, and Durkheim's critique of egoistic individualism focused on anomie and normlessness. Weber, in contrast, was concerned with disenchantment as a consequence of the increasing dominance of instrumental reason. The dominance of instrumental or 'occidental' reason meant that the rationalization of outcomes increasingly took precedence over ethical evaluation of the outcomes themselves. It also referred to the rationalization of all aspects of social life. This was not necessarily a temporary phase in the progress of modernity, and Weber supposed it to be a probable destiny.

Despite writing about capitalism, Weber did not afford it the same epoch-determining significance that Marx had. There was no 'givenness' to historical-epochal change. Rather, processes of rationalization had profound implications for the capitalist economy, and also for the spheres of religion, law and bureaucracy, because of historical contingencies (Dodd 1999). This view is partly derived from Weber's concerns with the cultural aspects of modernity and the cultural influences on social change. This had important implications for his envisioning of social analysis. While Weber discussed class with respect to labour-market position, for example, he also focused on the significance of social status. Social status is not reducible to economic resources, but depends also on social background, education, occupation and the like. This provided a more complex understanding of social stratification, power and politics (Bottero 2005). Economic class, this perspective argued, does not wholly determine social status and political interests. Neither could social change be reduced to economic relations and class conflict.

Whilst acknowledging the material dimensions of social change, Weber also illuminated the significance of cultural influences on capitalism and rational-bureaucratic modernity. Modern capitalism, he suggested, could be understood with reference to how the culture, ideas and values associated with particular religious beliefs had been profound motivating forces for social action. Weber elucidated this thesis – and the rationalistic orientations of modernity – in *The Protestant Ethic and the Spirit of Capitalism* (see Weber 2003). This challenged the idea that religion was the ideological reflection of the material foundation of society. Put briefly, Weber argued that religious ideas associated with the Calvinist doctrine of predestination in the seventeenth century were influential in fostering what subsequently became thought of as the capitalist ethos. The ethos of modern capitalism was partially rooted in Protestant beliefs and anxieties about predestination that promoted the disciplined generation and accumulation of wealth as evidence for being spiritually saved. Eventually capitalism became uncoupled from its religious roots and operated independently according to its inherited logic. What Marx had reduced to a question of economic relations – reflected in his argument that religion was the ideological opium of the people – Weber interpreted as an influential cultural movement whose ideas and values promoted distinctive approaches to economic and social organization. The culture of modernity, his analysis implied, was not merely an ideological reflection of its material underpinnings. Rather, cultural ideas and values – religious, political, economic and aesthetic – inform social action and have profound consequences for material conditions.

These ideas have broad implications for understanding human agency with respect to shaping modernity's direction and future. First, class struggle is rejected as the primary force that determines modern social change. Second, there is no one revolutionary class that is the agent of history. Social change is likely instead to be the consequence of combined interests and ideas. In terms of politics, Weber's analysis pointed to how social status, and the distinctions it was based on, was as likely to influence political alliance because it 'consists of our social position as viewed by others' (Dodd 1999: 41). Interests of power other than class and social status – such as the shared interests and conflicts of organizations of all kinds, including nation states – are also important in influencing social change.

This returns us to Weber's arguments about the progressive dominance of instrumental rationality in modern social life, and the pessimistic thrust of his analysis of modernity. Weber's argument suggests that modernity is defined by the infiltration of rational calculation into all aspects of social life, which promotes disenchantment. This implies the gradual but pervasive demise of 'magical' thought, the upshot of which is the loss of an overarching belief system and the 'breaking up [of] traditional worldviews into distinctive specialist areas of expertise: specifically, those of science, morality and art' (Dodd 1999: 41). This, combined with the drive towards bureaucratization in all areas of organizational life (and in social life more generally), is ultimately the basis for what some perceive as his 'bleak' view of progress, and the idea that a metaphorical 'iron cage' would dominate the human spirit or personal culture.

Modern fragments

While Weber's conception of modernity is often deemed the most pessimistic of the founding social thinkers, Simmel's analysis of the modern is also more pessimistic than Marx's and Durkheim's. Also, if Weber is the founding social thinker whose work most persuasively suggests that rationality and culture should be central to conceptualizations of the modern, Simmel (1858–1918) shared these concerns (see Calhoun *et al.* 2002b; Craib 2004; Frisby 2002; Turner 1999; Simmel and Levine 1973). There are a number of possible explanations for why Simmel's work has until relatively recently been overshadowed by other founding social thinkers. First, Simmel's combined interests in the social, cultural and psychological blurred the boundaries between sociology and other academic disciplines. This led to the problem of how to locate Simmel as a sociological thinker, which is evident in how he has been variously described as the first theorist of modernity, the first postmodern theorist, and the first major critic of modernity in classical sociology (Delanty 1999). Furthermore, some have argued that Simmel's work most powerfully expressed the dynamism of modernity because his approach to sociology was as in keeping with poetry as it was with science (Lepenies 1988). Finally, his focus on the 'fragments' of modern experience made it difficult to easily place him with respect to other modernist frames of social theory and sociology, as did his ultimate refusal to emphasize one overarching feature as the principal determining aspect or characteristic of modern.

Simmel's analyses overlapped with Durkheim's (where he emphasized implications of modernization for differentiation and social density); with Marx (where he analysed the money economy and emphasized the implications of modernity for alienation); and with Weber's (where he emphasized the growth of instrumental rationality and modernity's implications for the erosion of personal culture) (see Turner 1999). In his analyses of fragments of modern existence (city life, fashion, prostitution and the money economy) he focused especially on emergent socialities and modern socio-cultural forms. Together, these analyses highlighted the costs of modernity for diminished personal culture. In contrast to Durkheim's emphasis on the possibilities that social density and differentiation opened up for moral individualism, Simmel viewed the implications to be the erosion of subjective culture. The tendency in modernity, his work suggested, was for culture to become objectified and detached from the person. This concern, Delanty argues, links his various studies of city life with his work on the mature money economy: 'One of the distinctive features of the metropolis is the experience of distance between people . . . the money economy becomes dominant and shapes all social relations, bringing about a fragmentation of experience' (Delanty 1999: 43–4).

Turner (1999) argues that it is only recently that commentaries on Simmel's work have focused on the central theme of alienation. He notes that, previously, discussions undermined the 'theoretical backing' this work provided for subsequent explications of the alienation theme in Marx, and for Weber's analysis of the iron cage of modernity. The theme of alienation is evident in much of Simmel's writing on city life, but the difference between Marx's and Simmel's conceptions of alienation is important: the former's is tied to the exploitation of labour, while the latter's is focused on the objectification of culture (Delanty 1999: 44). Like Weber's study of the Protestant ethic, Turner (1999: 161) argues that Simmel's study on the money economy in *The Philosophy of Money* is a classic account of the roots of modernity and modern consciousness. It underscores, he suggests, the significance of Simmel's founding contribution to the sociology of modern*ism* – the culture of modernity (Turner 1999: 161). As pointed out earlier, however, the preoccupation with the psychological influences on human motivations and the absence of an overarching or principal dynamic that determined the social, combined with the focus on fragments of experience, have sometimes worked until relatively recently to obscure the relevance of his work to modernist *social* analysis.

Civilized modernity

Simmel's concern with the objectification of culture and the consequent impoverishment of subjective culture stems partly from the central importance afforded to psychological life in his analytical frame. This links to Freud (1856–1939), who is best known for his founding contributions to the study of psychology and psychoanalysis. While Freud's primary concern was to study and illuminate the subjective world, he also generated an influential analysis of modern – which Freud termed 'civilized' – society and culture (Calhoun *et al.* 2002b; Craib 2001; Freud and Bersani 2002). Freud's analysis of the relationship between personal life and civilized culture pointed to the significance of the psychological repression of human beings' 'animalistic' orientations, and was influential on a broad range of subsequent analyses of modern culture, including the Frankfurt School of critical theory (see Chapter 3), post-structuralist psychoanalysis (see Chapter 3), and modernist and post-modernist feminist analyses (see Chapter 6).

Freud explicitly articulated the centrality of ambivalence to modern culture through his focus on the tension that existed between the demands that civilized order made for repression, and the emancipation it afforded from 'natural' drives (see Smart 1998). The achievements and costs of civilized modernity were core features of his analyses of modern culture and of its implications for the formation of subjectivity. The energy and creativity of modern culture, he argued, were rooted in how it promoted the repression of basic human instincts towards aggression and pleasure. On the one hand, this enabled the realization of the most noble and creative cultural achievements. On the other hand, such achievements could not wholly compensate for the thwarting of basic human orientations towards pleasure. At the core of Freud's under-standing of civilized modernity was an evolutionary view of social and cultural progression. The nineteenth- and early twentieth-century European bourgeoisie, on some of whose psychic lives Freud's observations were based, experienced the gains but also the costs of civilized culture. The taming or repression of human beings' natural drives and instincts (for example, with respect to aggression and sexuality) was a key achievement of modern civilization. But it was also largely responsible for a sense of personal malaise. At the heart of the problem was one of Freud's most radical insights that was subsequently highly influential in debates about modern and postmodern subjectivities: that the subjective culture of modernity is defined by tensions and contradictions, which is related to how the human psyche is inherently split or divided (see Chapter 6).

Freud's work highlighted the issue of difference. On the one hand, his neo-Darwinian understandings of the development of modern (civilized) human life normalized the differences (with respect to gender, sexuality, civilized/uncivilized and the like) that were central to modern patri-archal, hetero-normative and colonial orders. On the other hand, by focusing attention on the splits within the human psyche, he cleared the ground for future claims about the significance of 'differences within' subjectivities which stemmed from how 'natural' human desires, instincts and drives had to be contained and redirected for the sake of civilized social order. Furthermore, he placed human relationships (especially those between children and parents) at the heart of his analyses of how subjectivity, identity and human psychology were structured. In doing so he laid the foundations for social explanations of the psychological (see Chapter 6).

Conclusion: constructing modernity and the sociological project

Overall, the work of Marx, Durkheim, Weber, Simmel and Freud indicate how the theme of the modern has been central to social thinking since its inception. Combined, this work influenced a constructive movement or 'moment' in conceptualizing modernity and in thinking about the interplay of economic, cultural, political and subjective forces that shape and are shaped by modern social life. This constructive movement had profound implications for sociology – the discipline to which the examination of modern social life is most integral (Giddens 1990: 3). It shaped the sociological preoccupation with the foundations of modern social order and the motors of social change. It also shaped the preoccupation with the threats and opportunities generated by modernity, and how social order is maintained and/or transformed. It bequeathed to modernist sociology a range of concerns that centred on knowing the direction of social change and the part that human agency played with respect to this. The idea that these *could* be known was itself influenced by philosophical ideas and epistemic principles (theories of knowledge) derived from Enlightenment thinking that emphasized the rational foundations of knowledge, truth and progress (see May 1996).

Marx, Durkheim and Weber developed their respective analyses in historical contexts where the anchors of tradition were loosening their hold on all aspects of life, and where technological, social, cultural and political developments were reshaping the world around them. In their different ways they attempted to comprehend the whole of the resulting change in terms of the underpinning or overarching processes that shaped these developments. Along with Simmel and Freud, they constructed narratives of the emergent social world that were sometimes, on the one hand, marked by ambivalence towards the modern (Smart 1998) but, on the other hand (with the exception of Simmel perhaps), attributed a certain direction, coherence and purpose to social change. In some cases, like Durkheim, they were the architects of strategies for comprehending and making tangible the reality of the social. In other cases, like

Marx, they were the architects of strategies for political action. In other cases still, like Simmel, they captured the distinctiveness of modern forms – or fragments – of existence, and gave expression to the textured experience of the modern and radical social change.

As Lemert (1997: 17) points out, Marx, Weber and Durkheim (and we should include Freud) were involved, in their different ways, in world constructing (or narrating) endeavours. They were involved in producing cultural-theoretical inventions that, in one way or another, were based on some kind of evolutionary or progressive understanding of social development. They also shared, as Lemert (1997: 16) puts it, a concern 'with the fall of the human back into the dark, murky slime of things'. As such, their work reflected nineteenth-century and early twentieth-century concerns with knowing the forces implicated in both fragmentation and order. They articulated these in their different ways as logics of progress. Collectively their work reflected optimism, pessimism and ambivalence towards the inevitability of social change (Delanty 1999; Smart 1998), and pointed to tensions between the opportunities and dangers they associated with it. These tensions were bound up with the disintegration of established orders and the emergence of new ones; with agency that was freed from dominating traditions but threatened by new forms of subjection; and with possibilities that arose for emancipation but also for the impoverishment of personal culture. The tensions expressed in these founding conceptualizations still permeate contemporary debates about modernity. They continue to be expressed in contemporary interpretations of social, cultural and political change and arguments about the ensuing implications for the sociological project. Deconstructive positions tend to focus on the increasingly intensified contradictions that emerge from these tensions, the implications for 'post' modernity, and the need to radically deconstruct the modernist sociological project. Reconstructivist positions, on the other hand, tend to focus of the radicalization of these tensions but emphasize more the implications for reconstructing modernity and a reconstructed sociology. As we shall see in the following chapters, deconstructivist theories tend to be more often identified with the more pessimistic spirit of founding social thinking, while reconstructivist theories often lay claim to its optimistic spirit.

3

THE DECONSTRUCTIVE
TURN

Introduction

The founding constructions of modernity considered in the previous chapter were infused with Enlightenment ideas about reason, truth and progress. Poststructuralist theories challenged the philosophical and theoretical bases of these constructions, and argued that the modernist ideals they promoted were unrealizable. Poststructuralists critically interrogated modernist social theoretical ideas to reveal the problematic assumptions they were based on, and poststructuralist arguments combined with the deconstructive ideas of radical difference theorists (feminist, queer, postcolonial and so on) to influence a sense of 'crisis' with respect to the legitimacy of sociological knowledge. Both poststructuralist and radical difference ideas influenced a further deconstructive movement that was focused on reflexive methodology. This latter movement argued the case for deconstructing the methodologies that underpinned modernist sociology to reveal its involvements with power. This chapter focuses on how these poststructuralist, radical difference and reflexive methodology arguments combined to promote a 'post' modernist sociology.

The first section of the chapter briefly introduces Frankfurt School critical theory, and the idea that modernity is an unfinished project. The second section considers poststructuralist arguments that imply that the project of modernity (as articulated by founding social thinkers) was always destined for failure, and that modernist constructions of social knowledge fail to fully grasp power. The radical difference arguments considered in the third section of the chapter argue that the sociological discourse of modernity is not a neutral one and, as is the case with modernist sociology more generally, fails to appreciate it own part in operations of power related to difference and otherness. The arguments about reflexive methodology considered in the fourth part of the chapter (sometimes related to critiques of modernity and sometimes not) agree that the methodologies underpinning modernist sociological frames should be interrogated with respect to the politics of knowledge and power. The core argument put forward in the chapter is that what is termed the 'deconstructive turn' in sociology is not reducible to post-structuralism – or even to theoretical postmodernism (see Chapter 4) – as is sometimes implied. Rather, to more fully comprehend this turn, we must also consider radical difference theories, reflexive methodology critiques and their arguments for reflexive sociology. Combined, these arguments shaped a deconstructive movement that radically disrupted grand narratives of modernity and modernist sociological claims about the social. They are crucial to situating and evaluating the reconstructive theories of modernity that are discussed in Chapter 5.

Critical theory

Between the founding theories of the modern and the deconstructive ideas considered in this chapter there were, of course, innumerable developments in social theory and sociology (see Calhoun *et al.* 2002a, b; May 1996). Of these, the 'critical theory' of the Frankfurt School provides a notable link between founding modernist and poststructur-alist thinking. Overall, the Frankfurt School combined Marxian, Weberian and Freudian ideas amongst others for an integrated under-standing of modernity. Theorists like Adorno (1903–69), Horkheimer (1895–1973) and Marcuse (1898–1979) sought to critique the culture of liberal capitalism and its ideological functions (see Bottomore 2002; Calhoun 2002b; May 1996). Rejecting scientific Marxism and critiquing the dominant positivist (the idea that social facts were out there to be observed and measured) and interpretivist (the idea that the social world could be known by focusing on humans' interpretations of it) epistemo-logical frames for legitimizing social knowledge, they sought to develop theory as a self-consciously political form of knowledge that would facil-itate emancipation. On the one hand, Frankfurt School theorists were critical of capitalist modernity and the kind of Enlightenment thinking that privileged instrumental rationality. Combined, they argued, these led to intense forms of human repression and subjection. On the other hand, they were critical of Weber's reduction of reason to the kind of rationalization associated with capitalism, and were ultimately commit-ted to the modernist project as it concerned developing theory that could articulate the conditions of emancipation. Of the contemporary descendants of critical theory, Jürgen Habermas is the theorist whose work has had the greatest impact (see Habermas 1986, 1989, 1998; Sitton 2003). His continuing commitment to modernity as an 'incomplete project' stood out amongst the social theory of the latter part of the twentieth century, which, as we shall see, was dominated by poststructuralist, radical difference and postmodernist critique. Habermas's work is best known for his arguments about communicative reason and ideal speech situations, which explicate the theoretical possibilities of emancipation through the development of universal ethical principles. Put briefly, drawing from Weber, Habermas argued that instrumental reason could not form an adequate basis for the values and beliefs necessary for an enriching culture or 'life-world' (broadly those aspects of life that are involved with socialization, such as the family, education and so on). Rather, these could only be developed via communicative reason – where the emphasis is on the principles that emerge through unfettered dialogue. The task for theory, from this perspective, was to challenge the increasing intrusion of instrumental values into the life-world, and to elucidate the conditions under which a kind of pure communication could become possible which would, in turn, generate the life-world values that could be universally ascribed to.

Poststructuralism and the logics of disintegration

In contrast to Habermas, the key thinkers associated with poststructuralism questioned the basis for any belief in modernity's unfinished project, and in their different ways demolished the idea of enlightened and emancipated social order that critical theory and Habermas promoted. While Jacques Derrida and Jacques Lacan's influence is not often explicitly incorporated into mainstream sociological debates, their work, combined with that of Michel Foucault, profoundly influenced the deconstructive movement with respect to modernity and modern theorizing that came into its own in the last quarter of the twentieth century. Combined, this work inspired subsequent deconstructions of the foundational philosophies and epistemologies (theories of knowledge) that underpinned previous theoretical understandings of modernity and modern conceptions of the social. Coming from the traditions of philosophy (Derrida), psychoanalysis (Lacan) and social theory (Foucault), this work directed analytic attention towards the cultural in a way that blurred the boundaries between humanities and social-scientific disciplines. It focused on language, identity and difference, and how discourse was involved in the production of social order and power.

Poststructuralist thinking is associated with the fragmentation of modernist frames and categories for thinking about the social, cultural, political and subjective. Under its influence many of the founding principles of modernist sociology were revealed as fictions or illusions. These included the self-evidential basis of social knowledge; the idea that history and social life had their own inherent logics; claims for the conceptual dominance of Western reason; and claims about the possibilities of social and subjective coherence. Further, neither these fictions nor the sociological knowledge that was derived from them were neutral. Rather, they were bound up in complex ways with power and with modern social and cultural order. An emphasis on the functioning and effects of language and discourse was one defining element of poststructuralism. Foucault, for example, viewed discourse as involving a relationship between knowledge and power. Turner describes Foucault's approach to scientific discourse thus:

> all narratives of science depend on various conventions of language . . . Narrative is a set of events within language and language is a self-referential system. Nothing occurs outside language. Therefore what we know about 'the world' is simply the outcome of the arbitrary conventions we adopt to describe the world.
>
> (Turner 1995: 11)

Under the influence of Foucault's ideas, sociologists like Turner interrogated how modern expert discourse – political, social policy, scientific narratives and the like – were implicated in the construction of particular versions of social reality (see also Rose 1996, 1999). This is also the case for sociology. Discourse is especially powerful when its shores up historical, social or political contingencies as inevitable or essential realities. Put another way, discourse involves a relationship between knowledge and power in how it promotes an understanding of the fictitious as real and contingent as given; and also in how it presents any state of social affairs or relations as pre-social and outside the scope of human influence. From the poststructuralist perspective, modernist understandings of the social, cultural and political are flawed when they adopt a teleological and normative orientation – a vision of how things will and should turn out. Discourse about modernity is itself bound up with the flow of knowledge-power when it narrates the discursively produced modern order as given or inevitable, and attributes a pre-determined direction to social change.

The insights of Derrida, Lacan and Foucault into the problems of modernist claims and principles were generated via their adoption of deconstruction as an analytical strategy. Each in their own way, for example, deconstructed the ideas of essential (or given) meanings and universal identities, and each also deconstructed coherent narratives or frames of meaning that were grounded in dualisms and binaries. A key insight of poststructuralism is that meanings, categories and identities are radically unstable, not only because they are context-bound and open to interpretation, but also because they are always constructed in relation to – and contain – their 'other' (for example, the category male is incomprehensible without its other – female). Whereas modernist philosophical and social theoretical frames emphasized order and coherence, Derrida's deconstruction, as Dews (1987: 47) remarks, emphasized systematic incoherence, instability of meaning, illusion and non-unity. Lacan also adopted a deconstructive approach to studying the role of culture and power in shaping psychic life. What he termed his 'return to Freud' emphasized the illusion and non-unity at the heart of subjectivity by focusing on the significance of language in the formation of psychic life (as opposed to the natural drives Freud focused on) (see Fuss 1989; Chapter 6).

Lacan's ideas should be understood in terms of the various schools of psychoanalytic thinking that developed in the twentieth century. For more sociologically inclined critics, the essentialist and universalizing assumptions underpinning Freud's work stretched credibility (see Chapter 6). Also, as Craib (2001) notes, the more sociologically compatible developments in psychoanalysis tended to shift the emphasis away from the tensions and conflicts within the human psyche, and work more closely to the surface of the psyche. They emphasized less the messy and potentially destabilizing unconscious processes that Freud was preoccupied with. While Marcuse, for example, had incorporated Freud's insights in theorizing the repressive implications of capitalist domination for sexual and relational life, he did so by ridding the theory of some of its universalizing and essentialist propositions. Object-relations theorists also emphasized more sociologically conducive aspects of psychoanalysis over the conflicts internal to the modern psyche (see Craib 2001; Chapter 6). Against this backdrop, Lacan sought to return Freud's most radical, complex and destabilizing insights to psychoanalysis, but without their biologistic foundations. He emphasized language instead of natural drives to illuminate the inherently fragmented and split nature of all subjectivities (see Chapter 6).

Modernity, order and governance

Foucault's concern with language is evident in his preoccupation with historically situated discourse. While the emphasis in his work changed over time, he was mainly concerned with analysing the emergence of modern technologies of governance, and with the micro-physics of power. Foucault's work centred on undertaking an 'archaeology' of knowledge which traced the historical and discursive origins of knowledge formations that dominated in modernity. His work focused on the transition from traditional to modern societies, and analysed how expert knowledge was bound up with the distinctive modes of governance associated with the latter. Of the major poststructuralist thinkers, Foucault's work stands out for its influence on social theory and sociology and its broad impact across the humanities and social sciences. One central theme in Foucault's work is how the emergence of modern institutions and discourses from the seventeenth century onwards promoted subtle 'disciplinary' modes of governance based on self-monitoring (see Chapter 6). These institutions and discourses (for example, relating to madness, illness, criminality, sexuality), he argued, came into their own by the nineteenth century, marking the consolidation of modern patterns of order. Overall, Foucault's work argues that the emergence of the modern order is not reducible to overarching developments associated with capitalism or rationalization. Foundational and critical theoretical frames for conceptualizing modernity (considered in Chapter 2), his work implies, fail to appreciate how knowledge and power operated with respect to modern social life.

Through focusing on modern discourses about madness, illness, criminality, sexuality and the like, and their associated institutions, Foucault showed how, in modernity, the body was the focus of knowledge and power, and regulated through 'governmentality' (Osborne 1994; Rose 1996, 1999; Turner 1995). Governmentality was concerned with a genealogy of the arts of modern government, and with 'all those more or less rationalized programmes and strategies for the "conduct of conduct"' (Rose 1996: 134). Rose describes this approach:

Government, here, does not indicate a theory, but rather a

certain perspective from which one might make intelligible the diversity of attempts by authorities of different sorts to act upon the actions of others in relation to objectives of national prosperity, harmony, virtue, productivity, social order, discipline, emancipation, self-realization and so forth.

(Rose 1996: 134–5)

Foucault's concern with the relationship between governance and the exercise of power led him to trace how modern surveillance was facilitated by knowledge focused on the body, which promoted self-monitoring to produce disciplined order (Turner 1995: 10). Modern medicine, criminal punishment, and expert concerns with sexuality, relationships and the like are all examples of the 'heterogeneous applications of discipline' (Osborne 1994: 31). Turner summarizes Foucault's perspective as follows:

The modern penitentiary, hospital, prison and school are elements within an expanding apparatus of control, discipline and regulations . . . which have secured order not through overt violence but through a micro-politics of discipline whereby people have been morally regulated into conformity. This system of social control has been, at least in part, made possible by the 'advances' in scientific medicine and by the emergence of new forms of knowledge: criminology, penology, sociology, psychology and so forth.

(Turner 1995: 12)

Foucault was concerned with how the body was the focal point for modern disciplinary power, as the ultimate site of political control, surveillance and regulation. Various kinds of expert knowledge that were focused on the body were crucial to the discursive construction of what the healthy, normal and moral person should be. This knowledge fed into a broad range of corrective and educational strategies aimed at producing healthy and productive individual bodies, but also a healthy social body. The issue of production is crucial for Foucault, and he proposes that we misunderstand how power is productive if we only view discourse, knowledge and discipline through a repressive lens. Rather, discourse and knowledge and the discipline they promote are productive – of ideas, social reality and personhood itself. For example, the idea of the individual is produced as an ideological construct through knowledge about what persons are and should be like. But the individual is also produced as a subject of discipline, meaning that knowledge and discourse about normal personhood is incorporated or internalized as the basis of self-monitoring. This self-monitoring becomes the basis for self-regulation in line with the norms and values of the culture that, in turn, produces social order. Medicine, for example, is one modern institution and discourse that focused on defining bodily 'norms', and the medical 'gaze' played a crucial role in ordering modern society. As Foucault puts it:

> Medicine must no longer be confined to a body of techniques for curing ills and of the knowledge that they require; it will also embrace a knowledge of *healthy man* that is, a study of *non-sick man* and a definition of the *model man*. In the ordering of human existence it assumes a normative posture, which authorizes it not only to distribute advice as to healthy life, but also to dictate standards for physical and moral relations of the individual and of the society in which he lives. It takes its place in that borderline, but for modern man paramount, area where certain organic, unruffled, sensory happiness communicates by right with the order of a nation, the vigour of its armies, the fertility of its people, and the patient advice of its labours.
>
> (Foucault 1989: 34–5)

Medicine is, however, just one way in which normative judgement takes place in modern societies. Foucault (1979a: 304) identifies various judges – such as the doctor judge, social worker judge, teacher judge and so on – who all have a crucial role to play in defining, measuring and policing norms. Medicine is therefore one part of an extensive system of moral regulation of populations through the disciplinary regime, but an especially instructive one. Turner (1995: 35) argues that the emergence of medical norms and deviance; the growth in the importance of the doctor; the development of medical institutions around the hospital, the clinic and the examination; and the organization of medical surveillance of society all represent 'components of a secularization' of modern cultures: 'Put simply, the doctor has replaced the priest as the custodian of social values; the panoply of ecclesiastical institutions of regulation . . . have been transferred through the evolution of scientific medicine to a . . . collection of localized agencies of surveillance and control' (Turner 1995: 35–6).

Enlightenment ideas about reason, truth and progress are radically demolished in Foucault's theory. Rather than being an expression and facilitator of modern progress, science and the knowledge it produces are viewed as being intrinsically bound up with power. Further, because power is at the core of the modern self and modern order, there is really no escape from it. There is no agency to be emancipated in modernity; rather agency is itself produced in the interests of power. In summary, Foucault's chief insights relate to how disciplinary power is not strictly repressive but *productive*: with respect to both modern subjectivity and social order. In remarking on Foucault's insights, Dews contends that while Habermas's work shifted towards a more optimistic evaluation of modern subjectivity than the Frankfurt School, Foucault (and poststructuralists more generally) move 'in the opposite direction' (Dews 1987: 155). Foucault, he suggests, views subjects as wholly constituted by operations of power, and 'draws up a balance unfavourable to the modern age' (1987: 157–8).

Critiquing poststructuralism

Poststructuralist theory has had a profound and dynamic impact across the humanities and social sciences. However, its critics have been declaring the demise of its deconstructive project since the early days of its inception. Peter Dews, for example, noted how in the 1980s philosophical versions of poststructuralist deconstruction were being superseded in France by a return to 'questions about the foundations of ethics, the nature of political principles, and the universal status of legal rights' (Dews, 1987: xii). With more hindsight and focusing on its broader impact, however, we might say that early predictions about the demise of poststructuralism were somewhat premature and over-influenced by wishful thinking. Poststructuralist approaches to the deconstruction of categories of meaning, subjectivity and identity have been influential across the humanities and social sciences and are now established as legitimate analytical strategies.

The influence of poststructural deconstructions represented a profound critical period for many humanities and social-scientific disciplines, because of the challenges they posed for the philosophical principles and conceptions of knowledge that such disciplines were founded on. For sociology, with its broad diversity of approaches to studying social life, and in which epistemological debates had been ongoing since its inception, poststructuralism introduced a new controversy, as it refused the legitimacy of social knowledge claimed on the basis of epistemic or political grounds. In doing so, it threatened to undermine the basis of all claims to social knowledge, and promoted the radical instability and heterodoxy of knowledge claims. The following quotation from Dews provides a strong sense of what poststructuralism's opposition to modernist understandings was generally taken to imply:

> an unqualified hostility to the universal in the domain of ethics and politics has a profoundly menacing – as well as emancipatory – aspect . . . a wilful self-restriction of analysis to the fragmentary and the perspectival [that] renders impossible any coherent understanding of our own historical and cultural situation.
>
> (Dews 1987: xiii)

Dews, like many other critics, was sceptical of the enthusiasm with which social and cultural theorists adopted what Habermas termed the 'avant-garde consciousnesses' of poststructuralism. He was critical of what he viewed as the parodied versions of modernist ideas, concepts and frameworks that poststructuralism sought to dismantle, and how poststructuralist versions of these were often taken at face value. Via Graff and Eagleton's arguments, Dews suggested that the ethos underpinning poststructuralism was, in fact, often continuous with modes of thought it aimed to disrupt. He quoted Graff's argument to highlight the undeconstructed politics that poststructuralism supported:

> It [has a] fundamental complicity with the real 'avant garde' [of] advanced capitalism, with its built in need to destroy all vestiges of tradition and orthodox ideologies, all continuous and stable forms of reality in order to stimulate higher levels of consumption.
>
> (Graff, quoted in Dews, 1987: xvi)

Dews acknowledged that it was not enough to argue against poststructuralism by 'moral appeal alone', as this left its core arguments intact. It was insufficient, he argued, to point out poststructuralism's passivity or dubious political complicities even if it 'prides itself on a reckless integrity and consistency, and . . . is therefore willing to brave all consequences' (Dews 1987: vi). A more effective critique, he suggested, would reveal how, for all its radical posturing, poststructuralist thinking is undermined by vulnerabilities that limit its potential as a truly *critical* theory. One such vulnerability is that while poststructuralist modes of thought are clear about the universalities, unities and ideas of progress they are against, they fail to articulate what they are for. Many critics viewed the radical posturing, pessimism and political irresponsibility that poststructuralism promoted as central to its popularity, but also its immaturity. In commenting on Foucault's work, Pierre Bourdieu made the following observation, underscoring this accusation:

> There is, it is true, a side of Foucault's work . . . which theorizes the revolt of the adolescent in trouble with his family and with the institutions that relay family pedagogy and impose 'disciplines' . . . Adolescent revolts often represent symbolic denegations, utopian responses to general social controls that allow you to avoid carrying out a full analysis of the specific historical forms, and especially the differential forms, assumed by the constraints that bear on agents of different milieux, and also of forms of social constraint much more subtle than those that operate through the drilling . . . of bodies.
>
> (Bourdieu and Wacquant 1992: 195–6)

Other deconstructions

The poststructuralist movement in social and cultural theorizing was one influential contributor to a broader deconstructive movement with respect to modernity and modernist sociology that emerged in the latter part of the twentieth century. It fed into, and combined with, the broader postmodern movement in theory (see Chapter 4) to influence a sense of crisis in confidence about foundational theories of modernity and the principles underpinning modernist sociology. But there were also other notable contributions to this broader movement. These included feminist, queer and postcolonial theory and sociology that sought to challenge theories of modernity and modernist sociology on the basis of radical difference (which sometimes incorporated poststructuralist ideas). Generally, they argue that the theory and sociology of modernity had historically privileged class relations to the determent of other kinds of subordination, and that through making invisible diverse experiences of modernity, supported patriarchal, hetero-normative and colonial interests. Put another way, the theory of modernity and modernist sociology had historically been concerned with exclusive (male, heterosexual, white European–North American) experience and had, as such, represented very particular political interests. They were founded on and promote phallo-, logo- and Euro-centric ways of knowing, were grounded in the experience of European patriarchal culture, and furthered the interests of socially dominant groups.

While there is no space in this book to go into much of the detail of the various arguments, they have been an important influence on the 'spirit' of deconstruction. They were one important way in which the interests of radical social and political movements have been brought into academic debates about modernity and modernist sociology. In the following sections of this chapter, the interests of this critical movement are considered briefly, as is their influence in deconstructive debates on reflexive methodology. In these debates the emphasis placed by modernist social science on the need for neutrality and objectivity to produce legitimate knowledge is problematized, and there is often an implicit or explicit rejection of modernist conceptions of knowledge and reason. The emphasis instead is on producing narratives of the social, cultural, political and subjective through reflexive approaches to sociological analysis. Like the poststructuralist arguments that have already been considered, reflexive methodology arguments have important implications for envisioning 'post' modernist sociology.

Radical difference

Feminist, sexuality, and 'race' and ethnicity theorists have long been critical of founding models of modernity, and of modernist sociology, on the basis of their exclusion of difference, and the tendency to reduce questions of power and inequality to class relations only. Social theoretical ideas about modernity and modernist sociology, they argued, tended to universalize male, heterosexual and white experience. Since the 1960s and 1970s, however, a wealth of theoretical and research endeavours have sought to incorporate gender, sexual and ethnic differences into sociology. Nowadays, the sociological inclusion of women's, lesbian and gay, and black experience is a widely supported project. Indeed, some argue the value of placing the experience of difference at the centre of sociological concerns, to illuminate modern dynamics of subordination and exclusion. This emphasis on difference often goes hand in hand with 'simple' forms of deconstruction that aim to reveal the exclusion of 'others'. Arguments about difference and otherness have led to the development of specialist areas of modernist sociology that are concerned with gender, sexuality, and 'race' and ethnicity. They have also promoted the incorporation of experiences that were previously made invisible into theories of modernity and mainstream sociology. The concern with difference raises identity as a key sociological issue, and many theorists of difference have sought to theorize the conditions for emancipating subordinated identities. While class was important, this perspective argued, the dynamics of subordination relating to gender, sexuality, and 'race' and ethnicity were not reducible to class relations. These arguments about difference were an important precursor to the deconstructive poststructuralist and postmodernist arguments considered in this and the following chapter.

However, it was often through the combining of concerns about difference with poststructuralist ideas that *radically* deconstructive feminist, queer and postcolonial theoretical movements developed. Rejecting the focus on identity and emancipation, these approaches sought instead to challenge essentialist thinking about difference and identity, and deconstruct the binaries (male/female, hetero/homosexual, black/white and so on) that underpinned it. In doing so, they sought to reveal how essentialist ideas about difference and identity were involved with discursive power, and how difference and identity were intertwined. Poststructural feminism, for example, interrogated gender categories, and revealed the categories of male/female, man/woman, and masculine/feminine to be social and cultural constructions that were potentially unstable (see Beasley 2005). From this perspective, previous efforts to reveal the 'truth' about women's experience and identity – and to theorize the conditions of women's emancipation – were problematic, as they were grounded in modernist ideas of coherent gender subjectivity, essence and progress that were ultimately fictions. These fictions worked to make multiple identities invisible (for example, white, black and lesbian women's identities). They also disregarded the multiplicity of identity itself (for example, one could be black and identify as lesbian or not in different situations and at different times of one's life). Further, they ignored the differences 'within' identity itself – the splits, conflicts and incoherence that poststructuralists argue were at the centre of identity – and undermined how identity always implied an 'other' (its 'opposite'). Poststructuralist feminists sought to disrupt universal notions of 'woman' and 'man' and to challenge ideas about femininity and masculinity as essence. They sought instead to reveal how such ideas were social and linguistic constructions and, in doing so, aimed to make visible the relationship between gender, discourse and power.

Deconstruction with respect to sexuality also focused on destabilizing sexual categories (homosexuality/heterosexuality, perverse/normal and the like) and aimed to reveal the social norms and cultural values that underpinned them (see Seidman 1996). In doing so, they challenged the binaries that give sexual categories their meaning, to reveal their relationships with power. Following Lacan and Foucault, for example, they suggested that sexual identities were historical and linguistic constructions that were intimately bound up with power. From Foucault, for example, queer deconstruction focused on how sexual categories and identities were the products of disciplinary discourse. Sexuality, from this perspective, was bound up with governance and regulation. The idea of sexual liberation was problematic because there is no essential 'sexuality' or sexual identity to be freed. Similarly, postcolonial deconstruction sought to challenge and destabilize the universalizing claims of Western modes of thought and the homogenizing categories (white/ black, First World/Third World and the like) they promoted (see Young 2003). These categories, it was argued, erased the differences between black, ethnic minority, and Third World people, and undermined the difference within each of the categories. They promoted fictitious universalities and unities that were, in fact, implicated in power. Such fictions were bound up with power because they were part of the legacy of European imperialism, and reflected the dominance of Western ideas. The views of the world they promoted were Euro- and logo-centric constructions that represented imperialist interests.

Taken together, these ideas about *radical* difference represented submovements that fed into the broader deconstructive movement with respect to theorizing modernity and modernist sociology. Drawing from the combined influences of the theory and sociology of difference and poststructuralism, they suggested that the modernist categories developed for social analysis – relating to gender, sexuality, 'race' and ethnicity and the like – were problematic, as were modernist frames from which they were generated. In shifting attention to how these categories and frames were constructions that privileged dominant interests over others, they pointed to how modernist social analysis left untouched the more subtle workings of power – especially with respect to language, discourse and identity. Further, they questioned the basis of belief in the idea that critical theory and sociology could produce enlightened knowledge that would facilitate emancipation. As identities were fictions, the idea of their emancipation was misguided. While some argued that the claiming of essentialist identities could be strategically useful – politically and subjectively – the idea that political and social movements based on identity could replace, or combine with, class actors as the radical agents of change (as some difference and social movement theory had implied) was based on misplaced faith in modernist ideas about liberation and political progress (see Hall 1996).

Poststructuralism, radical difference and sociology

The poststructuralist and radical difference arguments considered so far in this chapter raise crucial questions about the sociological project. These arguments radically disrupted the claims that were previously made for the sociological project derived from the founding propositions about modernity and the social (see Chapter 2). These propositions were, in their various ways, founded on ways of thinking that suggested the modern and social to be tangible and knowable. In contrast, poststructuralist and radical difference theorists implied that the social – if it could be said to exist – was more fragmented and less easily grasped. All knowledge claims should, from the latter perspective, be viewed with scepticism. Rather than simply expressing knowledge, the nature of language and discourse means that all knowledge claims are caught up in the flow of power. This implies acknowledging how all knowledge is contingent, as what is held to be true today may be revealed tomorrow as the play of discourse and knowledge-power. This does not pose fatal problems for the kind of deconstructive theoretical and analytical strategies that poststructuralism and radical difference promote. Rather, it entails viewing all knowledge (including expert, sociological and everyday life knowledge) as narratives or a text that can be deconstructed. The claims made on the basis of this are, of course, contingent and always open to contestation. There are, however, potentially fatal implications for the kind of sociological theory and empirical research that would claim unproblematic access to the social. In discussing the implications of poststructuralism (and postmodernism) for research Alvesson and Skoldberg (2000) quote Clifford's arguments about ethnography:

> The maker . . . of ethnographic texts cannot avoid expressing tropes, figures and allegories that select and impose meaning as they translate it. In this view, more Nietzschean than realist or hermeneutic, all constructed truths are made possible by power 'lies' of exclusion and rhetoric. Even the best ethnographic texts

– serious true fictions – are systems, or economies of truth. Power and history work through them, in ways their authors cannot fully control.

(Clifford, quoted in Alvesson and Skoldberg 2000: 170)

As Alvesson and Skoldberg note, Clifford's arguments apply also to the social sciences more broadly, including sociology. They also note Clifford's argument about four conditions that prevent ethnography (and by implication sociology) from depicting 'social phenomena' (Alvesson and Skoldberg 2000: 170–1). First, ethnographic and social analysis is always a matter of literary work 'contingent upon linguistic tools that portray "reality"'. Second, ethnographic and sociological writings cannot be objective, as they are determined contextually, rhetorically, institutionally, politically and historically. Third, they cannot represent the multiple voices that make up cultures. Fourth, cultures are continually changing so cannot be grasped once and for all. A key question arises: if the social cannot be known and cannot be depicted, should sociology be reconceived or abandoned? If it is to be reconceived, what should its reconstructed project be? Also, how should sociological analysis proceed? The short answer, from the deconstructive position, is that sociology must acknowledge that it is involved in narrative production, and that it is in the business of producing contingent knowledge that is open to contestation and, at best, can provide the basis for diverse interpretations of the social world. This moves sociology a long way away for the 'scientistic' aspirations it may once have had, but also challenges interpretivist approaches that assume knowing and knowable actors. Rather, sociologists must more radically recognize that they are involved in story productions. There are notable implications for the audience of sociological research, as Alvesson and Skoldberg point out, citing Brown:

The distinction between fact and fiction thus becomes blurred. An understanding of scientific texts as historical constructions means that claims to 'truth' are perceived as rhetorical expressions, which can be constantly opened up to alternative interpretations. This in turn means the reader becomes important. The text becomes an expression less of its own inherent character than that of the predispositions and creativity with which the reader approaches it.

(Alvesson and Skoldberg 2000: 171)

Poststructuralism and radical difference perspectives have notable implications for the producers of sociology. First, they imply that sociologists must relinquish their claims to any straightforward and unproblematic social knowledge, and become instead reflective sociological storytellers. Second, they suggest that ideas of objectivity and pure data (that were previously the bedrock of sociology) 'emerge as tantamount to mystification – or instances of naivety' (Alvesson and Skoldberg 2000: 171). Third, they suggest that sociologists need to incorporate within their narratives 'multiple voices, pluralism, multiple reality and ambiguity' (Alvesson and Skoldberg 2000: 171). While there is no one poststructuralist or radical difference model for what this actually means in practice, these arguments link closely with other deconstructive arguments about reflexive research methodologies.

Reflexive methodology and sociological practice

Debates about reflexive methodologies can be insightful with respect to the implications of poststructuralist and radical difference arguments for sociological practice. The debates considered in this section have been mostly framed in terms of empirical research, but are relevant to sociology more broadly. Like the perspectives considered in the previous section they also emphasize the view of the sociological researcher as a story producer. There are three broad positions with respect to reflexive methodology. First, there are constructive arguments about reflexive methodology and research methods whose primary objective is to produce 'better' knowledge than unreflective approaches. Second, more akin to (and sometimes influenced by) poststructuralist ideas, there are deconstructivist arguments for dismantling modernist methodologies on the basis of their involvements with power. Third, there are reconstructive approaches that deconstruct methodologies to address power, but aim for a reconstructed reflexive methodology that ultimately has faith in its claims to knowledge (for example, on the basis of feminist epistemology).

Reflexive methodology generally emphasizes the need for critical self-reflection on behalf of social researchers or analysts with respect the production of the sociological narrative, to acknowledge how their social, cultural and disciplinary positioning has shaped the narrative. It also promotes recognition of how such positioning combines with the contexts of research to shape knowledge on any given topic (Steier 1991). Deconstructive and reconstructive approaches to reflexive methodology acknowledge that academic narratives exist in the flow of power. From the reconstructivist perspective, feminist, sexualities and 'race' and ethnicity researchers have long emphasized that mainstream modernist methodologies worked to reproduce existing power relationships. The challenge, from this perspective, is to develop alternative research and sociological strategies that would incorporate an awareness of knowledge production as political practice. As Ramazanoglu (1992) remarked with regard to feminist methodology:

> Feminist methodologies are . . . new ways of knowing and of seeking 'truths', but they are also forms of political commitment to the empowerment of women . . . There is no alternative to political commitment in feminist or any other ways of knowing. Since knowing is a political process, so knowledge is intrinsically political . . . Other ways of knowing . . . are committed to other political goals.
>
> (Ramazanoglu 1992: 210)

Reflexive methodology argues that sociological projects involve complex sets of relationships and negotiations. Throughout the processes that constitute these projects, from the formulation of the topic to its final presentation, researchers negotiate with themselves and others the 'why', 'what', and 'how' of the project. It is through such interactions that the possibilities and limitations of the projects are set – as they impact on decisions regarding what constitutes interesting or appropriate aims, strategies, methods and narratives. In exploring this, some writers proposed seeing academic research as a form of story production that entailed story actions such as multiple 'conversations' and 'dialogues'. In doing so, they aimed to open up new possibilities of accounting for the diverse influences that shape the research (Mishler 1986; Steier 1991; Schrijvers 1991). Some reconstructive approaches to reflexive methodology also argued that the notion of a 'dialogical ideal' could help envision radical methodologies that could be aligned to 'political' or emancipatory projects, and that could challenge existing power relationships with respect to how social knowledge tends to be produced. Drawing from modern anthropology, Schrijvers (1991: 169) suggested that the notions of *dialogical* and *reflexive* research are interchangeable to a certain degree. In dealing with questions of power in terms of the researcher/researched relationship, Schrijvers uses the term 'dialogical' to refer to:

45

a specific, reciprocal manner of exchange and communication during research interaction, between the researcher and the subjects of research. It indicates a continuing process of actual communication between people who respect and value each other's contribution and in that regard are equals in their dialogical relationship. Throughout this communication the participants influence each other's points of view. This can lead to the transformation of the initial concepts and conceptions of the researcher and other participants.

(Schrijvers 1991: 169–70)

Schrijvers (1991: 170) distinguishes five aspects which characterize the dialogical ideal in research: *dynamic*, where the research focuses on change, and the results reflect the dynamics of life; *exchange*, where the terms 'researcher' and 'researched' lose their distinctive meanings; *ideal of egalitarian relations*, where researcher and research subjects become more acutely aware of power inequalities that separate them; *shared objectives*, where the objectives and priorities of research are determined by all participants; and *shared defining-power*, where all participants are empowered to determine the course and outcome of the research. Dialogical communication, it is suggested in this account, is necessary to reduce inequality in the research context. Further, the researcher both implicitly and explicitly acknowledges that s/he is actively engaged in various sets of power relations and, to some extent, a political endeavour: 'action-research involves activists who are struggling against existing power inequalities' (Schrijvers 1991: 172–3). There is a notable resonance between the model for reflexive methodology outlined here and the modernist ideas of 'pure' communication or ideal speech that theorists such as Habermas promoted. Like poststructuralist rejections of Habermas's arguments (see earlier discussion), deconstructive approaches to reflexive methodology would view the ideal dialogue that Schrijvers promotes as impossible. They would point out that it is the dominant party (the researcher) who is likely to set the terms of the dialogue in the first place, and whose version of events carries more political weight.

Deconstructive approaches to reflexivity more forcibly argue that ethnographers and sociologists construct the realities of the world they study and narrate. They point out that if, as Foucault argued, expert narratives exist in the flow of power, so do sociological accounts. While sociologists may not *aim* to engage in questions of power, in the production of sociological accounts (theoretical and empirical) they are explicitly and/or implicitly asserting, accepting or contesting what is rational, sane and true. In this sense, they are involved in the production (or reproduction) of 'truths', and in the production (or reproduction) of what Foucault (1979a) terms 'knowledge-power'. Deconstructive approaches to reflexive methodology adopt such arguments to acknowledge the constructed and contingent nature of claims to knowledge (Steier 1991). In attempting to account for their own involvements in the story actions that make up social knowledge, some argue the value of a different view of 'conversations' and 'dialogue' to the one that Schrijvers proposed. As Steier suggested:

> taking reflexivity seriously . . . is marked by a concern for recognizing that constructing is a social process, rooted in language, not located inside one's head . . . It is precisely through such an orientation to language that the self to whom our reflexivity refers is most clearly a social self, who become 'that' self precisely through participation with others, and allows research to become understood as a conversation (or, rather, several).
>
> (Steier 1991: 5–6)

From Steier's (1991) perspective, it was possible to recognize that multiple conversations are involved in constructing our sociological narratives that are, in effect, multiple realities – with no one being 'the real conversation'. Implicit in this was an acknowledgement that the writing and presentation of academic work involved editing in some realities and editing out others. The narratives that were eventually told never exhausted the wide variety of conversations that could have been focused on. Rarely did social analysts and researchers present, or were they aware of, the multiple realities that could be presented. For Steier (1991), the reflexive approach allowed contradictions and paradoxes to appear.

If accepted, the implications of poststructuralist and radical difference arguments for understanding and doing sociology are profound, as they are for 'undoing' modernist sociological practice. From this viewpoint the reflexive sociologist should allow the contradictions and paradoxes to be visible in the sociological narrative, and recognize and attempt to incorporate multiplicity, pluralism and ambiguity. However, as the deconstructive approaches to reflexive methodology emphasize, this means that the sociological story has no certain meaning and is open to wide and diverse interpretations. Despite the intentions and reflexivity of the sociologist, their involvement in narrative construction means they have no choice but to draw on the conventions of language and discourse. This, in turn, means their knowledge claims can never be neutral. It is on the basis of this kind of argument that sociological critics point to the relativism, pessimism and political complacency of post-structuralist, radical difference and radically reflexive conceptions of knowledge, and resist the deconstructive turn they promote.

Conclusion

This chapter has focused on poststructural, radical difference and reflexive methodology arguments that have contributed to the deconstructive turn with respect to modernity and modernist sociology. Combined, these movements have had radical implications for the founding models, frames and conceptions of modernity and the modern, and for envisioning a 'post' modernist sociology. Their arguments and claims are worthy of detailed and explicit consideration for a number of reasons. First, they raise fundamental challenges to theories and sociological understandings – past and present – of social, cultural, political and subjective life that are framed in terms of overarching and universal processes. In doing so, they generate critiques of universalizing arguments about modern social life. Second, they generate the themes, ideas and frames that reconstructivist theories of modernity and sociology are often strongly *against* (see Chapter 5). Poststructuralist, radical difference and reflexive methodological arguments have prompted critical and reflexive questioning about *what* sociology is or should be, and what and/or who is it for. They are thus implicated in promoting a critically reflexive orientation within sociology with respect to its own narratives and normative visions. Poststructuralist, radical difference and radical reflexive methodological arguments, in their different ways, promoted reflection on how sociological knowledge is potentially implicated in the workings of power.

Whilst poststructuralist and postmodernist critiques are often discussed as if they are one and the same thing, the following chapter suggests that arguments about postmodernity are worthy of exploration in detail in their own right, because they include diverse implications for how we comprehend social change; its implications for social, cultural, political and subjective life; and its implications for sociology. As with the arguments considered in this chapter, postmodernist ideas also focus on the blurring of the boundaries between self/other, public/private, personal/political and so on. They do so in a number of different ways that have distinct implications for understanding modernity, post-modernity and sociology. They also emphasize discontinuity, fragmentation, contingency and the like. But again, there is no one postmodern position on the implications of this for social life and sociology itself. Overall, however, they prompt sociologists to question how the ordered experience imagined in founding and critical theories of modernity underplay the complexity of contemporary social and cultural contexts. In emphasizing context, along with diversity and difference, they prompt the question of whose experience and interests are articulated and made visible and invisible in ordering narratives of modernity.

4

POSTMODERNITY AND THE CULTURAL TURN

Introduction

This chapter considers theories and arguments about postmodernity and their implications for conceptualizing contemporary social, cultural, political and subjective life. Postmodernist analytical strategies are often influenced by poststructuralist arguments, as considered in the previous chapter. They are associated with a rejection of modernist conceptualizations of the social, and emphasize instead culture, discourse and deconstruction. This chapter considers how theories about postmodernity and postmodern analytical strategies are, in fact, made up of a variety of conceptions and approaches that have different and distinct implications for envisioning the social and the sociological project.

The chapter begins by considering two accounts of the nature and implications of postmodernity. The first account, by Best and Kellner, argues the case for seeing the shift from modernity to postmodernity as an epochal one that has profound, but as yet unknown, consequences for all aspects of human life. From this perspective, contemporary developments in economic, social, cultural and political life are indicative of the demise of modernity as a distinctive historical era; and of the emergence of a postmodern one. This perspective argues that there is a related paradigm shift occurring with respect to knowledge that has profound implications for all academic and scientific disciplines, and that is influencing both deconstructivist and reconstructivist developments in social and cultural theory. The second account, by Charles Lemert, provides an account of postmodernity from a more sociological perspective. Lemert distinguishes between postmodernity and postmodern culture, and suggests how deconstructive (or postmodern) movements with respect to modernity and sociology can be conceptualized as a cultural turn in a way that does not entail abandoning the social. He distinguishes between three broad social theoretical approaches with respect to postmodernity: radical postmodernism, strategic postmodernism and radical modernism. This typology can be developed for considering the broad approaches that frame sociological engagements with the idea of postmodernity. To illuminate this, the chapter discusses Lyotard's arguments about contemporary incredulity towards meta-narratives and the atomization of the social, and Baudrillard's arguments about postmodernity as the hyper-reality or end of the social, as variations of radical postmodernist approaches. Following this, it looks at Bauman's arguments against the kind of sociology that Baudrillard's work promotes, and considers his strategic arguments for the sociological theory of postmodernity. The chapter also considers strategic arguments about 'social postmodernism' that attempt to reincorporate the social into postmodern theorizing. This lays the theoretical ground for consideration of key radical modernist arguments – in the form of reconstructivist approaches to modernity – in Chapter 5, whose implications for sociological understandings of social change and personal life are explored in depth in Chapters 6 to 9.

The postmodern turn

Best and Kellner (1997) propose that the kind of arguments considered in Chapter 3 should be viewed as part of more profound deconstructivist developments in theory, science and art that cut across disciplinary fields and boundaries. These developments, they argue, are part of a broader paradigm shift that is itself part of an epochal transition from modernity to postmodernity. If this is correct, it would imply the need to transform how we think theoretically in order to fully grasp and interpret the contemporary era, and it raises important challenges and questions for sociology more generally. Should the aim, for example, be to develop a postmodern sociology to comprehend and reflect the postmodern world? Or, should we distinguish between postmodern sociology and the sociology of postmodernity?

The idea of a postmodern world is in some ways consistent with the arguments about the demise of the modernist project that were discussed in Chapter 3. But while arguments about postmodernity often have their roots in disillusionment with theoretical fictions of modern progress and development, they also conjure up a powerful image of the disintegration of modern *society* itself that some poststructuralists would be cautious about. Sociologically, the idea of postmodern society can be understood in terms of processes of de-differentiation. As Dodd puts it:

the boundaries or distinctions created through social differentiation are blurred in post-modern society . . . the boundary
between high and low culture, reality and representation; politics, advertising, economic life and culture; production and
exchange; artificial and human intelligence or Western and
Eastern systems of belief.

(Dodd 1999: 131–2)

Poststructuralist ideas about fragmentation, together with the concept of
de-differentiation, as Dodd (1999: 132) points out, imply that it is no
longer possible to conceptualize society as the total or integrated system
as Marx and Durkheim did. The idea of fragmentation also challenges
Weberian ideas about the progress of instrumental rationality, and the
inevitable ascendancy of rational-bureaucratic organizations. While the
concept of postmodernity – or what some term 'postmodern society' – is
connected to poststructural concerns with fragmentation and sociological concerns with de-differentiation, it is also often used in a looser way
to talk about the destabilizing orientations of relentless socio-cultural
change, and its unfathomable and uncontrollable implications (economic, social, cultural, political and personal). This looser discourse of a
postmodern 'world' or 'condition' often appears to be especially pessimistic with respect to the possibility of human agency. What, if anything,
critics ask, does discourse about postmodernity offer in the way of a
vision or project for the future? What kind of sociology, culture and politics does it promote? In engaging with this debate it is important to take
note of Habermas's (1998) argument that no genealogy of postmodernity is neutral. But we might combine this point with the arguments for
reflexive sociology that were considered in Chapter 3, to suggest that
neither narratives of modernity nor postmodernity can simply be taken
at face value. In considering these narratives we need, rather, to be
attuned to the projects and interests they promote and challenge – intentionally or otherwise.

A postmodern paradigm?

Our contemporary situation . . . finds us between the modern
and the post modern, the old and the new, the traditional and
the contemporary, the global and the local, the universal and the
particular, and any number of other matrices. Such a complex
situation produces feelings of vertigo, anxiety, and panic, and

contemporary theory, art, politics and everyday life exhibit all of these symptoms.

(Best and Kellner 1997: 280)

In proposing the case for seeing the present in terms of a shift from modernity to postmodernity, Steven Best and Douglas Kellner (1997) conjure up a picture of the contemporary world that is all too familiar. They argue that the contemporary world is a 'highly conflicted' one that is marked by the unravelling of previously stable boundaries and social domains. Modern categories and experience related to gender, 'race' and class, they argue (1997: 263), are 'imploding into multicultural, consumer society', and inequalities and conflicts between and within groups are increasing. As evidence of increasing world crisis, they point to the growth of right-wing groups in Europe and North America, renewed fundamentalism worldwide and expanding global economic inequalities. Together with the demise of modern communist political blocs and the emergence of ever more sovereign states, there are inter-connected economic, environmental and energy crises and diminished possibilities for unified responses to them. The view that Best and Kellner offer (one-sided though it is) is one of global change *as* crisis. The world as characterized by them is one where all aspects of life are being reconfigured by dramatic developments and turmoil. We have entered uncharted territory between the modern and fully 'post' modern. They imply an epochal understanding of contemporary economic, social, cultural and political change that is at odds with other conceptions of the postmodern condition as an intensification of the processes associated with modernity (see Lyotard below). They imply the inevitability of a radical break with the past that will result from contemporary processes of change even if they admit that it is too early to predict what the fully 'post' modern will look like.

Taken together, Best and Kellner argue, a broad range of theories about postmodernity illustrate that contemporary societies are being reconfigured by new technologies, cultural forms and experiences that go hand in hand with economic, social and political transformations. These constitute 'a decisive rupture' with previously established ways of life and mark the end of the modern era. There is a double transformation taking place – the epochal one from modernity towards postmodernity, but also a transformation in social and cultural theory defined by a move towards a new paradigm for interpreting the world. Alongside the emergence of new technologies, new economic, social, cultural and political forms, and new identities and ways of living, there are related shifts in social and cultural theory (that are inclusive of poststructuralism but are not reducible to it). On the one hand, living between modernity and postmodernity means 'leaving behind the safe and secure moorings of the habitual and established' (1997: ix). On the other hand, living between modernities also requires letting go of our habitual and established ways of theorizing, and envisioning new modes of exploring and interpreting the world.

While there are numerous competing narratives of the postmodern, Best and Kellner suggest that there is also evidence that an emerging discourse of shared views and common features is consolidating into an emergent postmodern *paradigm* – albeit a highly contested one that is not yet dominant. In talking about a new paradigm they are, via Kuhn, referring to: 'a "constellation" of values, beliefs, and methodological assumptions, whether tacit or implicit, inscribed in a larger world view' (1997: xi). The postmodern paradigm, they argue, signifies shifts 'within virtually every contemporary theoretical discipline ... and the coalescing of these changes into a larger worldview that influences culture and society in general, as well as the values and practices of everyday life' (1997: xi). We can be sure we are witnessing a paradigm shift, they argue (1997: 255), by the quantity and nature of similar movements across different disciplines that challenge mechanistic and deterministic modes of thinking that underpinned modernist paradigms; and by the extent and depth to which postmodern ideas are reconfiguring established knowledge formations: 'It appears that the epistemological, metaphysical and ethical assumptions about the nature of the world are rapidly changing in all fields, creating new configuration of thought' (Best and Kellner 1997: 253).

Best and Kellner suggest that diverse debates and discourses about the postmodern, and the changes they posit or seek to resist, are themselves indicative of the realities of a paradigm shift. Many academic disciplines have entered periods of crisis that 'question the explanatory adequacy of the existing paradigm' (1997: 254). The transition to this new paradigm is a development 'whereby novelty rules and tacit assumptions, theories and techniques merge that are incommensurably different from what preceded' (1997: 254). The new paradigm, they note, suggests new research and raises new problems, but as it is in its early stages it is too soon to expect consensus about the nature of new knowledge (1997: 254).

In developing this argument, Best and Kellner (1997: 255–8) suggest four thematic similarities that cut across disciplines and break with modern concepts and themes. First there is the rejection of unities, totalities and universal schemes in favour 'difference plurality, fragmentation, and complexity'. This is often combined with an emphasis on the end of meta-narratives (such as those associated with theoretical or sociological 'grand' theories of capitalism, industrialism or instrumental rationality and so on). Second, there is a renunciation of closed structures, given meanings, and order in favour of 'play, indeterminacy, incompleteness, uncertainty, ambiguity, contingency and chaos' (reflected in social and cultural theory by the deconstruction of all kinds of essentialism and the rejection of historical determinism, given meanings of language or texts, and innate identities or subjectivities). Third, there is a rejection of realist and representational epistemologies and classical constructions of objectivity and truth, and an emphasis instead on 'perspectivism, anti-foundationalism, hermeneutics, intertextuality, simulation and relativism'. Fourth, there is an emphasis on transcending academic and scientific disciplinary boundaries. In social theory, for example, they argue that much of the best theorizing is transdisciplinary, citing the examples of the Frankfurt School, poststructuralism, cultural studies, feminism and so on. Indeed, they suggest, it is those academics and researchers who are stuck within the assumptions and paradigms of their discipline 'who are the regressive forces of the present'.

Despite the convergences on which they base their arguments about an emergent paradigm, Best and Kellner do acknowledge significant differences within this. In doing so, they distinguish between 'extreme' and more moderate theories (see 1997: 257–8). Extreme theories are those that not only deconstruct claims to truth, objectivity and given meaning, but that actively promote radical doubt, scepticism and relativism. Moderate theories include those that aim to reconstruct modern epistemological conceptions 'to provide new normative foundations for philosophy, social theory and critiques'. They describe reconstructive postmodern theorists in the following way: 'They temper scepticism with respect for mapping social structures, relations, and tendencies, attempting to develop theories adequate to conceptualize the developmental tendencies and emergent phenomena and trends of the present age' (Best and Kellner 1997: 258).

In suggesting the value of a tentative distinction between *deconstructive* and *reconstructive* postmodern theories, Best and Kellner argue that discourse about the postmodern should be viewed as contested ground between 'moderate and extreme postmodernists' (1997: 258). While these distinctions are useful as a way of pointing out that important differences *do* exist between postmodern theories, the distinction between 'moderate' and 'extreme' is an inadequate basis on which to evaluate theoretical and sociological arguments. Also, the deconstructive and reconstructive distinction undermines the concern with deconstructing modernist frames that *all* postmodern approaches share. Further, as Best and Kellner (1997: 260) acknowledge, there are other notable common elements in postmodern theorizing – not least the focus on the linguistic or discursive. Indeed, Best and Kellner are aware that it is postmodernists' *shared* concerns with deconstruction and discourse that has prompted the heightened reflexivity of contemporary theory: 'The linguistic turn . . . is the eruption into human consciousness of the perspectival, contextual, and contingent nature of all truth claims.'

While there are important distinctions to be made between different kinds of postmodern arguments, the bases on which Best and Keller suggest making these underplays how central deconstructive strategies are to all postmodern analyses. In the following sections of the chapter I consider Lemert's argument about more nuanced distinctions to be made between core contributions to debates about postmodernity, and the bases on which he suggests the core concepts in these debates can be clarified. Before this, however, it should be noted that while the distinction between deconstructive and reconstructive *postmodern* approaches has limited analytical value, the distinction between deconstructive and reconstructive approaches to theorizing modernity is a more analytically useful one. In this respect, this deconstructive/reconstructive frame is better suited to talking about the distinctions that exist between broadly postmodernist approaches (that tend to share some concern with deconstruction, and that are suspicious of theoretical unities, universalities and the like) and those contemporary approaches to modernity that self-consciously reject the concern with deconstruction and argue the case instead for theorizing new universalities and the like. Examples of the latter are considered in Chapter 5.

Postmodern distinctions: the cultural and the social

It is important, Charles Lemert (1997: xii) argues, to distinguish between postmodernism as a movement in culture and theory and postmodernity as something that is happening in the world. If postmodernism is about anything, Lemert (1997: xii) suggests, it concerns how the promises of the modern age fail to be convincing because, for the majority of people, there is no sound basis for believing that the world is improving. Social theoretical concerns with postmodernity concern a transforming world 'where real people live' (1997: xi). While postmodern is not necessarily the best name for it, Lemert argues, that 'something powerful, deep, and potentially far-reaching is going on [is] . . . beyond doubt' (1997: xi). The importance of the idea of postmodernity lies, therefore, in how it emphasizes that the modern world is changing:

> The cultural order that was founded in the colonizing sixteenth and seventeenth centuries, that achieved its grand political moment in the eighteenth, that revolutionized science and industry in the nineteenth, that perfected so many technologies in the twentieth is not what it once was.
>
> (Lemert 1997: 15)

If 'modernism' was the culture of the modern age (modernity), Lemert (1997: 21) points out, then postmodernism is about the breaking apart of modernism. The concern with postmodern*ism* is therefore a concern with culture. Social theory is increasingly concerned with postmodern-ism, not because the social is no longer important, but because *'culture is a particularly sensitive aspect of* [the] *social'* (emphasis added). Cultures, Lemert (1997: 21) argues, can be sensitive enough to indicate changes in the world (including its economic and political arrangements), especially where the changes destabilize modernity itself. This is important for understanding the relationship between the postmodern turn and what is often termed the 'cultural turn' in sociology. As Lemert's argument implies, the cultural turn does not necessarily mean – as some radical postmodernists propose, but modernist critics often fear that *all* post-modernists argue – that the social is no longer significant. Rather, it involves seeing the cultural as an aspect of the social. Lemert's definition of culture is insightful in this respect:

> the complex of *socially* produced values, rules, beliefs, litera-tures, arts, media, penal codes, laws, political ideas and other such diversions by which society, or any social group, represents its view of the world as its members (or at least the members in charge) believe it ought to be.
>
> (1997: 21, emphasis added)

Of postmodernity's cultural forms (or postmodernisms), Lemert notes, social theory itself is often the most contentious. Those who are most critical of postmodernism, he argues, tend to be most troubled by postmodern theories about social life. Postmodern social theories are often critiqued on the basis of their loose regard for sociological 'facts'. It is important, Lemert notes, to distinguish between a theory about the world and the facts related to world reality itself. Those engaging with social theory should first enquire into the nature of the world itself before accepting the theories about it, and postmodern theories should be evaluated against the 'facts' of the world. This may be near impossible, he acknowledges, as social theory often talks about things for which there is no factual proof. Also, as we have seen in Chapter 3, the idea that social knowledge can be articulated, presented and interpreted in any straightforward way is widely disputed. Nevertheless, Lemert suggests that there 'can be plausible social theories, even when the facts are not as robust as one might like, or one might think in the first place'. This argument resonates with those about reflexive sociology that were considered in Chapter 3, that suggest that sociology should be less preoccupied with the gold (but illusory) standard of objectivity and more with acknowledging that it is involved in the construction of narratives of social life that may be more or less convincing. In putting such narratives and arguments out into the world, and being explicit about why and how they were constructed, social theorists and sociologists become part of a broader dialogue about the social world and offer alternative interpretations of it. This implies, of course, that the audiences for sociology should be cautious about the stories that theorists and researchers narrate – especially because they continue to have the allure of authority that tends to be attached to academic knowledge.

We should be similarly cautious of arguments about postmodernity. Despite this, Lemert (1997: 35) points out that there are convincing arguments to be made about changes with respect to at least three of the fundamental features of the modern world. First, changes have taken place in the colonial system from which modernity's dominant states derived natural and labour resources. Second, there are changes in the organizational centres from which world politics and markets were overseen. Third, there are changes in 'the presumptive culture' (1997: 35) through which European–North American centres developed frames for justifying world history and order. The exact and long-term significance of these changes, Lemert argues in a similar way to Best and Kellner, cannot be known for certain. However, he suggests these changes are clearly destabilizing core structures of the modern world – 'structures that were built up . . . for nearly half a millennium'. In terms of post-modern culture and politics, Lemert notes that while the notions of a unified and universal world culture were part of the modernist ideal, they are now widely and actively resisted. New social movements (such as feminist, 'race' and ethnicity, and gay rights movements) and re-emerging ethnicities are now, he suggests, a primary source of social distinction. These developments combine with religious fundamental-isms to form a powerful body of opposition to the dominance of European–North American modernist cultures. Modernity's claim to 'be the universal culture of human progress', Lemert (1997: 37) argues, no longer has the legitimacy it once had. Coupled with this, he suggests, there are other notable points of correspondence between the 'actual' structure of the world and the main contentions of postmodern theories:

> Where the modern world was allegedly well organized along a linear history yielding straightforward meanings, the post-modern world is thought to be poorly organized in the absence of a clear, predictable historical future without which there are, at best, uncertain, playful and ironic meanings.
>
> (Lemert 1997: 36)

Like Best and Kellner, Lemert emphasizes that postmodernism in its social theoretical form is comprised of different orientations, and there are three different approaches in postmodern theory that he distin-guishes. The first, radical postmodernism, considers modernity to be exhausted, and sometimes characterizes the present as hyper-real. The second, strategic postmodernism, is defined by openness to seeing the world as transformed. The third, radical modernism, acknowledges change but refuses to see this as the end of modernity. Radical post-modernism includes the work of Lyotard and Baudrillard, the former because of his defining of the postmodern condition as incredulity towards meta-narratives and his concern with the fragmentation of the social, and the latter because of his position as the high priest of post-modern sociology who argues the end of the social. Strategic postmod-ernism agrees with aspects of radical postmodernist and radical modernist positions, and will be discussed in the following sections by focusing on Bauman's work. Bauman argues against postmodern sociology and for a sociological theory of postmodernity. Radical modernism, Lemert argues, like postmodernism, wages war on totality, and under this heading he includes the work of Habermas, Giddens and

Bourdieu. Giddens' and Beck's radical modernist ideas will be considered in Chapter 5.

Postmodern differences

Radical postmodernism

Radical postmodernist positions should not be confused with the argument that postmodernity is a new epoch. Jean-François Lyotard, for example, sees the postmodern condition as the exhaustion of modernity as a project and does not envision a postmodern society as such. His contribution to the debate about postmodernity came to the fore through his work in *The Postmodern Condition: A Report on Knowledge*, whose argument is summarized in the statement: 'Simplifying to the extreme, I define *postmodernity* as incredulity toward meta-narratives' (1984: xxiv, original emphasis). This work was a discussion of scientific paradigms that focused on the problems of legitimating knowledge in technologically advanced societies. Lyotard used the term 'postmodern' to address this problem, and in doing so aligned himself with critics who use the term to refer to 'the state of our culture following the transformations which, since the end of the nineteenth century, have altered the game rules for science, literature, and the arts' (1984: xxiii). Adopting the linguistic or discursive approach common to postmodernists, Lyotard conceptualized contemporary transformations with respect to the status of knowledge as narrative crises. He noted how science – with its claims to objective truth based on the rational pursuit of knowledge – has historically been in conflict with narratives, and how it legitimated itself by defining itself *against* stories and myths. Modernist critical theory and sociology, Lyotard implied, legitimated itself by invoking meta-discourses and grand narratives: 'the dialectics of the Spirit, the hermeneutics of meaning, the emancipation of the rational or working subject, or the creation of wealth' (1984: xxiii). In other words, science (including critical theory and sociology) has historically legitimated itself by claims to be the bearer of truth and emancipation, and distinguished itself from other narratives by invoking principles derived from Enlightenment thinking. He argued:

> For example, the rule of consensus between the sender and addressee of a statement with truth-value is deemed acceptable if it is cast in terms of a possible unanimity between rational

minds: this is the Enlightenment narrative, in which the hero of knowledge works toward a good ethico-political end – universal peace. As can be seen from this example, if a meta-narrative implying a philosophy of history is used to legitimate knowledge, questions are raised concerning the validity of the institutions governing the social bond: these must be legitimated as well. Thus justice is consigned to the grand narrative in the same way as truth.

(Lyotard 1984: xxiv)

The postmodern condition, as incredulity towards meta-narratives, challenges modernist knowledge claims as it reveals these to be powerful fictions. This means that science (including critical theory and sociology) must therefore downgrade its claims, and acknowledge its part in language games. The demise of grand narratives (for example, any over-arching 'structural' or 'systems' narrative about social, cultural and political processes) and meta-discourses that legitimate knowledge (the ideas about knowledge as the basis for truth and progress, on which grand narratives are founded) is partly a product of scientific scepticism turned in on itself. But it is mostly a consequence of the crisis in the universal claims of metaphysical philosophy (1984: xxiv). The narratives on which claims to knowledge were based have begun to fragment:

Thus the society of the future falls less within the province of a Newtonian anthropology (such as structuralism or systems theory) than a pragmatics of language particles. There are many different language games – a heterogeneity of elements. They only give rise to institutions in patches – local determinism.

(1984: xxiv)

How, after the demise of meta-narratives, Lyotard asks, can knowledge be legitimated? On the one hand (1984: xxv), the primary criteria for evaluating contemporary modes of knowledge production is performativity – the logic of maximum performance: a technological criteria that concerns efficiency and productivity, but does not provide any basis for evaluating what is true or just. On the other hand, neither can legitimacy be grounded in the consensus that Habermas's theory of communicative reason promotes (see Chapter 3). Unlike Habermas's emphasis on ideal speech situations as a route to agreeing universal values, Lyotard argues that 'to speak is to fight, in the sense of playing' (1984: 10). The

61

consensus that Habermas envisions is misguided. The breaking up of meta-narratives and grand knowledge claims means that we must recognize the diversity of knowledges and diverse ways of knowing. These can be conceived as diverse language games which demolish the aspirations to universal values based on consensus through dialogue:

> Such consensus does violence to the heterogeneity of language games. And invention is always born of dissension. Postmodern knowledge is not simply a tool of the authorities; it refines our sensitivity to differences and reinforces our ability to tolerate the incommensurable. Its principle is not the expert's homology, but the inventor's paralogy.

Lyotard conceptualizes the social bond as comprised of 'language moves'. Several developments combine to promote the breaking up of the social into smaller configurations of 'flexible networks of language games' (1984: 18). These include the factors already discussed (the end of meta-narratives, technological developments and the concern with performativity), but also the resurgence of liberal capitalism and the demise of a communist alternative. But this fragmentation should not be confused with arguments about the disintegration of the social bond into 'a mass of individual atoms'; rather social bonds are observable in smaller configurations of language games. Lyotard is arguing against theories like Habermas's that promote a vision of total systems. Totalities have historically been inseparable from terror and incompatible with social justice. For Lyotard, the answer is to 'wage a war on totality; let us be witness to the unrepresentable; let us activate the differences' (1984: 82).

In contrast to Lyotard's concern with the breaking up of the social, Jean Baudrillard's radical postmodernism is often associated with a more pessimistic kind of theorizing that suggests the end of the social. Baudrillard is best known for his argument that postmodernity is a post-social world of hyper-reality. From this perspective, postmodernity implies a world dominated by the images and signs produced by the electronic mass media. The realities of modern social life have been superseded by the saturation of electronically generated images and signs. The idea of social reality is becoming redundant because 'simulation' dominates in cultural life and replaces social life. Images and signs produced by the electronic media relate only to other images and signs, and their relationship to the 'real' objects has dissolved. Like Lyotard, Baudrillard

argues that the meta-narratives derived from Enlightenment philoso
and invoked by modernist theory (Marxian and the like), no longer f
an adequate basis for knowledge and critique. In the era of hyper-rea
sociology must acknowledge that it is impossible to distinguish between
the virtual and the real (see also Chapter 6). Simulation has radical
effects in emptying social of its content and emptying modern categories
of their meaning.

While Lyon (1999) cites Alain Touraine as admitting that Baudrillard
is honest about the loss of social references, Baudrillard's sociological
critics more often express dismay at how detached his analysis is from
what they argue to be very real – and often very harsh – social realities
(see Bauman below). Lyon (1999: 22) argues that Baudrillard's position
can be summarized thus: 'the social has disappeared in the cracks
between instrumentality (corporations, governments, working in markets) and culture (meaning is just subjective, unshareable)'. This decline
of the social goes hand in hand with the dominance of the symbolic
order, where signification – not communication – is the key issue. The
social, according to Baudrillard, is constructed by the mass media in
their own image, robbing it of any authenticity and neutralizing social
relations (Baudrillard, cited in Delanty 1999: 111). Delanty points out
the consequences of the argument that the social has no substance of its
own. Social transformation, he notes, therefore becomes a meaningless
idea, as there can only be different kinds of simulation. Increased information and communication does not generate more socialization but
promotes the disappearance of the social, and its survival in a merely
simulated form means that an adequate theory of social change is impossible (1999: 112).

Postmodernity and sociological strategy

In Baudrillard's hyper-reality, Zygmunt Bauman (1992a: 151) suggests,
claims to truth are not only deconstructed, but 'made irrelevant'. Like
other commentators, Bauman argues that Baudrillard's analysis is deeply
pessimistic, because simulation dominates and ultimately cannot be
opposed. Bauman (1992a: 151) argues that Baudrillard's position
reduces human agency to 'the bovine immobility of the masses' which
uncritically consumes the signs and images produced by the electronic
media. He points out that, for many people, real life is far from simulation, as reality 'remains what it used to be: tough, solid, resistant
and harsh' (1992a: 155). Like many other critics, Bauman is critical of

Baudrillard's approach to theorizing that itself adopts a postmodern style – including hyperbole, irony and contradiction. In contrast to this, he proposes an altogether different agenda for the sociological theory of postmodernity. Before discussing this, however, it should be noted that Bauman in his most recent work has shifted away from using the vocabulary of postmodernity. Nowadays he talks about 'liquid modernity' for reasons that will be considered in Chapter 5. Despite this, many of his arguments about liquid modernity are consistent with those he developed in relation to the sociological theory of postmodernity.

Prior to his later focus on liquid modernity, Bauman (1992a: 187) argued that the term postmodernity accurately conveyed the defining elements of 'the social condition that emerged throughout the affluent countries of Europe and of European descent in the course of the twentieth century and took its shape in the latter part of that century'. Postmodernity, he argued (1992a: 187), was an appropriate term as it pointed to continuity and discontinuity as two sides of the 'intricate relationship between the present social condition and the formation that preceded and gestated it'. 'Modernity' should be understood with respect to the foundational models of society, and the social condition of the modern they proposed (as considered in Chapter 2). Postmodernity, in contrast, talked to the continuing presence of the modern, but also to how certain key characteristics that were associated with it were now absent. Principally, while modernity disembedded from tradition it more or less fully re-embedded through new social forms. Postmodernity, on the other hand, disembeds from modern forms but without fully re-embedding. Also, postmodernity, Bauman argued, could be interpreted as modernity that was more or less fully developed. It was modernity that was aware of and acknowledged its own unintended consequences. Postmodernity, from this view, was modernity recognizing and conscious of itself. Modernity, Bauman suggests, sought order, commitment, universality and homogeneity. In doing so, it viewed difference, contingency, ambivalence and uncertainty with suspicion, and as something to be rectified. Postmodernity, in contrast, is the recognition – or institutionalization – of diversity, uncertainty and ambivalence. In this respect, the postmodern condition is modernity freed from its false envisioning of itself, and is a new social condition marked by the explicit recognition, acknowledgement and institutionalization of the characteristics modernity sought to eradicate or sequester.

For Bauman (1992a: 188), the differences between modern society and the postmodern condition were of sufficient import to necessitate a distinctive sociological theory of postmodernity. This would involve a departure from inherited modern categories, conceptions and models of society and the social. It would ultimately involve developing new ways of conceiving the world and a new vocabulary for doing so. The foundational models of modernity, Bauman noted, shared a concern with progress. Despite their differences (as outlined in Chapter 2) they shared the view of modernity as movement with a direction. This principle, Bauman suggested, did not hold in light of postmodern experience: 'the master metaphor of progress with a pointer is redundant'. Crucially, Bauman (1992a: 188) argued that it was mistaken to view postmodernity as a temporary departure from or crisis of 'normal' modernity. Rather, it was 'a self-producing pragmatically sustainable and logically self-contained social condition defined by distinctive features of its own' (1992a: 188). Bauman was adamant that the adequate theory of postmodernity could not simply be a reworked theory of modernity that focused on modernity's losses. Rather, it needed to be forged in a new conceptual space, with a focus on postmodern issues. Further, the distance between new concepts, ideas and concerns and those promoted by discourses of modernity would be one basis on which to judge the insights it generated. In arguing for a sociological theory of postmodernity, Bauman implies that while we might focus on how the social is being reconfigured, we should not wholly abandon the idea of the relevance of the social as does Baudrillard. This is a theme that is also addressed by other postmodern theorists who wish to reintegrate the social.

Reintegrating the social

Postmodernist theories have prompted sociology's critical reflection on itself. Despite this, many sociological critics note the rarity of efforts made by postmodernist theorists themselves to explicitly and critically reflect on the problems of the cultural, linguistic or discursive emphases they promote. In this section I consider briefly one critical account of postmodernism from 'within' theoretical postmodernism that attempts to revision postmodernists' relationship to the social. This account is noteworthy because it is indicative, some argue, of a movement towards acknowledging that postmodernism's own energies have become exhausted (see Delanty 1999), and that the postmodern project of deconstruction is being replaced with a reconstructivist orientation in many disciplines. While reconstructivist narratives of modernity are considered in Chapter 5, the narrative considered here is more properly a reconstructivist move *within* postmodern theorizing itself.

Linda Nicholson and Steven Seidman (1995) argue that there are many stories of postmodernism that could be told. Some narratives emphasize the importance of 'changes in systems of production, technology, and information systems', while others 'underscore the importance of deterritorialization or globalization' (1995: 7). They suggest that a narrative could also be told of how the encounters of new social movements and Marxism and liberal Enlightenment traditions were a crucial axis on which postmodern theories developed. From this latter perspective, Nicholson and Seidman note how their own commitments to postmodern theorizing were grounded in a conviction that postmodern theory had generated resources for rethinking social theory and politics. Despite this, they recognize that postmodernism has also had its problems, not least, they suggest, because the linguistic and discursive emphasis associated with it meant that postmodernism (and poststructuralism) became associated with a critical approach to textual analysis (1995: 8):

> At times, the social was collapsed into the textual, and critique often meant 'deconstructing' texts or exposing the instability of those foundational categories and binaries which structured texts and which were said to be the ideological carriers of meaning.
>
> (Nicholson and Seidman 1995: 8)

While recognizing deconstruction as an important strategy for politicizing language and knowledge, Nicholson and Seidman suggest that the 'textualizing' turn of the postmodern also meant that issues that should be of central importance to social theorizing were sometimes neglected. The study of institutions, social class, political organizations, economic processes and social movements especially, they argued, often remained in the hands of Marxist and other modernist theorists (Nicholson and Seidman 1995: 8). Because of this, they suggest, there was a separation of the 'postmodern' and the 'social' that impoverished theories of both postmodernity and the social. The implications of this separation, they argue, are illuminated by postmodernist engagements with new social movements. Such engagements were often based on critiquing how that latter essentialized or naturalized identity categories (such as woman, homosexual, black and so on), and aimed instead to demonstrate how these were historical and cultural products (see discussions of radical difference theories in Chapter 3). These endeavours often lost sight of the social:

> By focussing on what was wrong in the understanding of specific categories of identity, our attention remained fixed on the individual categories themselves. We were paying little attention to the ways in which the genealogies we and others were constructing intertwined with each other. Many of us had abandoned broader, systematic, and integrating perspectives on social processes and dynamics.
>
> (Nicholson and Seidman 1995: 9)

In short, Nicholson and Seidman (1995: 8) argue that postmodern critique was often too narrowly focused on knowledge and representation without attending to their social contexts. Coupled with this, they echo the arguments of critics of theoretical postmodernism by suggesting that one of the reasons for the turn away from the social was the sustained 'negative and critical' orientation of postmodern theorizing. The impetus to avoid totalizing and essentializing analyses, they argue, made the analysis of the interrelation of social patterns a difficult one. The critics of theoretical postmodernism, they acknowledge, viewed this as indicative of analytical and political weakness. While postmodernism was clear about what it was against, it had difficulties articulating what it was for: 'After all, was it not impossible to generate strong political [and intellectual] movements, while also deconstructing the categories such movements were based on?' (1995: 9).

Nicholson and Seidman argue that it is now important for postmodern thinkers to correct their previous neglect of the social by focusing on institutions as well as texts: 'to think about the interrelations of social patterns without being essentializing or totalizing, and to create constructive as well as deconstructive analysis of the social' (1995: 9). It is crucial, they suggest, to begin a process of imagining what postmodern *social* analysis could look like, and how postmodern agency could be conceptualized. They argue that this is a difficult but not impossible task, as postmodernism 'as a way of thinking about knowledge, self, society and politics has its roots in the struggles of social life that have been at the centre of many Western societies in the past decades' (1995: 34). For this perspective, it is important to advocate a certain *kind* of postmodern perspective: one that is perhaps more conducive to sociological incorporation. This would seek to acknowledge and over-come the limits of poststructuralist and postmodernist thinking (as considered in this and the previous chapter) whilst also acknowledging its importance in pushing for critical reflexivity with respect to social knowledge. The aim therefore is for an analytical strategy that integrates deconstruction while incorporating 'some of the analytically synthe-sizing and expansive hopes of the modernist tradition of social theo-rizing' (1995: 53).

Conclusion

Postmodern theorizing encompasses diverse approaches to social and cultural thinking. Best and Kellner argue that we can broadly distinguish between more *deconstructive* and *reconstructive* approaches, and Lemert distinguishes between radical and strategic postmodernist and radical modernist approaches. Coupled with this, Bauman suggests the need to distinguish between postmodernist theory and the sociological theory of postmodernity. Nicholson and Seidman further suggest the need to distinguish between the kinds of theories of postmodernity that reject the social and those that attempt to incorporate it. The possible distinctions between postmodern theories should be kept in mind when engaging in what tend to be overly dichotomized debates about moder-nity and postmodernity, and the modern and postmodern in sociology. As will become clear in the following chapter, while reconstructive theo-ries of modernity are often constructed *against* the dominating themes and orientations of postmodern theorizing, there are also important commonalities in terms of the social and cultural changes – and the implications of these – they are concerned with.

5

LATE MODERNITY AND THE REFLEXIVE TURN

Introduction

The postmodern challenge, at least in it post-structural form, now no longer sets the terms for debate, for its radical claims have been more or less accepted, having been to an extent realised in social practice today . . . In a way we are all now postmodernists . . . Postmodernism is exhausted because its work has been done . . . recognising heterogeneity and differ- ence in homogeneity and unitarian concepts; fragmenting oppressive subjectivities; dissolving the power of identity and ideology and self-legitimating doctrines of knowledge.

(Delanty 1999: 181)

Since the early 1990s the sociological interest in modernity has been reinvigorated, partly due to new confidence in radical modernist theo- rizing that rejects poststructuralist, radical difference and postmodernist arguments. The work of Anthony Giddens and Ulrich Beck has been especially influential in shaping new interest in what is variously charac- terized as 'reflexive', 'late', 'advanced', 'second', or 'global' modernity – which is sometimes discussed as risk society or reflexive modernization (see Beck 1992, 1999a, 1999b; Beck, Giddens and Lash 1994; Giddens 1990, 1991, 1992, 1999). Key concerns in the new theory of modernity overlap with postmodernist ones about living with uncertainty and contingency, and moving beyond the binaries that have hitherto framed social thought (such as structure/agency, domination/freedom and so on). However, the new theory of modernity rejects the idea of a post- modern era or condition. It argues instead that the current period of modernity (that will be discussed mostly as 'late' or 'reflexive' modernity in this chapter) is distinguished by the reconfiguration of modernity's institutions and its social, cultural and political forms through processes associated with globalization, detraditionalization and individualization. Poststructuralist and postmodernist analytical approaches, as discussed in Chapters 3 and 4, were often accused of ignoring the social in favour of the cultural, being over-preoccupied with fragmentation and deconstruction, and promoting theoretical and political pessimism. In contrast, the new sociology of modernity tends to be concerned with radical social developments; the interconnected reconfiguring of the global and the local; the mutual shaping of the institutional and the personal; the emergence of new universalizing tendencies and commonalities in experience; and agency and politics in 'post-emancipatory' settings. Indeed, some commentators argue that these new theories of modernity, and especially that of Giddens, have reintroduced the theme of agency in a particularly powerful way through theorizing the heightened reflexivity (or self-awareness) of the current period of modernity.

The major impact of theories of late or reflexive modernity in contemporary social theory – and sociology more generally – warrants that serious attention be paid to their arguments and implications. The radical implications of their understandings of global and institutional change for conceptualizing power and agency will be considered in depth in the following chapters, especially with respect to personal life. There is a powerful emphasis in this work on the implications of the demise of tradition and individualization for social, cultural and political life, and the following chapters explore in depth these implications via discussion of the subjective and the personal. Theories of late or reflexive modernity suggest that a diversity of uncharted 'sub-political' and 'life-political' endeavours are taking place, which will potentially redefine society in the twenty-first century. Some sociologists have drawn on these to argue that there is 'a radical, pluralistic, democratic, contingent, participatory politics of human life and difference in the making' (Plummer 1994). The following chapters will ask if the analyses of new political forms that emerge in discussions of reflexive personal lives in late modernity convincingly warrant a shift to the kind of 'post-emancipatory' theory and sociology that new theories of modernity promote. Other questions will also be asked, including: Do these theories adequately account for possibilities and limits with respect to agency that are defined by and in defiance of existing social, cultural and political structures? What and whose realities do theorists of reflexive modernity draw on and make invisible in envisioning or constructing the world? How should the performativities of the theory of reflexive modernity be understood with respect to how it brings into existence some experiences as late modern, and refuses others.

Overall, the aim in the following chapters is to consider the light cast by possible answers to these questions into the reconstructive orientation that radical modernist theories adopt, and the sociology they promote. Prior to this, it is necessary in this chapter to introduce the frames, ideas and vocabulary that have emerged for talking about, articulating and giving shape to the reconstructivist theory of reflexive modernity. This is essential for evaluating the claims that reconstructivist theories make for new understandings with respect to the interplay of the global, local, institutional, political and personal. The next section begins by first of all explicitly situating theories of reflexive modernity with respect to their theoretical and sociological 'other' – the theory and sociology of postmodernity. Following this, the chapter considers Giddens' arguments about late modernity and how they overlap with Beck's arguments about risk society. The chapter then discusses both theorists' ideas about institutional and social reflexivity and how this links to their arguments about the heightened reflexivity of the current period of modernity, and considers the understandings of globalization, detraditionalization and individualization that underpin these ideas. There are notable commonalities in these theoretical accounts with respect to the new challenges and universalities that the current period of modernity is thought to promote, but there are also some notable differences in how they interpret the potential social, political and personal implications. Overall, Giddens' interpretation is more optimistic than Beck's. The latter's interpretation is left more 'open'. Despite this, both theorists agree that late or reflexive modernity has crucial implications in terms of the need to rework the basic premises of modernist sociology.

Rethinking postmodernity

By the last decade of the twentieth century, the energy and appeal of theoretical narratives of postmodernity had, some commentators argue, become exhausted (see Delanty 1999). Some theorists, like Bauman, who had previously vigorously argued the case for the sociology of postmodernity began to lose faith in the analytical potential offered by the concepts associated with postmodernity, largely because the terms postmodernity and postmodernism had become the subject of wide and diverse interpretations and confusions in sociology (but see Chapter 4). Also, arguments about postmodernity had sometimes been associated

with radical posturing for its own sake, and because of this many sociological critics were quick to pronounce symptoms of their demise. In
defence of arguments about postmodernity, however, theorists like
Barry Smart (1998) argued that the concerns associated with postmodernity were more deeply rooted in sociology's history than was often
acknowledged. He also suggested that sociology could not afford to
ignore the issues that it raised: not least how the legislative reason
through which sociology had historically understood and justified its
own project was, as Lyotard and Bauman had pointed out, undermined.
Smart pointed out that the search for universal foundations or epistemology through which legislative reason could be claimed was now
widely recognized as a futile one. Also, there was widespread recognition of the silencing and exclusionary dynamics of totalizing theories and
categories. Sociology's limits, in these respects and others, were now
evident and visible and should be reflexively acknowledged.

Smart further defended postmodern perspectives by suggesting that
their preoccupations might be more in tune with the challenges presented
to contemporary social analysis, the social processes they try to comprehend, and the complex interrelationship between the two, than many
of their critics acknowledged. These challenges included the analysis of
living in and *with* transition, and avoiding the problematic nature of
inherited assumptions about the social. The value of postmodern perspectives, Smart suggested, could only be fully appreciated when
postmodernity itself was rejected as a primarily historicizing term, and
viewed as an expression of the radical questioning of modernity. Put
another way, debates about postmodernity should be seen as part of the
reflexive process of critical reflection on the modern project itself, and as
a notable *expression* and *method* of modernity's reflexivity or self-
consciousness. Viewing the postmodern as the recognition of living
without guarantees and illusions, and living with contingency, uncertainty and ambivalence, Smart suggested that sociology should take
postmodern critics seriously by acknowledging that many of the core
assumptions, expectations, and objectives historically taken up by sociology were now inappropriate and unrealizable.

Despite Smart's incorporation of Bauman's work into his defence of
postmodern orientations to sociology, Bauman himself more recently
stopped framing his own theoretical project in terms of the sociology of
postmodernity. In *Liquid Modernity* (2000a), *Liquid Love* (2003) and
Liquid Fear (2006), for example, Bauman has instead framed his
analyses of contemporary social, cultural, political and day-to-day life

in terms of liquidity. For Bauman, liquidity speaks better to how the contemporary era is marked by both disjuncture and continuity with respect to modern processes, and is a better way of talking about how current modernity is distinguished from 'solid' modernity. Modernity, he argues, always disembedded social forms, relations and identities from their established bases. However, it also re-embedded them through disciplinary processes such as those described by Foucault. Liquid modernity disembeds without re-embedding. Also, the terms 'postmodernity' and 'postmodernism', Bauman argues, are often conflated in a way that rids them of their analytical precision (see Bauman and Tester 2001). A key problem, as Bauman sees it, is that despite how theorists of postmodernity aim to talk about disjuncture *and* continuities, 'post' implies the end of modernity. But in many ways, he suggests, 'we are as modern as ever – modernizing anything we can get our hands on' (Bauman and Tester 2001). While postmodernity once seemed a convincing way of talking about the reordering of modernity, as a general term for the kinds of transformations shaping contemporary society it has lost its analytical salience.

The metaphor of liquidity, for Bauman, better grapples with the combined continuities (melting and disembedding orientations) and discontinuities (the lack of resolidifying and re-embedding mechanisms) that mark the current phase of modernity, and can better help to conceptualize continuity and change. However, while the metaphor of liquidity may be a useful one for sidestepping the confusions and deadlock that many perceive to define debates about 'modernity/postmodernity', it does little in the way of transcending them. There is a consistency in Bauman's analyses of postmodernity and liquid modernity that places a question mark over the degree of improved analytical purchase that the latter concept affords. Some critics might view the shifting vocabulary of Bauman's work as signifying that theories of postmodernity are now a spent force (cf. Delanty 1999). But it also coincides with a more pessimistic turn in his work from a previously overarching concern with the possibilities of postmodernity (and especially postmodern ethics, see Bauman 1993) to an increasing preoccupation with the demise of social, political, ethical, subjective and relational possibilities.

As is acknowledged by Bauman, and was discussed in Chapter 4, several of the key theorists associated with the postmodern turn had already talked about postmodernity as the continuation or intensification of modern processes, and had highlighted the disembedding character of modernity. Although Lyotard's work is often associated with theorizing postmodern rupture, it did not talk about a new epoch or order as such (see Chapter 4). Best and Kellner talk about an emergent postmodern order and paradigm, whose identity is not yet fully known (see Chapter 4). In charting the postmodern turn, they are attempting to articulate the 'uncharted territory' between the modern and the fully 'post' modern. Further, as Nicholson and Seidman's work illustrates, postmodern theorists are not always arguing the case for a complete analytical break with modern frames and concepts as is often feared by their critics (see Chapter 4). Indeed, in explicitly arguing that case for reincorporating the social into postmodern theorizing, Nicholson and Seidman are implying the significance of social continuities. In this regard, there are notable areas of convergence between aspects of the arguments proposed by some variations of postmodern theorizing and those proposed by radical modernist theories of reflexive modernity. The latter theories are discussed with reference to Giddens' and Beck's work in the following sections.

Reframing modernity

Beck has sidestepped the debate about postmodernity by talking about 'second modernity', whereas Giddens employs the term 'late modernity'. While Bauman deems the former to be better than the latter, he argues that it is in many respects an 'empty container that invites all kinds of content' (Bauman and Tester 2001). The term 'second modernity', Bauman argues, does not indicate anything about the distinctions between it and the first. Late modernity, as Giddens uses it, implies acknowledging contingency but, Bauman argues, in this respect there seems to be little difference between late modernity and postmodernity. Like postmodernity, he argues, 'late' implies that modernity proper is now drained of its energies and can be regarded as a whole retrospectively. Despite their terminological preferences, however, all three theorists point to the perceived need to shift away from what Beck, Giddens and Lash (1994) characterize as the now futile debates about postmodernity, and from privileging deconstruction as an analytical strategy. They argue instead for a move towards recognizing explicitly the continuities in modernity and its current period, whatever it is termed, as well as the differences. The following sections consider how Beck and Giddens do this in similar (but also slightly different) ways by talking about reflexive modernity, implying that the reflexive reordering of modernity might provide the basis for modern renewal.

Late modernity

For Giddens, as Penna *et al.* (1999) note, 'late modernity' talks to developments in electronic media and communications technologies; developments in the world economic order, especially the mobility of capital; changing global and local patterns of political action; changing relationships between work and the domestic; and changes in public and personal life. But, most importantly, late modernity speaks to an *integrated* frame for understanding these developments and changes. In addressing modernity and its institutional forms as a sociological problem, Giddens (1990, 1991) argues the need to rethink the nature of modernity and some of the basic premises of sociological analysis. In doing so, he argues, it should be recognized how modern institutions are distinguished by their dynamism; their undermining of traditional patterns of social organization, relations and practice; and their global impact. While modernity should be understood at an institutional level, he argues, how developments associated with modern institutions connect with day-to-day life should also be incorporated into the frame. In general terms, Giddens suggests, modernity refers to the 'the institutions and modes of behaviour established first of all in post-feudal Europe, but which in the twentieth century have become world-historical in their impact' (1991: 15). Its four institutional axes are industrialism, capitalism, surveillance, and controls of the means of violence on an industrial scale. In viewing modernity's institutional axes thus, Giddens combines what were previously emphasized as the discrete overarching dynamics of modernity into a more holistic frame (see Chapter 2; Foucault in Chapter 3; Elias in Chapter 8). The nation state that is associated with boundaried histories of industrialization, capitalism, surveillance and controls on violence is, Giddens points out, one of modernity's distinct social forms. It is an example of the centrality of organized control to modernity: 'Who says modernity says not just organizations, but organization – the regularized control of social relations across time-space distances' (1991: 16). 'Society' and the nation state are often imagined as one and the same thing in modern sociological thought. However, in late modernity transformations with respect to the organization of social relations are afoot, so that it makes more sense to talk about society in global terms – not a world society as such, but one that is marked by universalizing tendencies.

Modern institutions, for Giddens, make a definitive break with premodern cultures and ways of living, and the dynamic nature of modernity – it is like an unstoppable juggernaut – is key to understanding its profound implications for reconfiguring social relations, practice and modes of behaviour. This dynamism is related to three interconnected movements: the uncoupling of time and space so that social relations are stretched across broad – nowadays global – spans of time-space; the disembedding of social institutions through the 'lifting out' of social interaction from particular locales (through the printed and electronic media, expert systems and symbolic tokens such as money and the like); and far-reaching – nowadays chronic – reflexivity, where knowledge about social life systematically feeds back into social life itself (for example, via the media in the form of expert knowledge), influencing change and transformation (Giddens 1991: 20). Institutional reflexivity implies the monitored or self-conscious nature of modernity. On the one hand, this is partly the product of rational thought as promoted by the Enlightenment: science and expert knowledge have provided the basis for awareness of the material and social world as it has been shaped by human activity. On the other hand, rational thought has not produced the control, certainty and order that it was thought it would. Rather, the reflexivity of modernity is partly the product of how rational thought turned on itself undermines the certainty of knowledge and truth – there is general awareness that what we know today may be undermined by new knowledge tomorrow; what was thought to be true today might be revealed as flawed knowledge tomorrow. In this sense, there is a distinction to be made between the simple reflexivity that is associated with modernity in its earlier form – where reason provided the basis for the partial demystification of pre-modern bases of authority, legitimate knowledge, hierarchy and social order (for example, myths, religion, monarchy and aristocratic privilege and the like) – and the double reflexivity of late modernity where rational thought interrogates and questions itself. In doing so, the latter promotes a culture of radical doubt where all kinds of knowledge, including expert knowledge itself, are only valid until further notice.

For Giddens, there is a transformative drive inherent to modernity that unleashes reflexivity. The issue of reflexivity is also relevant to how he views modernity as an era of radical mediation. To begin with, Giddens argues, practically all human experience is mediated as everybody is subject to socialization, especially through the acquisition of language (but Giddens does not share the poststructuralist or postmodern deconstructive concern with language). Coupled with this, modernity has its own media – initially the printed text and then electronic communication. The intertwined development of mass media and electronic communication is crucial for understanding late modernity (Giddens 1991: 25). The electronic and mass media as we know them today are mechanisms and expressions of the disembedding and globalizing tendencies of modernity. Time and space is reorganized through them, and they play a crucial role in constituting modern institutions (1991: 26). But while Giddens acknowledges that the media do not simply communicate or reflect reality – they contribute to it – he is clear that we should not conclude, as Baudrillard does, that the media create an 'autonomous realm of hyperreality where the sign and image is everything' (1991: 27; see Chapters 4 and 6). In a further criticism of radical postmodernist frames, he argues:

> It has become commonplace to claim that modernity fragments, dissociates. Some have even presumed that such fragmentation marks the emergence of a novel phase of social development beyond modernity – a postmodern era. Yet the unifying features of modern institutions are just as central to modernity – especially in the phase of high modernity – as the disaggregating ones. The 'emptying' of time and space set in motion processes that established a single 'world' where none existed previously . . . late modernity produces a situation in which humankind in some respects becomes a 'we', facing problems and opportunities where there are no 'others'.
>
> (Giddens 1991: 27)

As this quotation makes clear, whereas postmodernity is synonymous with fragmentation, Giddens rejects this as *the* central feature of late modernity in favour of analysis that emphasizes instead movements towards new universalities and new forms of global connectedness. Indeed, because of radical doubt, people and agencies are nowadays connected by the uncertainties they face. They are potentially brought together by common concerns – such as the risks posed to the environment, health crises such as HIV/AIDS, or the threatened collapse of financial markets – that all have global implications. They are brought together by risks and crisis, but also potentially by the opportunities for responding to these. It is in this context that Giddens' arguments about subjective and personal life are important, as he contends that globalization and self-identity are 'two poles of the local and global in the conditions of high modernity', and that for the first time in history the self and society are interrelated in a global context (1991: 32; see Chapter 6).

The global media and information and communication technologies, along with all manner of expert systems (like financial systems, scientific expertise, health and environmental expertise and the like), are centrally involved in the institutional ordering of late modernity, but expert systems are also involved in personal life – not least because they provide resources for the constitution of lifestyles and self-identities (for example, through discourse on lifestyle, health and well-being, financial advice and so on) (1991: 33, see Chapter 6). The conditions of late modernity are therefore not simply about fragmentation. Rather, mediation and the interconnectedness of the global and the local (and the institutional and the personal) are central to late modern forms of social organization and order where, for Giddens, opportunities and risks are balanced 'in equal measure' (1991: 34).

There are several ways in which Giddens' ideas about late modernity overlap with postmodern analyses. Not least, he shares with many theorists of postmodernity the concern with implications of living *with* contingency. However, contrary to the poststructuralist and radical postmodernist positions that argue the case for seeing the project of modernity as exhausted, Giddens' analysis implies that modernity is in many ways being reinvigorated or renewed. On the one hand, he agrees that the project of modernity as it was associated with Enlightenment ideas about reason as the basis for certainty and truth, and as the basis of some inevitable future social order, has been revealed as myth. Rather, reason has been the source of institutionalized doubt in late modernity. On the other hand, Giddens sees globalization, and the institutional changes it involves, as offering a new framework for thinking about new universalizing tendencies that theories of postmodernity underplay or do not grasp. Globalization also offers a new framework for political responses to issues and problems that are global themselves. In this way, as Dodd (1999) notes, Giddens *retains* the universalism of the modern project, but on the basis of empirical not philosophical and theoretical reasons.

Giddens' rearticulation of the universalism of the modern project, it will be argued in the following chapters, has important consequences for the kind of sociology that his work – and the theory of reflexive modernity more broadly – promotes. This is not reconstructivist in the sense of returning to the epistemological principles or meta-narratives that influenced founding social thought, but it is reconstructivist in its return to a concern with universalisms and commonalities in experience that poststructuralists, radical difference theorists and postmodernists critique in their various ways. The social theoretical interpretation it offers is, it could be argued, powerful because of its appeal to empirical correspondence – to well-documented changes and developments that are happening in the world. Also, the attraction of this reconstructive approach to modernity is understandable in terms of the reconstructed social and political – and *sociological* – possibilities it talks to. But its costs in terms of the differences and other 'realities' it puts aside and makes invisible are also important. These are highlighted in the following chapters. First, I consider how the primary themes of Giddens' theory of late modernity overlap and link with Beck's arguments about risk society and reflexive modernity.

Risk society

The disembedding mechanisms associated with modernity, Giddens (1990: 124–37) argues, generate both the basis for increased levels of security and new forms of risk. Risks associated with nuclear or chemical warfare, human interventions in the material environment, financial and investment markets, food production, air travel, energy generation and the like are all 'man-made' products of modernity. They are generated by expert systems, and lead to globalized and intensified risk combined with an increased awareness of it. These risks provide new dangers for everyone and, via Beck, Giddens notes that they are often universal in that they transcend borders and the divisions between different economic, social, cultural and geographically based groups. These kinds of risks become the backdrop to everyday living. They have profound implications for the institutions of modernity, and for individuals and agencies, but go hand in hand with new possibilities for engagement at a global level.

Beck provides a more detailed analysis of 'risk society' that centres on the argument that 'at the other side of the obsolescence of industrial society is the emergence of risk society' (1994: 5). For Beck, there are two stages to be distinguished in the development of risk society. The first is where 'self-threats' are systematically produced by industrial society, but are justified as risks that come with progress and are not a central focus of public, political and personal concerns. The second is when the self-threats of industrial society start to dominate in public, political and personal life. The issue here is how modernity produces risks and threats it cannot control, and how core features of industrial modernity itself become social and political problems:

> On the one hand, society still makes decisions and takes actions according to the patterns of the old industrial society, but, on the other, the interest organizations, the judicial system and politics are clouded over by debates and conflicts that stem from the dynamism of risk society.
>
> (Beck 1994: 5)

For Beck, the transition from the industrial to the risk period of modernity is one that is unforeseen and comes about in response to industrial society's unwanted side-effects. Industrial modernity was dominated by consensus about progress and justified its hazards in term of the 'goods' (for example, economic growth, employment, improved quality of living, social security systems) it produced. With risk society disputes over how these goods are distributed – which were at the heart of modern labour conflicts and the like – are overlaid by disputes about the 'bads' produced by industrial modernity, and whose responsibility they are. The latter disputes are evident in debates about how the risks associated with nuclear and chemical technologies, genetics, health and environmental threats and the like should be 'distributed, prevented, controlled and legitimatised' (1994: 6). Risk society talks to the current period of modernity in which an awareness of the bads and threats produced by industrial modernity dominate. These threats are not wholly calculable and knowable. Risk society is therefore modern society confronted with the limits of its own project and its concept of progress.

For Beck, the concept of risk society implies an epochal transformation in the relationship of industrial modernity to the natural resources *and* social relations (for example, the division of labour between men and women, with the latter as unpaid domestic labourers) that were crucial to its development. There is also an epochal shift in the relationship of society to the threats and problems produced by it – these are no longer justifiable on the basis of progress. There is a further shift with respect to those modernist categories of meaning related to social class, family, community and the like. These do not have the grounding they once had, and people are being released from social ties that characterized industrial modernity 'into the turbulence of global risk society'. This entails a kind of individualization that is distinctly different from the sort that the founding thinkers of modernity envisaged. People nowadays are not being released into a confrontation with the kind of risks (extreme exploitation, poverty, dehumanization, anomie and the like) that dominated in early modern industrial societies. Rather, they must live with a 'broad variety of different, mutually contradictory, global and personal risks' (1994: 7). Like Giddens and many postmodernists, Beck is partly concerned with how uncertainty is returning with a vengeance. Risk society, brings into view the previously unseen or unacknowledged side-effects of modernity and is ultimately about institutional crises that go to the heart of modernity itself. It entails recognizing the unpredictability of the threats that go hand in hand with modern development. This in turn entails the need to rethink the foundations on which modern social order was sought and modern conceptions of reason as they were tied to progress. On the one hand, risk consciousness in the 'triumph of instrumentally rational order' (1994: 9) as risk consciousness is the recognition that action *must* be taken. On the other hand, risk consciousness signifies a post-rational order (with respect to instrumental rationality) because it does not say *what* action to take: 'The salient point here is that the expansion and heightening of the intention of control ultimately ends up producing the opposite' (1994: 9).

Beck argues that risks imply decisions and action, but in risk society there is no established or legitimate bases – at institutional and individual levels – for understanding what the most appropriate actions are. Via Bauman, he argues that this leads to the recognition of ambivalence. Risk issues are tied to questions of order in that they appear to demand intervention. However, they have come about because of the modern bases on which order was sought – the instrumentally rational logic of control. Recognizing this, Beck argues, implies a new conflict at the centre of the current period of modernity about the established foundations of rationality. This stems from how these were the bases on which modern order was imagined and actively sought, but have turned out to produce an unimagined risk. There is therefore a seemingly irresolvable tension with respect to instrumental rationality as the basis of progress that takes place at the very heart of the institutions of modernity. This is not the critique of rationality previously associated with the modern margins, or is not reducible to the Habermasian concern with the intrusion of instrumental reason into the life-world (1994: 10). Rather this is a core conflict stemming from not knowing how the future of modernity should be imagined and on what basis it should proceed. Modern institutional and organizational forms, and modernist ethical and political principles, are confounded by the radical uncertainty, contingency and uncontrollability implied. There are profound implications for social science: 'it is true that social science categories and methods fail in the face of the vastness and ambivalence of the facts that must be presented and comprehended' (Beck 1994: 10).

Like Giddens, Beck emphasizes the new universalities that emerge in risk society. Social development in risk society is not conducive to control, and thus there is a breaking up of 'regional, class specific, national, political and scientific jurisdictions and boundaries' (1994: 11). In the case of the kinds of risks posed by nuclear catastrophe or global warming not only is 'everyone' at risk, but everyone is encouraged to share a sense of responsibility with respect to risk, and to monitor it. Risk society, Beck's analysis suggests, promotes an orientation towards a kind of self-critiquing society where 'everyone' is engaged in this. The key question for Beck is what this ethic of critique will produce on institutional, political and personal levels. While it appears difficult if not impossible for things to go on as they previously did, the outcome is – as yet – unknown. This leads us to the differences between his and Giddens' theories of reflexive modernity.

Reflexive modernity

While some of Giddens' ideas about the reflexivity of modernity have been discussed earlier, it is important to note how they are rooted in his earlier work on structuration that sought to theorize how structure and agency mediate each other. This latter work theorized how social action was monitored by its participants to reproduce social relations in a structured fashion over time. Giddens' concern in theorizing structuration was to transcend the 'structure or agency' debate, by focusing on how human agents reproduce social order through their social practice. Social actors are not therefore merely 'subjected' to structure, but are actively involved in reproducing it in a potentially open way. In doing so they draw on resources in the form of knowledge necessary for being a social actor – or 'rules' as Giddens terms them – to mobilize their practices. Reflexivity in this context refers to the monitoring of social action that is necessitated to reproduce it. But key to the openness of social practice is its potentially transformative nature with respect to social relations and structure. In contrast to Foucault, who viewed institutional and personal monitoring as governmental techniques crucial to the production of a disciplined social order (see Chapter 4), Giddens sees monitoring as the mobilization of knowledge and resources necessary for engaging in social life and potentially reconfiguring it. As will be seen in Chapter 6, there are notable overlaps and tensions between Giddens' concerns with the reflexivity of modernity and Foucault's disciplinary discourses. But, for the moment, it is important to note how reflexivity in Giddens' theory of modernity relates to (and includes) the idea of agentic monitoring. The reflexivity of late modernity, for Giddens, refers to modernity's institutional reflection, awareness and self-consciousness and the mutually transformative relationship between this and the reflection, awareness and self-consciousness of social actors in day-to-day life (see Chapter 6).

Also crucial to Giddens' ideas about the heightened reflexivity of late modernity is the idea of detraditionalization. This implies that traditional bases for social action are no longer simply given. Rather, they are increasingly undermined by the dynamism of modernity, and the social institutions that previously gave social actions their meanings are now being reconfigured. This implies that social, political and personal life in late modernity must, in significant ways, take the form of experiments. In this context, the heightened reflexivity of late modernity is related to uncertainty and contingency, but what postmodernists might term the sense of intense crisis that pervades contemporary social, political and personal life (and that is highly destabilizing) Giddens sees as a contemporary challenge to be engaged with. Reflexivity, in this sense, allows for an analytical focus on how expert knowledge and cultural resources in their broadest sense are crucial for such engagement – as they provide the 'material' through which modernity's self-reflection and consciousness is shaped and becomes possible. While the institutional reflexivity of modernity has its roots in how expert knowledge promotes radical doubt, this reflexivity is itself the basis for re-envisioning order and security.

While Beck uses reflexivity to talk about modernity's awareness and confrontation with itself in risk society, the concept is, for him, more in keeping with the idea of *reflexion* than reflection: confrontation that has come about as a reflex reaction to risk and uncertainty. There is, for Beck, an important distinction to be made between reflexivity as it might refer to 'the increase of knowledge and schematization in the sense of self-reflection on modernization' and the reflexivity that refers to 'autonomous, undesired and unseen transition from industrial to risk society' (1994: 6). While the transition from first to second modernity may ultimately lead to reflection as a response to the risks modernity has produced, this should not 'obscure the unreflected, quasi-autonomous mechanism of the transition' (1994: 6). In this respect, Beck's discussion of reflexivity emphasizes more the contingencies associated with contemporary modernity, and conjures up more the unknown, erratic and open implications of the processes that underpin it than does Giddens' analysis. While Beck is in agreement with Giddens, for example, that social, cultural, political and personal life become experiments in second or late modernity, he emphasizes more the potential conflicts that arise in these experiments. Also, whereas Giddens emphasizes the expert resources that are generated in late modernity, and the possibilities they open up for reconstituting modernity's institutions, and social, political and personal life, Beck is far less committed to professing the possibilities of new order, and more to setting out the challenges, contradictions and tensions that modernity's confrontation with itself implies. For Beck, reflexivity as reflexion concerns the unknown and unknowable. He argues that we have unwittingly been placed in the position of having to make decisions for ourselves without recourse to certain knowledge or sources of legitimacy and authority. Coupled with this, many of modernity's social and institutional forms (such as the family, community, social class and so on) are becoming 'zombie categories' – they are in many ways dead, but live on as there are not yet new social and institutional forms to replace them.

Globalization and individualization

Both Giddens' and Beck's arguments concern what they envision as global processes and tendencies. Both are concerned with globalization in the sense of highly developed global media and communications systems, global financial markets and the like, and both are concerned with the relationship between the global and the local. While globalization is often discussed as a phenomenon 'out there', they are concerned with how it involves the 'right here'. Globalization, in this sense, implies an increasing global connectedness, where the contingencies and hazards associated with distant places can have profound effects on diverse locales. Globalization means that social, political and personal activities 'here' can have profound implications out 'there'. But globalization also has consequences that penetrate to the heart of personal life itself. Despite the similarities in their approaches, Giddens talks about the implications of globalization in a most explicit way. From his perspective, globalization does not lead to the relativization of values, as some argue, but to a shared global concern with ethical and moral issues (see discussion of life-politics below). Globalization cannot simply be viewed as the extension of the dominance of Western systems, because it leads to a world where there are no 'others'. Globalization is about the incorporation of the voice of others: not merely in the sense that the other 'talks back', but that 'mutual interrogation becomes possible' (1994: 97). Knowledge of the world at large is promoted by electronic communications media, and the global media imply that in some respects we all 'inhabit a unitary framework of experience' (1991: 5). This means that the perspective and outlook of different cultures have not become increasingly plural, but in some ways more singular (1991: 27).

Globalization implies global risks and, as noted earlier, Giddens emphasizes how such risks are an aspect of common experience, and provide the opportunities for global responses. But in his concern with how 'the global insecurities we face as individuals tend to unify rather than divide us' (1990: 149), Giddens touches explicitly on the deep implications that globalization has for self-identity and personal life. Key here is how the worldwide spread of the institutional dynamics underpinning modernity, along with its disembedding and detraditionalizing tendencies and its implications for uncertainty and contingency, presents profound challenges – or insecurities – at the level of self-identity and personal life on a global scale. Modernity undercuts the traditional 'given' bases for self-identity and personal life, and in late modernity even the modern bases for self-identity and personal life (social class, occupation, community, family and so on) are undermined. Therefore the bases on which a sense of self and relational and personal security are founded become more open.

Traditional and modern sources for self-identity (for example, class or religious affiliation), as well as traditional and modern conceptions of life stages or trajectory (a path incorporating transitions through family, school, occupation, marriage, parenting, retirement and so on), are undermined as the foundations or scripts for personal life in late modernity. Amongst the implications of this there are important ones for a potentially heightened sense of personal or existential insecurity. Unlike societies that are organized around religious belief systems, modernity does not provide adequate answers to moral issues that emerge with respect to questions about the meaning of life and death. Such questions are especially likely to arise when people encounter existentially troubling issues or events (such as those relating mortality, the beginning or end of a relationship, serious illness and other critical life moments). However, the open nature of self and personal life in modernity means that people are increasingly likely to encounter existentially troubling issues in their day-to-day living. In late modernity the prevalence and awareness of risk issues also increases the likelihood of encountering such issues. Heightened threats to existential insecurity become the backdrop to everyday life, and a shared common experience in an increasingly global world (see Chapter 6).

Giddens' arguments about globalizing tendencies in late modernity should be viewed in terms of broader debates about globalization that have occurred in social theory since the 1990s (see Featherstone and Lash 1995). As Featherstone and Lash point out, these debates were the successors of modernity/postmodernity debates in significant respects, and were crucial in shifting the emphasis in social analyses from a temporal to a spatial one. Debates about globalization mark a shift in the analytical preoccupation with national institutions towards a concern instead with global flows in 'mediascapes, ethnoscapes, finanscapes and technoscapes' (Featherstone and Lash 1995: 2). The upshot of this is that 'international social, political and cultural (for example the media) organizations are standing alongside and beginning to replace their national counterparts' (Featherstone and Lash 1995: 2). But, in rebuking the kind of analysis that Giddens promotes, Featherstone and Lash argue the more postmodern case for being attentive to the differences within globalization by talking about 'global modernities'. This acknowledges the varying and different histories of modernity that exist in the world, and how these influence different contributions to and experiences of global flows. Put another way, globalization is not as uniform or neutral in its flows and effects as Giddens implies. This raises the issue of the universalizing terms in which Giddens' analysis is framed, and the extent to which his account of global experiences is skewed in terms of a specifically Western – or dominating – vision of globalization. While his arguments about global risks, challenges and opportunities may be partially convincing, his arguments about the opportunities that global modernity offers for mutual interrogation, the demise of 'otherness' and difference, and the unifying potentials of global insecurities are less so (see Chapters 6 to 9).

While Giddens has emphasized the implications of globalizing modernity for heightened existential insecurities, Beck has emphasized how globalizing modernity goes hand in hand with individualizing modernity. In collaboration with Beck-Gernsheim, Beck argues that the kind of sociology that is stuck in its concerns with modernist 'zombie' categories (such as family, class and social status, community and the like) cannot see the realities and contradictions of globalizing *and* individualizing modernities (see Beck 2000; Beck and Beck-Gernsheim 2002). If the concept of globalization, Beck and Beck-Gernsheim (2002) argue, challenges the tendency for social thinking to be entrapped in national-territorial conceptions of society, then the focus on individualization highlights the problems of being entrapped within the collective bias of social analysis. Individualization, as Beck and Beck-Gernsheim theorize it, is concerned with 'institutionalized individualism'. First, individualization means the disintegration of previously existing social forms (such as those related to the zombie categories above). Second, it refers to how in modern societies the individual is the focal point – or institutional reference point – of a vast array of new demands and controls from the labour market and the welfare state and the like. These produce something akin to what Bauman (2000a) via Elias terms the 'society of individuals'. Contrary to neo-liberal conceptions of the free-market individual who freely negotiates choices, and postmodern conceptions of pick-and-mix identities, individualization refers to institutional pressures to construct a do-it-yourself biography that incorporates and becomes the focus of various – often contradictory – demands, rights and responsibilities. On the one hand, there are the demands and responsibilities that come with respect to basic social, civil and political rights that are increasingly focused on the individual and not the group. On the other hand, there are the commitments with respect to participation in the labour market, which nowadays demands flexible individualized workers.

Individualization, in this sense, is not about freedom of choice, but is instead about the ways in which the self is always incomplete – there is always more to do in constructing it. To the extent that institutional pressures are taken on board by individuals, and each constructs a flexible biography to fit the demands of the labour market, there is a 'spiral' of individualization that undermines the established foundations of social life. In this respect, Beck and Beck-Gernsheim's analysis of individualization echoes other accounts of how second or liquid modernity disembeds without re-embedding (Bauman 2000a). In second modernity, Beck and Beck-Gernsheim argue, the individual is becoming the 'basic unit of social reproduction', and individualization is becoming 'the social structure' of second modernity itself. This does not necessarily imply a selfish society, but one where social reproduction involves everyone engaging in *separate* do-it-yourself biographies. It implies that the individualized society promotes individual – or biographical – solutions for systematic problems. In second modernity, for instance, the economic and social inequalities that were previously conceived in terms of the collective experience of class are now individualized into separate biographies. The concept of class, Beck and Beck-Gernsheim (2002) argue, underplays how currently there are increasing inequalities *without* collective ties. This raises profound implications for social analysis, and especially for sociology. Sociology cannot begin to comprehend the implications of individualizing tendencies of modernity without reworking or reimagining its established frames, vocabularies and routines for social analysis. These invariably overemphasize the collective in a way that does not grasp developments with respect to individualization. Combined with the globalization framework, the individualization framework presents a powerful challenge for sociology, but also the opportunity for its reconstruction.

Life-politics and personal life

One of the striking features of Giddens' and Beck's analyses of late and reflexive modernity is how the 'personal' is brought centre stage. Personal life is explicitly addressed in depth in Giddens' *Modernity and Self-identity* (1991) and *The Transformation of Intimacy* (1992). Personal life is the central concern of Beck's collaboration with Beck-Gernsheim in *The Normal Chaos of Love* (1995) and a key concern in *Individualization* (2002). Both Giddens' and Beck's concern with personal life follows long and varied traditions in modernist sociology that have put identity, family, community and the like at the centre of their analytical concerns. Functionalist sociologies, for example, have long placed personal life at the centre of their explorations of the logics of social order. Critical sociologies (including Marxist and feminist approaches and combinations of these) have also focused on personal life in their explorations of social order and power. Combined with this, the cultural and postmodern turns emphasized personal issues in a distinctive way by focusing on how gender and sexuality were bound up with discursive power, and how combined with 'race' and ethnicity they blurred the boundaries between the public and the private, the personal and the political. Amongst the various ways in which personal life is discussed in the theory of late or second modernity, two are noteworthy here. First, personal life is employed as a way of talking about the interconnections between changes at the institutional level of modernity and developments in day-to-day life, and to illuminate human agency and the reach and depth of contemporary social and cultural change.

Second, it is employed as a way of talking about core life concerns that were put aside or sequestered as 'private' in modernity, but that come to the fore – as public and political issues – in reflexive modernity. This, Giddens argues, has potentially profound implications that previous approaches to personal life have not fully grasped.

With respect to the first way in which personal life is discussed, both Giddens and Beck are arguing that if late or second modernity can be understood as reflexive modernity, then personal life – especially as it concerns self-identities and personal relationships – should also be understood as reflexive. But the differences between Giddens' and Beck's understandings of reflexivity in this respect are also important. For Giddens, reflexive self-identity implies agency through self-monitoring and the ongoing construction of a narrative of self-identity (see Chapter 6). From this perspective, the reflexive narrative of the self offers distinct possibilities with respect to self-making, and is also indicative of the opportunities for self-empowerment that are routinely available in late modernity. Contrary to postmodernist critiques that posit the fragmented and split nature of the self, Giddens emphasizes the coherence that the reflexive self can achieve through its engagement with the kinds of resources that expert systems provide (for example, through lifestyle discourse; see Chapter 6). Reflexive relationships also imply monitoring and creativity on the part of their participants (see Chapter 7). Intimate and personal relationships, Giddens argues, are nowadays entered into and negotiated by social and economic equals. Because of this, they must be actively worked at. When they no longer satisfy the needs of one or the other partner they are likely to be disbanded. This implies a new contingency in intimate and personal life, but it also promotes a movement in personal life towards a kind of dialogical intimacy and democratic form of relating where men and women (in heterosexual and same-sex couples) explicitly communicate their desires and concerns within the relationship. Reflexive and democratic relationships, Giddens argues, have potentially profound implications for the institutions of modernity as a whole (see Chapter 7).

In line with his different conception of reflexivity, Beck (with Beck-Gernsheim) sees reflexive self-identity and relationships in a different way from Giddens. As was discussed in the previous section, he conceptualizes identity as a 'do-it-yourself' biography: a kind of reflex reaction to the loss of given bases of identity and to institutional pressures that promote separate as opposed to group-based biographies. Chief amongst these pressures is the requirement of flexibility demanded by the labour market. Unlike Giddens' approach, this analysis implies that the reflexive biography is as likely to be faced with conflicts and tensions as it is with opportunities: it is highly burdened by conflicting responsibilities. There are important implications for reflexive relationships that are related to this. Beck and Beck-Gernsheim envision reflexive relationships as a kind of reflex response to the competing demands that are made on two individual biographies. Like Giddens, Beck and Beck-Gernsheim suggest that a new equality in men and women's labour-market participation is shaping relational reflexivity. Unlike Giddens, they emphasize the consequences in terms of conflicting demands on both men and women in relationships to construct separate flexible biographies. Couple and family life can no longer rely on the gender roles of the past and this, combined with conflicting biographical demands, sets the scene for intimate conflicts or battles. The outcomes – other than an increased contingency in personal life – are as yet unknown (see Chapter 7).

This brings up the personal concerns that were put aside or sequestered under the private in modernity, but that are coming to the fore as public concerns in reflexive modernity. Giddens addresses this as an aspect of an emergent life-politics. Life-politics is a post-emancipatory politics that partly stems from the reflexivity and openness of self-identities and relationships. On the one hand, the challenges that reflexive relationships bring up, especially as Beck and Beck-Gernsheim present them, clearly prompt new 'political' questions about how couple relationships could and should be organized. On the other hand, the issues they raise are *life-political* (as opposed to political in its established meanings), to the extent that they are concerned with moral questions that modernity has traditionally not provided answers for. These include the question of how we should live, and the moral basis on which this should be decided. Life-political issues are also intrinsically related to the existential questions that death raises (see Chapter 8). Human mortality is an existentially troubling issue that has, along with issues like madness, illness, sexuality and the like, been hidden away as 'private' in modernity. These experiences are sequestered because there are not enough answers to the moral questions they raise. As a consequence of the contingency and reflexivity of late modernity, however, existential questions threaten to return with a vengeance (see Chapter 8). Personal life is precisely where life-political issues come to the fore, and the moral issues that life-politics feeds into the public sphere are potentially radical because they demand the remoralizing of social life.

Conclusion: the sociological project of reflexivity

Against the kind of postmodernist theories that argue the demise of modernity and the end the social, Giddens and Beck both provide a radical re-envisioning of modernity, and a theoretical basis for reconstructing sociology that would focus on the reflexivity of modernity and its social, cultural, political and personal forms. Both theorists reject deconstructive orientations to modernity and modernist sociology. They argue instead for a reconstructed understanding of modernity that acknowledges its 'late' or 'second' stage, which is characterized by reflexivity. Reflexive modernity talks to challenges and opportunities that, they claim, cannot be recognized if stuck within modernist and postmodernist frames. Modernity has changed, and globalizing and individualizing developments warrant the rethinking of modernity and how sociology previously tended to conceive it. Risk and uncertainty are defining aspects of contemporary global culture, and Enlightenment principles relating to reason, truth and progress can no longer be relied on to generate order and security. Rather, the current period of modernity, both argue, is marked by radical doubt as a consequence of reason's reflection on – or confrontation with – itself. This generates uncertainty that hits at the heart of modernist sociology itself.

In contrast to the postmodern concern with fragmentation, Beck and Giddens point to new universalizing tendencies in a global world. They theorize these differently, but emphasize in their different ways the new commonalities in experience that emerge in societies being reconfigured by globalization and individualization. These changes imply an experimental society at social, political and personal levels. Giddens and Beck agree that sociology must rethink its established frames and dualisms to grasp the current situation, and to interpret the challenges and opportunities that come with reflexive modernity. Giddens especially emphasizes the opportunities, and Delanty's (1999) suggestion that we can see his concern with reflexivity as one of mediation is insightful in this respect. It is the case that Giddens' work from structuration onwards has long been preoccupied with developing a theory and sociology of mediation. For example, his analysis of structuration is focused on how structure and agency mediate each other; his analysis of late modernity foregrounds how electronic communications mediate global and local experience; his analysis of self in late modernity focuses on how mediating expert systems generate resources for self-identity; and his analysis of intimacy emphasizes how relationships are mediated in the sense of their negotiation according to an egalitarian ideal.

This points to one notable difference between Giddens and Beck: the extent to which the latter is less preoccupied with theorizing the possibilities of *mediated order* than the former, and talks instead to challenges and potential conflicts whose outcomes are unknown and possibly unknowable. This difference is partly due to the differing normative thrust driving the respective analyses – the vision of how things *should* be (with Giddens' analysis being more clearly shaped by this). While these differences are important, the similarities in Giddens' and Beck's theories are significant because of the emergent project they articulate for a reconstructive theory of reflexive modernity. The implications of this for 'thinking' and 'doing' a reconstructed sociology become clear when we look at their specific arguments with respect to contemporary social change and personal life. Personal life is of central importance to the theory of reflexive modernity because of the connections between institutional and personal reflexivity. Personal life is reconfigured on a global scale by institutional developments in late modernity, but personal life is also where moral issues emerge that give rise to life-politics. Life-politics has profound implications because of the radical responses it demands.

The following chapters take up this theme of personal life to compare the insights into social change that the theory of reflexive modernity claims to generate with those derived via other modernist and post-modernist frames. In doing so, they illuminate how problematic and contestable reconstructivist interpretations are. Reconstructivist arguments about new universalities may be (relatively) convincing when they are focused on the more abstract details of working out the reflexivity of modernity. However, they are less convincing when the theory is brought down to earth and compared to other perspectives on social and personal life. In these latter perspectives, otherness and difference are centrally important – locally and on a global scale – to shaping personal life and day-to-day experience.

6

RECONSTRUCTING
SELF AND IDENTITY

Introduction

'Fragmented', 'brittle' and 'fluid' are terms that have been employed by postmodern and radical difference theorists in analysing contemporary selfhood, and some poststructuralist theorists have characterized the modern self as docile and disciplined. Some modernist psychoanalytic accounts have viewed the contemporary self as narcissistic, while others focus on how its formation is central to the reproduction of difference and power. Poststructuralist psychoanalytic analyses have argued that the idea of coherent self or identity is illusory, while some modernist approaches to classed identities have viewed the self as an ideological construct. In the theory of late modernity, self and identity are viewed as reflexive achievements. This chapter considers different modernist, post-modernist and late modernist frameworks for understanding self and identity, and the different insights they generate for the implications of social change with respect to personal life.

The chapter begins by outlining Giddens' theory about reflexive self-identity in late modernity. Giddens suggests that self-identities can be viewed as individual projects that emerge from the negotiation of risks and choices in everyday life. Viewed in this way, the topic of self is said to illuminate the increased power that reflexive modernity affords to individuals over their own lives, and the mutually transforming relation-ships of agency and structure in detraditionalized settings. Giddens' ideas about social change and self-identity are underpinned by a set of arguments that relate to human beings' essential needs for a sense of ontological security, and the constant self-monitoring that individuals undertake in day-to-day life. He is concerned with how nowadays indi-viduals reflexively engage in the construction of biographical narratives of the self, and the implications of this for an active engagement with life-politics. A number of questions can be asked about Giddens' analysis, and the understandings of contemporary personal life it promotes. First, to what extent does it overplay new possibilities that are open for individual agency in relation to the self? Second, to what extent does it construct an overly coherent conception of the self? Third, in what ways does it undermine the significance of resources for shaping the different possibilities that exist for self and identities in contemporary social contexts? Fourth, to what degree does it present an overly optimistic account of social change? Finally, to what extent does Giddens' account of reflexive selfhood overemphasize universal subjective experience, and what are the consequences of erasing subjective differences for sociology?

An adequate response to these questions requires consideration of other frameworks that provide alternative understandings of the economic, social, cultural and psychological processes that shape the modern or postmodern self. The remainder of the chapter explores psychoanalytic theories that highlight the significance of difference to the self as developed by Chodorow and Lacan; Foucault's theory of the modern self as a product of disciplinary power; postmodern theories of 'surface', 'fragmented' and 'consumer' selves and identities; and modernist arguments about the significance of resources for the self. These frameworks provide a range of perspectives on how difference and power work in relation to the self and identity. They combine to provide some considerable basis for scepticism about the reflexive self and the significance it is afforded in the reconstructive theory of late modernity, and the reconstructed sociology that the latter promotes.

The project of self-identity

Giddens' starting point is the need for a theory of self-identity that can capture the dynamic and mutually influencing nature of individual experience and the institutions of late modernity. He challenges overly deterministic analyses of social life that overemphasize social structure and undermine human agency, and is critical of overly pessimistic accounts of the postmodern self as fragmented, brittle and fluid. Giddens is concerned with the increasing interconnection between the two extremes of 'extensionality' and 'intentionality': 'globalizing influences on the one hand and personal dispositions on the other' (Giddens 1991: 1). He argues that structural and poststructural analyses of social life misconceive the flow of power and agency in the post-traditional global world.

While the former conceptualize social life and institutions in a static way, the latter overemphasize disintegration, fragmentation and discontinuities in the postmodern world. Both kinds of analyses conceptualize the self in overly passive terms, and fail to grasp new mechanisms of self-identity which are shaped by – and shape – the institutions of modernity (1991: 2).

For Giddens, individuals actively participate in forging their self-identities, and in doing so contribute to social life in a way that has global implications (1991: 2). Contemporary self-identities, he argues, are projects that demand and promote individual agency. As discussed in Chapter 5, Giddens' concern with self-identity is part of a broader rethinking of basic premises of sociological analysis that he argues is necessary for understanding the development of modernity and its institutional forms. He draws on a range of sociological and psychological concepts in developing his analysis, and on examples from the social-scientific and self-help literature on key life experiences to illuminate the developments that concern him. These works, he argues, are not merely illustrative of the social processes at play in late modernity, but also constitute them. On the one hand, the social sciences play an important part in modernity's reflection upon itself, and influence its self-understanding and self-making. On the other hand, the social sciences influence and generate cultural resources that individuals employ in making sense of their own experiences and negotiating their self-identities.

Self-monitoring and existential questions

Giddens' analysis of the reflexive nature of self-identities begins from the premise that all human beings possess an awareness of what they are doing and why they are doing it. Individuals, he argues, continuously monitor their everyday activities in producing and reproducing social conventions. This self-monitoring operates in discursive ways (through the internal conversations an individual has), but 'practical consciousness' is also crucial in how people go about day-to-day life. For Giddens, practical consciousness refers to non-conscious, almost habitual, ways of being. It is an important aspect of reflexive self-monitoring and forms a sense of rootedness in everyday life that allows individuals to go on as normal. Practical consciousness involves day-to-day routines, and plays an essential role in providing an emotional grounding in a sense of everyday reality. Central here is the idea that social reality is not given as such, but is constructed and given meaning through the day-to-day activities of individuals. Our sense of social reality is therefore 'simultaneously sturdy and fragile' (1991: 36). People go on 'as if' the social world was real and social conventions were given. However, as Giddens puts it:

> The social world . . . [is] one in which each person is equally implicated in the active process of organising predictable social interaction. The orderliness of day-to-day life . . . is not one that stems from any sort of outside intervention; it is an achievement on the part of everyday actors in an entirely routine way.
>
> (Giddens 1991: 52)

If social reality is not given, the capacity of individuals to go on as normal in everyday life implies that individuals acquire and maintain a sense of ontological security: a secure sense of the reality of things and other people, or as Giddens defines it: 'a sense of continuity and order in events, including those not directly within the perceptual environment of the individual' (1991: 243). A sense of ontological security, Giddens argues, further implies that individuals have the capacity to deal with fundamental existential problems (1991: 47). These include questions about the nature of existence itself, human finitude, the existence of other persons and self-identity, which are largely addressed through the routines of day-to-day behaviour (1991: 47). The individual's ability to deal with these questions is central to Giddens' argument about human agency (as will be discussed in the following section). The significance he affords these questions also highlights core assumptions of his theory as they concern fundamental psychological and social processes. They are, therefore, worthy of detailed exploration.

For Giddens, questions about existence are initially answered in early psychological development when infants discover a sense of external reality, and later people give meaning to their existence by the kinds of activities they engage in. Human finitude and mortality can, however, present psychic challenges for the individual. While self-consciousness means that human beings are aware that they will die, the death and non-existence of the self is something that individuals cannot fully conceive or comprehend. Non-being presents a fundamental psychic threat to the individual and must be put aside in day-to-day living. People therefore act as if human life will go on indefinitely. However, the precarious nature of social reality means that existential anxieties can threaten to overwhelm the individual at times of personal crisis where life routines are disrupted. As will be explained in the following section of this chapter, how individuals respond to personal crises, and the threats these pose for psychic security, forms a key component of Giddens' argument about power and agency in late modern contexts. It is first of all necessary to consider the remaining issues that he identifies as crucial to understanding the self.

The issue of trust forms an essential component of Giddens' theory of late modern social life, and it is central to his understanding of the significance of other persons for self-identity. Subjectivity, Giddens argues, emerges through relationships with others, and 'learning the qualities of others' in infancy is connected with the 'first stirrings of what later become established as feelings of self-identity' (1991: 51). Developing a sense of trust is an essential aspect of early life experience, and trust established in early life is an essential basis for ontological security. Trust in others, as Giddens puts it, 'is at the origin of the experience of a stable external world and a coherent sense of self-identity' (1991: 51). The trust that the child vests in its parents (or caretakers) forms a kind of protection against existential anxieties that could potentially threaten to overwhelm the individual in adult life. 'Basic' trust initially emerges from the absences of the carer, and is the coping mechanism the infant develops for dealing with such absences. It provides the basis for a sense of autonomy, and is a condition of the 'elaboration of self-identity'. In adult life, Giddens argues, trust, interpersonal relationships and a sense of ontological security are profoundly interrelated (1991: 52). The capacity to trust is therefore a core component of a 'normal' sense of psychic order.

The elements discussed hitherto, Giddens implies, form an essential underpinning for 'normal' and 'stable' self-identities. Self-identity is not, however, simply reducible to these, and neither is a set of personality traits. Rather it is a biographical narrative that is constructed by the individual: 'a self as reflexively understood by the person in terms of her or his biography' (1991: 53). Self-identity, for Giddens, presumes the active individual, and a normal self-identity is where a person 'has a feeling of biographical continuity which she is able to grasp reflexively and . . . communicate to other people' (1991: 54). For Giddens, the reflexive and monitoring self must also be recognized as embodied, as the production and reproduction of social relations requires that competent agents 'exert a continuous, and successful monitoring of face and body' (1991: 56).

The universalizing terms in which Giddens discusses the existential dilemmas and the social and psychological processes underpinning so-called normal self-identities are noteworthy. What therefore are the distinguishing features of self-identities in late modernity? The answer for Giddens lies in the disembedding dynamics that are inherent to modernity (see Chapter 5), and the ensuing consequences for threats to a coherent sense of selfhood. In traditional settings, social life was more tightly bound up with a given sense of reality. Religious belief systems, for example, provided a sense of the natural order of things, and social relationships were grounded in boundaried time and space and in face-to-face relationships. Modernity, in contrast, involves a break from the certainties of tradition and the sources of personal meaning it provided. The post-traditional order is increasingly characterized by contingency and radical doubt. There are few, if any, given authorities, and multiple (and often conflicting) sources of expertise mean that all claims to truth are open to revision. Individuals are therefore faced with a multiplicity of competing 'truths' on any given issue, and there is no one framework that explains the meaning of things, or tells people how they should live. Further, developments in technology mean that ours is a global world characterized by the mediated nature of personal experience. Mass communication has made the world more unified with respect to time and space. This implies that individuals must invest a high degree of trust in non-face-to-face relationships. These factors, together with other dynamics considered in the following section, mean that personal stability and meaning can become heightened problems in detraditionalized settings.

Self-identity, reflexivity and empowerment

Modernity by its nature is future-orientated. In late modernity, Giddens and Beck argue, this entails consideration of the risks that modernity itself produces (see Chapter 5). Technological advances (in food production, global travel, nuclear technology and the like) combine to produce unforeseen global risks and man-made disasters. Risk awareness, and planning in relation to risk, require and facilitate institutional reflexivity. For Giddens, an orientation to the future, and consideration of the potential risks entailed in future possibilities, are issues that are also relevant to individual experience. Self-identity in late modernity, he argues, implies heightened self-reflexivity. In late modernity thinking in terms of risk is a fairly constant exercise, as is the negotiation of choice. What to be, how to act and who to be are questions that people must address on a fairly constant basis. However, while modernity may confront people with many choices, it offers us little guidance about the choices we should take up (see also Beck 1992, 2000). Of the consequences that follow from this, Giddens suggests, there are particular implications for lifestyle: 'because of the "openness" of social life today, the pluralisation of contexts of action and the diversity of "authorities", lifestyle choice is increasingly important in the constitution of self-identity and daily activity' (Giddens 1991: 5).

The more tradition loses its ability to provide a secure and stable sense of identity, the more individuals must negotiate lifestyle choices, and attach importance to these choices. Indeed, Giddens argues, the more post-traditional the setting in which the individual moves the more issues of lifestyle concern the very core of self-identity. Lifestyle, in these terms, is directly connected to individuals' needs to establish a meaningful and reliable sense of self in post-traditional contexts, where personal meaninglessness is a fundamental psychic problem. In modernity, Giddens argues, there is a direct relationship between how personal meaninglessness is kept at bay and the institutional exclusion or 'sequestration' of elements of life experience that raise existential or moral problems:

> The term 'sequestration of experience' refers here to connected processes of concealment which set apart the routines of ordinary life from the following phenomena: madness; criminality; sickness and death; sexuality and nature . . . the ontological security which modernity has purchased, on the level of day-to-day routines, depends on an institutional exclusion of social life from fundamental existential issues which raise central moral dilemmas for human beings.
>
> (Giddens 1991: 156)

What is at issue here is the institutional exclusion of issues and forms of behaviour that are potentially disturbing at a psychic level from everyday life (see also Chapter 8). Such exclusion cannot, however, wholly protect individuals from encountering situations that raise existential and moral crises. This is especially the case in late modern societies where there is a heightened awareness of risk. For Giddens, life crises are illustrative of how overwhelming the threat of personal meaninglessness can be for individuals in late modernity. However, they are also illustrative of the possibilities that are increasingly open to individuals to actively participate in shaping their self-identities and lifestyles, and of the opportunities for 'empowerment' and agency that exist in late modernity. These opportunities and possibilities become clear in Giddens' (1991) working out of the challenges that individuals face when dealing with critical moments in their lives such as the birth of a child, the start or end of a relationship, the diagnosis of illness, bereavement and so on. Giddens terms such life-changing events 'fateful' moments, and describes them in the following way:

> Fateful moments are times when events come together in such a way that an individual stands, as it were, at a crossroads in his existence . . . There are, of course, fateful moments in the history of collectives as well as in the lives of individuals. They are phases at which things are wrenched out of joint, where a given state of affairs is suddenly altered by a few key events.
>
> (Giddens 1991: 113)

As Giddens (1991) puts it, these moments bring individuals and collectives up short. For the individual, fateful moments imply that he or she is faced with a changed 'set of risks and possibilities' (Giddens 1991: 131). Fateful moments are threatening for the 'protective cocoon' that defends individuals against ontological insecurity, and often involve aspects of experience that are institutionally sequestered in modernity. They represent a key moment for the return of moral and existential questions which modernity provides no immediate answers to, a situation that the individual can experience as overwhelming. Yet, for Giddens, such times can also mark periods of 'reskilling' and even empowerment.

During fateful moments individuals must 'sit up and take notice of new demands as well as possibilities' (Giddens 1991: 143). These, Giddens stresses, are transition points which have major consequences for the individual's future conduct, lifestyle and self-identity. However, through reskilling the individual is also provided with opportunities. At fateful moments he or she can reskill and be 'empowered' through an engagement with expert systems (through engaging with counselling, self-help, lifestyle discourse and so on), and ultimately can become 'a different person' in a significant sense. The extent to which individuals can be active agents in these self-'reinventions' is related to the degree to which empowerment is routinely available to people as part of the heightened reflexivity of late modernity:

Coupled to disembedding, the expansion of abstract systems creates increasing quanta of power – the power of human beings to alter the material world and transform the conditions of their own actions ... In any given situation, provided that the resources of time and other requisites are available, the individual has the possibility of a partial or more full blown reskilling in respect of specific decisions or contemplated courses of action.

(Giddens 1991: 138–9)

Critical or fateful moments could theoretically illustrate the deskilling – and the disempowerment – that comes with advanced modernity. Giddens, however, employs such moments to illuminate the empowerment that is afforded to individuals, and to explicate new and emerging forms of politics in late modernity: life-politics. Life-politics, he argues, is a politics of choice and life decisions and of self-actualization. Life-political issues 'place a question mark against the internally referential systems of modernity' (1991: 223), and concern 'precisely those moral and existential questions repressed by the core institutions of modernity' (1991: 223). They demand the remoralizing of social life and 'a renewed sensitivity to the questions that the institutions of modernity systematically dissolve' (1191: 224). Self-identity is of central importance to life-politics:

Thoroughly penetrated by modernity's abstract systems, self and body become the sites of a variety of lifestyle options. In so far as it is dominated by the core perspectives of modernity, the project of the self remains one of control, guided only by a morality of 'authenticity'. However, concerning as it does the most intimate human sensibilities, this project becomes a fundamental impetus towards remoralising social life.

(Giddens 1991: 225–6)

Several critics are sceptical of the self-monitoring, self-making and 'empowered' individual that Giddens describes, and the implications this is said to have for life-politics (Adkins 2002; Heaphy 1996; Skeggs 2003). His analysis, it can be argued, conceives contemporary self-identities in overly rationalistic terms, and overplays individual agency. It also overplays the possibilities for empowerment that are generally available to people in modernity, and fails to fully engage with the question of how power works in relation to the self. His analysis ignores issues of difference that have been a predominant feature of other theoretical discussions of self and identity. On the one hand, there are the differences that exist between self-identities, such as those related to class, gender and ethnicity. On the other hand, there is the more complex 'difference' at the core of self and identity that has been the subject of psychoanalytic, radical difference and poststructuralist analyses. Theorists from a number of different perspectives have explored how difference is central to how self and identity are ascribed to individuals, and the play of power in relation to this. Others have explored how differential access to material, social and cultural resources works to shape diverse conceptions of self, and unequal possibilities for agency. These issues are considered throughout the remainder of this chapter. The following section turns to psychoanalytic conceptions of self and identity to consider the centrality of (gender and sexual) differences in these accounts of subjectivity.

The difference within: self and psychic structure

While Giddens' theory of self-identity is infused with social construc-tionist insights, his theory ignores the more radical insights that social constructionist theories provide into the complexity of selfhood. In particular, it ignores the potential messiness of self-identity, the differ-ences between and within subjectivities, and undermines the content of subjectivity (cf. Lash 1993). Despite his engagement with psychological theories, Giddens has relatively little to say explicitly about the complexity of psychic structures as explored in psychoanalytic theory, and especially the workings of the unconscious. While Giddens talks about the institutional 'repression' of existentially troubling issues in late modernity, he pays little attention to the concept of repression as it is related to the unconscious in psychoanalytic theories of subjectivity. While these ideas raise other problems, they provide some sense of the messiness and complexity of subjectivity and identity. They can help us to think about the limits of the rationalizing and self-mastering subject that Giddens' reconstructive theory of reflexive self-identity implies. They can also alert us to how the self is shaped by broader cultural values, and the extent to which difference is inherent to identity, in ways that fail to be explicitly recognized in the theory of reflexive personal life.

Psychic structures and repression

In contrast to the autonomous and self-mastering subject that was assumed in Enlightenment thinking, Freud, in some ways, presented a theory of more troubled selves or subjects (Craib 2001; Calhoun *et al.* 2002b; Freud and Bersani 2002). His psychoanalytic theory argued that unconscious ideas were a fundamental component of the human psyche, and that an individual's desires, actions and emotions were profoundly influenced by the unconscious. Far from being a primarily rational self guided by clear motivations and judgements, the human subject in Freudian theory is driven by unrecognized conflicts and passions. These stem from childhood experience and are shaped by the norms of the broader society. As discussed in Chapter 2, the concept of repression is central to Freud's analysis of the structures of the human psyche, and connects the human psyche to the internalization of cultural values.

As Craib (2001) puts it, Freud explored the relationship between biological impulses and mental representations. He was concerned with physical and psychic drives, and the way 'that the social enters into our heads' (Craib 2001: 19). The most important drive for Freud was sexuality, and he argued that it profoundly shapes psychological development. It is fundamental to 'the energy for psychic life' and plays a crucial part in the formation of psychic structures (Craib 2001: 20). One of the most controversial elements of Freud's theory concerns early childhood sexuality. He argued that childhood sexual fantasies were central to selfhood and identity formation. Childhood sexuality is the source of often terrifying fantasies that must be repressed, and thus leads to the development of splits in the psyche.

Summarized briefly and very simply, Freud argued that an infant's psychological development – and normal sexual and gender development – emerges through a set of processes that involve fantasy relationships with its parents. The original sex aim, or object, is the parent. A key stage of identity development is the Oedipal complex where the infant's love object, or the focus of desire, is the mother. This desire brings boys into a fantasy conflict with the father, which is experienced as a threat to the penis – castration. Through a laborious process the boy child resolves the conflict with the father through compromise, and re-directs his desires towards more appropriate female partners in the future (see Craib 2001). Girls, in their desire for the mother realize their 'castration', and interpret this as punishment for desire. The girl must accept her 'inferiority', and her desire is displaced through a complex set of processes, which ultimately leads to the redirection of desire towards male partners in the future (see Craib 2001). These fantasies, desires and aggressions form the ideas that are split off and repressed to form the unconscious.

As noted in Chapter 2, Freud (see Freud and Bersani 2002) was also concerned with the connections between the values of 'civilized' society and individual subjectivities. Civilized society, he argued, requires the repression of human natures. On the one hand this 'protects' human beings from their nature. On the other hand, it is also responsible for human misery. He identified three parameters of civilized sex, where society denies sexual expression of love between parents and children, denies children's sexuality per se, and curbs the erotic object choice of mature adults (excluding people of the same sex, kin and so on). Such repression allows for a redirection of energies towards cultural creativity. However, it is also the source of dissatisfaction, craving and neuroses. Adult sexual relationships cannot fully compensate for the loss of the original object of desire (the parent), and even they are repressed through cultural values and norms (such as monogamy and other commonly accepted restrictions) that limit sexual pleasure.

Despite what appear to his many critics as its idiosyncratic elements, Freud's theory has a number of important implications for understanding subjectivity. First, the notions of the unconscious and repression point to important, though unobservable, dimensions of human experience. They highlight the irrational motivations for human action, and the limits of human mastery over the self. The unconscious works in complex ways to influence emotions and feelings, and to shape behaviour. It does not operate according to the rules of rational life, and represents important limits for individuals' rational reflexive decision-making capacities. While its effects are constantly felt, it is not subject to rational intervention. Hence, it also places important limits on individuals' self-making capacities (see Craib 2001). Second, the emphasis on civilization and repression highlights the role of cultural values in shaping and limiting human experience. This highlights the centrality of ambivalence to human experience, and the tensions that exist between 'freedom' and 'order'. Such ambivalence and tensions are reflected in a number of other theories of modernity. Smart (1998), for example, has argued that ambivalence has historically been a central feature of theories of modernity, and Bauman (1992a) has emphasized that ambivalence is central to postmodern experience. Third, Freud's theory places sexual difference at the centre of his theory of subjectivity, and influenced later theories of the gendered self as dynamic achievements that had unstable roots. As noted earlier, Freud's own thinking was influenced by a kind of biologism, and his work was infused with notions of natural and inherent drives that give his theory of self-development a normative quality. It has therefore been left to Freud's followers to develop the more radical implications of psychoanalytic theory for the self. While the centrality of sexual difference to his theory has allowed his work to be taken up in some feminist analyses of gendered subjectivities and power, the theme of the unstable self has been more fully developed in poststructuralist analyses. The following sections consider two distinct developments of psychoanalytic ideas on the self: first, Nancy Chodorow's merging of psychoanalytic and sociological ideas in her 'structural' analysis of the formation of gendered subjectivities in modern patriarchal societies; and, second, Lacan's influential reworking of Freud's ideas and its implications for poststructuralist conceptions of the fragmented self.

Gendered subjectivities and patriarchal structures

Many critics have challenged Freud's assumptions about the universal necessity of repression for social order and the universality of the Oedipal complex in self and gender development. Unsurprisingly, some of his fiercest critics have focused on the gendered assumptions underpinning his analysis of the Oedipal complex. Some commentators argue, however, that his analysis inevitably reflected the patriarchal values of his time. Despite being highly critical of Freud's assumptions about gender, Chodorow employs psychoanalytic object-relations theory within a sociological framework to explore the connection between the patriarchal structuring of society and men's and women's gendered subjectivities. Craib (2001) notes that, compared to more orthodox Freudian theory, the object-relations approach works 'a little closer to the surface of the psyche'. It tends towards regarding 'the external world . . . [and] the way the baby is treated, as being as important as, or more important than, the internal process' (2001: 165). As such it is especially amenable to sociological analysis.

Chodorow (1978/1999) explores the processes that influence men and women in developing and valuing different self-identities. She asks a number of questions that are relevant to gendered subjectivities in Western patriarchal contexts: Why are women more relationally focused while men adopt an independent stance? Why is it that women psychologically invest in mothering when it leads to a less valued social position? Why are men so psychologically invested in masculinity? She argues that it is the relationship with the mother that is the most significant one in the process of self-identity development. Central to her argument is the notion that the early relational sphere is different for boys and girls. Mothers, as the primary carers, have different interactions with, and expectations for, male and female children. Put simply, the mother views and interacts with her daughter as an extension of her self. Girls identify with the mother, and this identification continues in a modified form into adulthood. Boys must separate from the mother and develop a different form of identification to achieve a masculine identity, and repress their early connection with her.

Men and women, Chodorow asserts, gain strengths from the relationship with the mother, but are also is some ways damaged by this. Women's selfhood is relational and a positive dimension of this is the capacity to form attachments to other people. On the other hand, they do not easily develop a distinct or separate sense of self. Masculinity, on the other hand, requires the repression of early connections with the mother. This provides a basis for autonomy, but is a more insecure basis for self-definition. Masculine identity is formed in reaction against the mother, and men gain autonomy at the expense of caring capacities. Chodorow argues that the fact that it is mostly women who adopt the social role as mother has profound implications. On this hangs the self-hood of men and women. While women's self-identities are orientated towards caring for others, and towards repeating the mothering they received, men's are orientated towards independence and dominance.

The sociological framing of Chodorow's analysis allows her to avoid accusations of essentialism that are often levied at psychoanalytic theory. As Craib (2001) notes, the focus on Western patriarchal structures also avoids the universalizing tendencies of psychoanalytic thought. Her work has added to the insights that feminist theory provides into how gendered ideologies and practices shape *gendered* subjectivities and self-identities. There are also clear political implications that emerge from Chodorow's analysis that are consistent with its feminist grounding. This would include greater inclusion of men in the mothering (as a social role) and the challenging of hegemonic values and practices as they relate to the child-rearing process. Overall, Chodorow's analysis points to self-formation as a gendered process in patriarchal cultures. Subjectivity, her argument suggests, is not inevitable or neutral, but involves social power. While she acknowledges the possibility of subjective changes over time, there is a sense in which the formation of a gendered self in early psychic life lays a foundation that is beyond the touch of reflexivity. The freely choosing, agentic and self-making self that Giddens talks about seems to have more in common with independent masculine subjectivities as characterized by Chodorow than feminine subjectivities that are more likely to be tied to others.

There are, however, critiques of Chodorow's work that should be noted. Chodorow's departure from more orthodox psychoanalysis has been criticized by some critics, and it is sometimes argued that her analysis conflates social roles with psychic structures (Craib 2001; Elliot 2001). Craib (2001:169) argues that in rejecting the significance of biological impulses she loses 'some of the drama and agonies of the differences between the sexes'. He is more critical, however, of 'the ease with which psychodynamic horses are hitched to sociological carriages that have relatively little to do with them' (2001: 169). For those who are sceptical of the more surface-level analyses of the self that object-relations psychoanalytic thinking promotes, accounts such as Chodorow's risk losing sight of Freud's original insights. This is not a criticism that could easily be made of Lacan's reworking of Freud's theories, which has radical implications for theoretical understandings of the fragmented nature of subjectivity and self-identity, but is orthodox in its return to the basic principles of Freudian theory.

The decentred self

One of the key themes to emerge in theoretical discussions of the self in the latter part of the twentieth century is the extent to which subjectivities and self-identities – gendered and otherwise – can no longer be viewed in essentialist terms and are inherently unstable (see Chapters 3 and 4). Fuss (1989) notes that psychoanalysis is nowadays often viewed as the anti-essentialist discourse par excellence, as it challenges unitary notions of subjectivity and posits gendered and sexual difference as something to be explained. Lacan is especially associated with the psychoanalytic decentring of the unified and rational subject, and anti-essentialist understandings of self and identity (see Chapter 3). While he is in many ways an orthodox Freudian, his emphasis on the role of language and culture in constituting the self has been highly influential on poststructuralist thinking about subjectivity.

Lacan argued that all conceptions of the self as unitary and coherent are illusory, and emphasized the role of language in how people were subjected to cultural norms and values. In his analysis of early childhood experience, he argued that the infant initially exists in a relationship with the mother as if they were one. The child gains its first but illusory sense of wholeness through the 'mirror stage' where it mistakes its reflection as representing a unified or whole being. The conception of a coherent and authentic self is therefore imaginary from the beginning. A child's sense of separateness is not fully achieved until the acquisition of language. Language, Saussure argued, is a relational system of signs, where signs have no given and essential meanings or properties. Rather, meaning is derived from the differences between signs. Lacan developed this notion to argue that the acquisition of language is fundamental to a separate sense of self as it provides the basis for distinguishing between 'self' and 'not self'. Selfhood, therefore, can only be defined in relation to what is not self, and at the heart of selfhood is the definitional relationship to 'the other'.

Through acquiring language and a sense of separate self, Lacan argued, the child becomes located in the Symbolic Order. Language is a relay route for the norms, rules and moral codes of the culture. These are internalized by the child, and mark the entry of the social into the psyche. During the Oedipus complex, Lacan argues, the child imagines the incest taboo to be imposed by its father. The child is subjected to the Law of the Father – the cultural laws and prohibitions of the culture – represented by the male parent. The absence or presence of the phallus is the basis for the recognition of sexual difference, and the taking up of a social self as masculine or feminine. The internalization of the incest taboo implies that the desire for the mother must be repressed. As with Freud, this repression requires a splitting off that forms the basis for the unconscious. Subjectivity, illusionary from the start, is fragmented, split and conflictual. There remains, however, an unconscious (illusory) idea of the wholeness that has been lost, and there is an unquenchable desire for this and the 'other' that was given up for a sense of separate self. However, given their illusory foundations, such desires can never be fully satisfied.

Ultimately Lacan attempts to explain how subjectivity is bound up with the internalization of culture and the subjection to cultural laws and prohibitions. The processes and forms of subjection he analyses bear little resemblance to the reflexive self as envisioned by Giddens. In the latter's account, the self uses and employs cultural resources to shape themselves and the world around them, and is relatively unencumbered by cultural laws and prohibitions. Language is viewed in a fairly straightforward way as something that is employed to narrate self-identity.

There are, of course, criticisms to be made of Lacan's work. His critics have pointed out that despite his influence on deconstructionist theory, and his association with radical anti-essentialism, he is in some ways the most orthodox or 'authentic' of Freudians. Fuss (1989) notes that Lacan strategically employs linguistics to clean Freud's house of biologism. However, she suggests, his analysis remains infused with assumptions about the essential role of language in the production of subjectivity, and the universal production of the subject in the Symbolic (Fuss 1989). We might also ask what the possibilities of human agency are if the human subject is so thoroughly subjected to cultural forces (Craib 2001; Elliot 2001). Despite this, the emphasis on divisions within the psyche, the importance of the symbolic over the real, and the imaginary dimension to our sense of self has been an important source of inspiration for deconstructive or cultural analyses of the self in social theory (see Elliot 2001). The following section considers Foucault's influence on theories of socially constructed subjectivities, which is critical of psychoanalysis as a discourse, and provides a basis for conceptualizing power with respect to reflexive selfhood.

Inscribing selfhood: discipline and power

While psychoanalytic theory has been influential on conceptions of the fragmented and non-unitary self, many critics are unconvinced by its reliance on unobservable and universal psychic processes. The emphasis on human sexual drives at the heart of much psychoanalytic theory is often viewed suspiciously as a form of theoretical essentialism. It is also often viewed as a framework that operates with an inadequate conception of power, especially in relation to its own normative categories and concepts. A radically alternative framework for understanding the cultural production of subjectivities and self-identity, and the play of power in relation to this, is provided by Foucault's work (see Chapter 3). Foucault was concerned with the history of ideas and discourse, and especially with power–knowledge relationships in 'disciplinary' society. His theory suggests that an adequate understanding of modern subjectivities requires attention to their construction in historical terms. Power, he argued, is at the heart of self and identity in modern contexts. Power is inherent in knowledge about the mind and body, and knowledge focused on the body (and resistances to it) shapes and produces certain forms of subjectivity and self-identities.

Disciplined subjects

Foucault's work can be seen as a fecund source for much recent work on identity and subjectivity (see Best and Kellner 1997; Hall 1996; Webb 1997). His earlier work (1979a, b) provides a distinctive analysis of the ways in which selfhood and subjectivity are bound up with the workings of power in modernity. Foucault rejected psychoanalytic explanations of how modern selfhood was shaped and produced, and instead emphasized the relationship between discourse and power-knowledge. As discussed in Chapter 3, Foucault's early work focused on various forms of expert knowledge and their application in hospitals, prisons and schools from the eighteenth century onwards. He viewed this in terms of the emergence of new technologies of power, and presented a picture of the production and subjection of individuals through social institutions, discourses and practices. In effect, he presented a picture of subjectivities that were the products of disciplinary power. In doing so, Foucault argued that power must not be understood purely in negative terms, but also in terms of its productive nature.

In *Discipline and Punish*, as discussed in Chapter 3, Foucault (1979a) presented a study of the 'micro physics' of power as they operated within the institutions of prisons, schools and hospitals. Discipline is identified as one of the primary techniques that serves as a relay route and support for power–knowledge relations that subjugate human bodies by turning them into objects of knowledge. Through discipline, as it is linked with normalization strategies, the individual is not merely observed and regulated but 'carefully fabricated'. Discipline is tied up with normalization strategies through its focus on the body, the ultimate goal being the elimination of all social and psychological irregularities and the production of useful docile bodies. For Foucault the individual subject is an effect of political technologies through which its very identity, desires, body and 'soul' are constituted. He argued:

> it should not be forgotten that there existed . . . a technique for constituting individuals as correlative elements of power and knowledge. The individual is no doubt the fictitious atom of an 'ideological' representation of society; but he is also a reality fabricated by this specific technology of power that I have called 'discipline'. We must cease once and for all to describe the effects of power in negative terms . . . In fact, power produces; it produces reality; it produces domains of objects and rituals of

truth. The individual and the knowledge that may be gained of him belong to this production.

(Foucault 1979a: 194)

This theme is further considered in the first volume of *The History of Sexuality* (Foucault 1979b), where again the modern individual is both the object and subject of knowledge. Here Foucault again emphasizes the productive nature of power, and power relations and their technologies are viewed as open strategies. In this scheme the individual is not repressed, but is shaped and formed within matrices of scientific disciplinary mechanisms. The 'homosexual', for example, can be viewed as a product of medico-scientific and psych-scientific knowledge. The notion of 'the homosexual' subject or identity initially emerged as a category of deviance – of abnormality – in expert medical, psychological and sexological knowledge in the nineteenth century. This category was applied to people who had sexual desires for members of the same sex, and was mobilized in the development of medical and psychological techniques to correct perverse behaviours. Eventually, however, the category was taken up by people to make sense of their own desires and identities. While homosexual behaviour may have always existed, the idea that people could identify as homosexual subjects only became possible after the category was created. As such, homosexual identities are historical productions that have their roots in expert knowledge.

As Best and Kellner (1997) point out, drawing from Dews' (1987) analysis, the subject for Foucault has a double meaning: subject to someone else by control and dependence, and tied to one's own identity by a conscience or self-knowledge. Self-knowledge in this sense is a strategy and effect of power, whereby one internalizes self-control or monitoring. Foucault's earlier work can be seen, in part, to be concerned with posing a challenge to the notion of identities as pre-given, neutral, unified and fixed. Indeed, as Best and Kellner (1997) suggest, a key assumption in Foucault's work is that strategies of resistance would have to attempt to destroy the prisons of received identities and challenge hegemonic discourses to encourage the proliferation of differences of all kinds.

Discipline/reflexivity

As noted in Chapter 3, Foucault's concern with the relationship between expert discourse (medical and psychoanalytic discourse, for example) and the exercise of power is developed within a broader project that

111

aims to trace the development of surveillance as an aspect of governmentality (whereby the self-monitoring individual internalizes surveillance) (see Chapter 4). In contrast to Giddens, who argues that modern institutions such as the hospital and the prison are crucial for the institutional exclusion of existentially disturbing experience in modernity, Foucault viewed these as central to, and indicative of, disciplinary mechanisms of power. From a Foucauldian perspective, psychoanalysis (which refers to a form of therapeutic practice as well as a theory), is also bound up with disciplinary power, and is one of a number of interrelated discourses that construct and judge our conceptions of normality. Therapeutic knowledge, including psychoanalysis, is a supreme example of surveillance, as it produces and regulates psychological norms and deviance. For some Foucauldians, the growth in the importance of the therapist in contemporary cultures, and the growing hegemony of therapeutic knowledge in explaining personal and social problems, would all be indicative of how thoroughly effective the psychological surveillance of society is.

Foucault's work has been criticized for conflating human experience with male experience and for refusing to engage meaningfully with feminist analyses of subjectivity (see Chapter 7). Critics have also pointed to the unlikely cohesion that the discursively constructed self achieves in Foucault's analysis, and the extent to which the ambivalences and desires of the subject are undermined (Elliot 2001). Some critics argue that his view of the docile subject epitomizes the soullessness of determinist analyses, and his reduction of human agency to the micro-politics of 'resistance' in his earlier work is generally viewed as problematic. The micro-politics of resisting received identities is often viewed as a weak form of agency. How, many critics ask, if discourse and knowledge-power are all-pervasive, does such a politics work? While he does explore the relation of 'the self to the self' in his later works, the insights for agency remain opaque (see McNay 1992, 1994).

In terms of the contemporary relevance of Foucault's analysis of modernity, Bauman (2000a) suggests that Foucault had mapped the significance of disciplinarity to modern societies as it became less central to social organization. What disciplinarity was to modernity, it could be argued, reflexivity is to late modernity. As Lash (1993) points out, what Foucault views as disciplinary discourses, Giddens sees as expert systems that ward off threats to ontological security. Lash employs Foucault's insights in developing a critique of Giddens and Beck and exploring the limits of reflexivity. For Lash, modern subjectivity should be understood as only capable of subsuming a limited amount of content under the reflexive self. Contradiction and contingency, he suggests, are far more characteristic of the contemporary self than Giddens' theory of reflexivity will allow. Lash reminds us that what Foucault characterized as disciplinary discourses that discipline and normalize individuals, Giddens sees as 'expert systems' that ward off contingency. Where Giddens wants expert systems to impose order in the face of chaos, Lash suggests, Foucault is on the side of flux and difference, and opposed to the ordering properties of discourse. Lash further points out that what appears as freedom of agency for the theory of reflexivity is just another means of control for Foucault, as the direct operation of power on the body has been displaced by its mediated operation on the body through the 'soul'.

Consuming postmodern identities

Both Lacan's and Foucault's theories has been influential on the idea that self and identity are unstable categories, and have been drawn upon to argue that postmodern identities are becoming increasingly fragmented, brittle and fluid (see Best and Kellner 1997). Some theorists have also celebrated the theoretical and micro-political deconstruction of identities as a form of resistance to the operations of power that Foucault described. A number of queer theorists, for example, have drawn on Foucault to argue for a politics of transgression that is centred on the instability and fluidity of sexual and gender identities (see Seidman 1996). This, they argue, would entail 'queering' our notions of normal sexual and gender identities through gender parody, and could include parodying stereotypical performances of gender through practices such as drag. Playing with gender and queering it, they argue, can reveal given gendered identities – and indeed all identities – as fictions. While this argument, on the surface at least, appears to imply that individuals can intentionally resist imposed gender identities, in arguing for a performative conception of gender (where gender is produced through the constant discursive reiteration of gender as a real and tangible thing), Butler (1990, 1993) argues that there is no subject or 'doer' behind the gendered deed or the troubling of it. In this sense, subjectivity and self-identity are wholly mythical.

From a very different perspective, Baudrillard has argued that 'we are all transsexuals now'. We are, he suggests 'symbolically transsexuals . . . where nothing is either masculine or feminine' (cited in Segal 1999).

However, as opposed to celebrating the 'liberation' from the tyranny of received gendered identities, Baudrillard is concerned with the crisis of postmodern selfhood. Whereas the maintenance of a sense of social reality is central to Giddens' notion of the project of the self, Baudrillard (1998, 1999) argues that the postmodern self exists in the age of simulation and hyper-reality (see Chapter 4). The postmodern era is one where simulations appear more real to the individual than reality itself. In the hyper-real world the search for the reality and truth of our selves is a futile one. Self and identity, he argues, is now about the surface and no longer about depth, as it is surface reality that defines postmodern society.

For Baudrillard, the world of hyper-reality is the world of mediated experience and mediating technologies (see Chapter 4). The increasing dominance of media and communication technologies means that communication itself is more important than the message or content. The dominance of the media means that we live in a world of internally referential signs and images, where signs are related only to each other and there is no real meaning behind them. The question of what is real or true is therefore one that is nowadays impossible to answer. In the world of simulation, the notion of an authentic self has no purchase. The modern self for Baudrillard was, as Elliot (2001: 141) puts it, 'constructed around subjective elements, such as passions, guilt, conscience ... against this backdrop meanings were attached to identity as concealed or hidden, with depth of the self or interiority a key theme'. In contrast, the postmodern self has little content or depth. Rather, it is preoccupied with surface and style. It is a self that is endlessly consuming images but, like the messages themselves, is detached from meaning and alienated.

As noted at the beginning of this chapter, Giddens is highly critical of characterizations of the postmodern self as a passive entity. Radical postmodernist analyses like Baudrillard's, he suggests, fail to acknowledge the demands that exist for individuals to actively engage with the world around them. Giddens is also critical of Christopher Lasch's (1991) influential (but equally pessimistic according to Giddens) account of contemporary selfhood. Lasch is concerned with the rise of the 'narcissistic' self that lacks a strong sense of connectedness with others. This is a self that is increasingly preoccupied with itself, and is socially and historically disconnected. For Lasch, consumer capitalism furthers narcissism, as consumer society is one that is dominated by appearances. Giddens describes the argument thus:

114

Consumption addresses the alienated qualities of modern social life and claims their solution: it promises the very things the narcissist desires – attractiveness, beauty and personal popularity – through the consumption of the 'right' kind of goods and services. Hence all of us, in modern social conditions, live as though surrounded by mirrors; in the search for the appearance of an unblemished, socially valued self.

(Giddens 1991: 172)

For Lasch, the self that is preoccupied with itself is one that struggles with feelings of inauthenticity, which it is encouraged to remedy through consumption. Analyses like those produced by Baudrillard and Lasch, Giddens argues, underestimate the possibilities that exist for individual agency in relation to self-identity in late modernity, and overplay the extent to which emptiness and passivity are becoming the defining characteristics of the contemporary self. Despite this criticism, both theorists touch on a theme that is often central to discussions of contemporary (postmodern) selfhood that Giddens' arguments about the reflexive self mostly ignore, but is worthy of further discussion: the extent to which postmodern identities are consumed. The following section considers Bauman's work on identity in postmodernity, and the consumer ethic that, he argues, underpins it.

Do-it-yourself identities

As discussed in Chapter 4, Bauman is concerned with how post or liquid modernity disembeds without re-embedding, and how the 'patterns, codes and rules' to which people could conform are nowadays in short supply (2000a: 7). Bauman argues that liquid modernity is in many ways post-Panoptical modernity, where the surveillance that Foucault had observed is no longer the prime integrating (or disciplining) mechanism for the majority (2000a: 13). He is also sceptical of the extent to which the self-reflexivity that Giddens observes provides for 'a genuine self-constitution' (2000a: 34).

Contingency, Bauman argues, is the hallmark of the current era, and heightened or radical contingency is the key characteristic of contemporary identities. Processes of individualization, he suggests, means that human identity has been transformed from a 'given' to a 'task'. This implies that human beings are no longer simply born into identities, and people must now take on the responsibility of making their own (2000a:

31–2). Self-made identities must be solid enough to work as identities. However, they must also be flexible enough not to limit future movements in 'constantly changing, volatile circumstances' (2000a: 50). Bauman is concerned with the consumer ethic that permeates all aspects of contemporary social life, and its influence on the task of self-making. Postmodern society, he argues, engages its members as consumers as opposed to producers, and whatever we do 'is an activity shaped in the likeness of shopping' (2000a: 73). Postmodern 'pick-and-mix' identities are always left open to revision. In contrast to the stable and coherent self-identities that Giddens emphasizes, Bauman conjures up an image of identities that are much more fragile:

> Identities seem fixed and solid only when seen, in a flash, from the outside. Whatever solidity they might have when contemplated from the inside of one's own biographical experience appears fragile, fragmented, vulnerable, and constantly torn apart by shearing forces which lay bare its fluidity and crosscurrents which threaten to rend in pieces and carry away any form they might have acquired.
>
> (Bauman 2000a: 83)

For Bauman, identities nowadays are intrinsically volatile and unfixed, and the ability to 'shop around in the supermarket of identities' (2000a:83) becomes central to the pursuit of identity. This implies only holding on to one form of identity until another is desired. However, while the 'freedom' of the consumer is paramount in contemporary cultural contexts, it provides an ambiguous framework for human existence and action. In this sense, the all-pervasive ethic of consumer freedom also implies the burden of choice. In a way that resonates with Giddens' analysis, he argues that in postmodern contexts there is no recourse to a universally agreed framework for making moral decisions. There are multiple sources of moral authority, and individuals are therefore responsible for moral decision-making and negotiating choices. In contrast to Giddens, however, Bauman emphasizes the implications of this for individuals who are thrown back on their own resources, and must live with the consequences of their decisions. In post or liquid modernity, the authority of traditions and modern institutions dissolve, leaving individuals highly attuned to the consequences of their actions. In such contexts, moral choices are highly problematic as the resources for guiding them are not given. There is a privatization of experience that raises existential anxieties (of the kind discussed by Giddens) in a profound way.

Unlike Giddens, Bauman emphasizes the centrality of resources to the 'freedoms' of identification offered in the era of the consumer ethic. Resources, he suggests, allow some people the freedom to choose how to live and who to be, but also protects them from the consequences of making the wrong choices (2000b: 218). The well-resourced can fully embrace the ethic of consumption in all areas of personal life, and its centrality to identity, because when mistakes are made they employ their resources to move on. The poor and the powerless, however, whilst also subject to the consumer ethic, do not have the resources to make choices so freely, and are subject to – and must live with the consequences of – the choices of others. As far as choice and control over one's identity are concerned, Bauman suggests that while the dynamics that Giddens identifies might imply empowerment for some, the consequence for others is disempowerment. He argues: 'the ability to deal with this deeply uncomfortable sense the brittleness, haziness, temporariness and overall unreliability of identity rebounds in two sharply distinct experiences' (2000b: 214). On the one hand, there is the exhilaration and pleasure that is dependent on being well resourced. On the other hand, there are the threats to identity that are experienced by those without access to resources. For Bauman, there is a new social hierarchy that 'stretches from choice to no-choice; from the autonomy of self-identification at the top to the dependency on assigned identities at the bottom' (2000b: 214). This highlighting of resources, together with a generally less optimistic view of the consequences of social change, marks an important distinction between Bauman's and Giddens' analyses. The next section of this chapter discusses further the issue of resources.

Self-reflexivity and resources

In discussing Giddens' analysis of self-reflexivity, May (1997) points to the necessity of exploring the 'natural' history of the subject more closely, and considering the limited visions of everyday possibilities that are open to individuals. Such a critique, May (1997: 48) suggests, would emphasize the 'opacity and naturalness of everyday experience'. It would further consider the ways in which discourses and structures, which deliver these opaque features of everyday life to subjects, place limits on the ways in which it is possible to think about the world. In other words, while there are some possibilities opened up in late modernity for agency in relation to the self, we must also consider the limits of agency. A key challenge in accounting for the possibilities and limitations of agency is to account for the *different* possibilities that are available to people for the self-reflexivity that Giddens theorizes. This theme of difference is taken up by Beverly Skeggs (2003) who argues that Giddens' analysis of the reflexive self ignores the significance of class-based differences (and the economic, social and cultural resources that different groups of people have access to) in defining the possibilities open to people in any given social context. Resources, Skeggs suggests, are crucial in influencing the extent to which individuals are allocated certain kinds of selves and subjectivities or actively participate in the self-defining and self-creating processes that Giddens describes. She argues:

> All the new debates that take perspectives on self-production, -responsibility, -monitoring, -reflexivity, etc., are premised upon the availability of, and access to, discourse and cultural resources, and the techniques and practices necessary for producing, but also knowing, a self.
>
> (Skeggs 2003: 20)

Analyses like Giddens', Skeggs notes, provide no sense that having a self is a classed, raced or gendered issue. The self as described by Giddens, she argues, is a category of personhood that is only applicable to the privileged few, and neither is how individuals construct their personal biographies as neutral a method as Giddens implies. Citing Savage, Skeggs further argues that the globalizing forces that Giddens sees as the systemic background feature of late modernity, might be more properly conceptualized as characteristic of the possibilities that are open to particular types of socially located individuals. The kind of sociology that Giddens produces, she suggests, could be viewed 'as part of a symbolic struggle' for authorizing middle-class experience and perspectives. Class, Skeggs argues, is still important, but erased in the sociology of the reflexive self that reflects well-resourced middle-class ways of being. We should turn our attention, she suggests, to how classed selves are reinscribed in theories of reflexive modernity. Rather than viewing the world from a position of the privileged, and assuming individualization, reflexivity and choice, we should instead ask what interests lie behind theories that posit these processes as universal. It is important to do so, she suggests, to avoid providing only a partial analysis of life experience – and theorizing only the conditions of the middle classes.

Conclusion

Giddens rearticulates the contemporary self as a reflexive project, and in doing so affords the contemporary self an empowered agency. Instead of fragmenting, he argues, contemporary self-identities are constantly remade and produced by subjects themselves. Central to Giddens' argument is the idea that self-identity is for 'everybody' becoming open and malleable, and that individuals nowadays have little choice but to participate in self-making. In arguing this case, he emphasizes new universalities and commonalities with respect to self-identity. In doing so he mobilizes a number of interlinked arguments about the *essential* and universal aspects of psychic life and experience. Modernist and post-modernist positions of self and identity highlight the problems with Giddens' argument about self-identity in late modernity, and the sociology of self-identity this promotes. They point to a number of problems in his analyses relating to the overemphasizing of agency with respect to self-identity and lifestyle; the overly coherent view of the reflexive self; the denial of how significant resources are for determining the different possibilities that exist with respect to self-making; and the overly optimistic view of social change that is presented. Modernist and post-modernist arguments about self and identity tend to foreground issues of difference and power. In doing so they provide a number of bases for scepticism about theories of reflexive self-identities, and point to the problems inherent in the universalizing arguments and essentialist assumptions that underpin them. Combined, these also provide a considerable basis for scepticism about the significance afforded the reflexive self in the reconstructive theory of reflexive modernity, and the reconstructed sociology of self and identity it promotes.

7

REFLEXIVE RELATING
AND INTIMACY

Introduction

This chapter considers the insights that modernity's 'emotional history' is said to provide into the democratization of social life in late modernity. Chapter 6 considered the possibilities that reflexive modernity is said to present for the individual project of self-identity. According to Giddens, when traditional ways of living lose their value individuals face pressing questions about who and how to be. People negotiate their identities by making practical lifestyle decisions about everyday issues, including their relationships with others. Furthermore, in the insecure and risky world of late modernity, intimate life is identified as the place where security is most intensely sought and cherished, but it is also where radical insecurities and contingencies can be encountered in powerful ways. The topics of relating and intimacy are therefore deployed by reconstructivist theorists to provide insights into the implications of the social and cultural developments associated with late modernity.

While many sociologists recognize that relationships are not what they used to be, attempts to understand how and why they are changing, and the implications of these changes, have led to contentious debate about the nature of power, agency and social structures in contemporary settings. Much of this debate has focused on changing gender orders. Giddens and Beck suggest that intimate relationships between men and women are becoming more equal. Interrelated (economic, social and cultural) developments, in Giddens' view, result in a drive towards democratic sexual and emotional relationships, which has far-reaching implications for modern institutions. Others put forward a counter-argument that theories of democratic relational life have an inadequate understanding of how power works in relation to gender and intimate relationships. They suggest that relationships continue to be shaped by social and economic inequalities and that there are limited possibilities currently available to women and men for constructing egalitarian forms of relating. The chapter begins by outlining how Giddens and Beck (with Beck-Gernsheim) approach the issue of reflexive relating and intimacy. It then explores how their ideas converge and differ, and considers the implications and criticisms of their work. The remainder of the chapter considers a number of postmodernist and modernist theories of sexuality and gender relations that are crucial to understanding the operations of power and gender inequalities that Giddens and Beck imply are being overcome in contemporary social contexts. The concluding sections of the chapter consider themes that have emerged in research that point to the ways in which gendered differences and inequalities in relation to both paid work and intimate life are more resilient and complex than theories of reflexive intimacy imply. Crucially, this research points to how demands to be reflexive with respects to gender and relating are not neutral.

Transforming intimacy

Giddens (1992) develops his ideas about the changing nature of contemporary relationships in *The Transformation of Intimacy*. He argues that intimacy in its late modern form implies a radical democratization of the interpersonal domain, which 'might be a subversive influence upon modern institutions as a whole' (1992: 3). Giddens' argument is developed with reference to changes in sexual mores and behaviours in Western societies. First, there have been significant developments in heterosexual approaches to sexuality and intimate relationships over the past few decades. For example, women nowadays assert their sexual desires in a more explicit and vocal way than ever before, and generally have greater sexual experience than previous generations. For men *and* women sexual pleasure is a key requirement of married or couple life. Second, there have also been significant developments in the non-heterosexual world. In particular, homosexuality is no longer considered a 'perversion', and is increasingly viewed as an 'alternative' – and increasingly valid – lifestyle.

Meanwhile, the growing importance attached to a relationship in contemporary societies is something that cuts across the heterosexual and homosexual dichotomy. For both heterosexuals and homosexuals sexuality is a key feature of who we are – an aspect of the self that can be developed in self-realization. It is a prime 'connecting point between body, self-identity and social norms' (Giddens 1992: 15). A key issue for Giddens is a new commonality in heterosexual and homosexual experience. He argues that:

> Gay women and men have preceded most heterosexuals in developing relationships, in the sense that the term has come to assume today when applied to personal life. For they have had to 'get along' without traditionally established frameworks of marriage, in conditions of relative equality between partners.
>
> (Giddens 1992: 15)

Giddens is suggesting that heterosexual and homosexual relationships are becoming more and more similar. Nowadays, all relationships can be considered everyday experiments. First, as non-heterosexual relationships are constructed and operate outside established (heterosexual) norms, they lack institutional support and cultural guidelines. But this is increasingly the case for heterosexuals, as old models of relational life no longer hold under the pressures of detraditionalization. Second, as non-heterosexual relationships are not grounded in the gender differences that have traditionally structured heterosexual relationships they are – in theory – relationships between equals. Equality, however, is increasingly an expectation (if not a reality) in relationships between men and women. Changes in the economic conditions of women, and their emotional and sexual expectations, mean that women are no longer trapped into economic dependence on men, and no longer perceive their position as one of servicing men's needs, domestically, sexually or otherwise. Third, Giddens argues, the absence of solid guidelines has meant that individuals in same-sex partnerships have had to be particularly creative in forming relationships from scratch. But as they are relationships between equals, the creation and everyday operation of same-sex relationships also require the negotiation of a mutually satisfying relationship. This, he contends, is the situation that many heterosexual relationships find themselves in today.

Plastic sexuality, the pure relationship and confluent love

To understand the dynamics that underpin changing patterns of intimacy, we can look at three of Giddens' key concepts. First, the notion of *plastic sexuality*, which expresses the severance of sexuality 'from its age-old integration with reproduction, kinship and generations' (1992: 27). This began in the nineteenth century when new forms of contraception meant that, for women, 'sexuality could become separated from a chronic round of pregnancy and childbirth' (1992: 26). Today, reproductive technologies mean that this differentiation is complete:

> Now that conception can be artificially produced, rather than only artificially inhibited, sexuality is at last fully autonomous. Reproduction can occur in the absence of sexual activity; this is the final liberation for sexuality, which thence can become wholly a quality of individuals and their transactions with one another.
>
> (Giddens 1992: 27)

For Giddens, plastic sexuality is the outcome of the 'deep-lying and irreversible' structural changes and processes of institutional reflexivity (see Chapter 5). It is the precondition, not the result, of the sexual revolution of recent decades which heralded female sexual autonomy, and the flourishing of forms of homosexuality. Contrary to Foucault's view that expert discourses on sexuality are a means of disciplinary power and regulation (see below), Giddens sees them as resources for the creation of reflexively ordered narratives of the self, which open up processes of institutional reflexivity. An increasing acceptance of sexual diversity demonstrates how institutional reflexivity becomes an almost inherent democratizing drive within modernity.

Second, this democratizing impulse is stimulating the emergence of a new form of relationship in late modernity – the pure relationship – which is 'in some ways causally related to the development of plastic sexuality' (1992: 58). For Giddens, the pure relationship:

> refers to a situation where a social relation is entered into for its own sake, for what can be derived by each person from a sustained association with another; and which is continued only in so far as it is thought by both parties to deliver enough satisfactions for each individual to stay within it.
>
> (Giddens 1992: 58)

The pure relationship is part of a generic restructuring of intimacy, which can be traced in relationships today, including marriage (Giddens 1992). Pure relationships are sought and entered into only for what the relationship can bring to the contracting partners. The guiding justification of the pure relationship is that it should survive only as long as the commitment survives, or until a more promising relationship offers itself. For women this is only truly possible when they are not economically dependent on male partners. Women's economic autonomy, therefore, is a key factor in the increased pressure for a wholly equal and reciprocal relationship – as economic independence implies the freedom to leave. This freedom is central to Giddens' notion of confluent love:

> Romantic love has long had an egalitarian strain . . . However, [it] is skewed in terms of power. For women, dreams of romantic love have all too often led to domestic subjugation. Confluent love presumes equality in emotional give and take, the more so the more any particular love tie approximates closely to the prototype of the pure relationship. Love here only develops to the degree to which intimacy does, to the degree to which each partner is prepared to reveal concerns and need to the other and be vulnerable to that other.
>
> (Giddens 1992: 61)

Nowadays, Giddens argues, love does not presume a permanent relationship. Confluent love, and the pure relationship, involves a high degree of instability, and a new contingency in personal relationships. Once taken-for-granted roles, behaviours and commitments must be continually negotiated, with couples being explicit about how they want things to be. As each partner is engaged in the process of developing their own self, there is a distinct possibility that different agendas will emerge over time – and the relationship cannot be presumed to continue. Hence, partners must constantly assert, reassert and negotiate their commitment and what they want.

In short, Giddens is arguing that intimacy today assumes that the individual is the maker of his or her own life and that there is equality between partners. Men and women have freedom to choose lifestyles and forms of partnership, and also the freedom to leave relationships, choice being the ideological motif. The drive to find a satisfactory relationship is personal affirmation, and marriage and couple relationships are sustained only for as long as they provide emotional satisfaction from close contact with others and from intimacy (Giddens 1992). Marriage becomes less of a status transition, more a symbol of commitment, as potent as that which lies at the heart of many other forms of relationship, including non-heterosexual ones. The emphasis on individual autonomy and choice provides a radicalizing dynamic that makes the transformation of personal life possible.

Intimate battles: biographies, relationships and work

Beck develops his analysis of the changing nature of relationships in the context of his theory of individualization in second modernity (Chapter 5). In *Risk Society*, Beck describes individualization as 'a structural, sociological transformation of social institutions and the relationship of the individual to society'. It releases men and women from their traditional roles and unleashes the potential to create new and democratic forms of living and relating. In *The Normal Chaos of Love*, Beck and Beck-Gernsheim examine the dynamics and effects of these developments in marriage and family life. In contrast to Giddens, the degree to which their investigation is framed in the traditional language of family and marriage is striking. On the one hand, theirs is an analysis of radical change; on the other, it is fairly narrowly confined to 'traditional' (heterosexual) forms of relating.

As discussed in Chapter 5, individualization has radical implications for individual identities and family life, as people are liberated from taken-for-granted roles and cut loose from traditional securities, such as religious faith and familiar forms of belonging. Women, freed from the fate of compulsory housework and economic dependency on their husbands, place a strain on traditional family ties and a 'negotiated provisional' family begins to emerge, where there is no given set of obligations or opportunities, and the relationship between men and women cannot be copied or modelled on what went before. Intimate life becomes a contingent mix of freedom and insecurity, full of possibilities and pitfalls – where structure and rules have to be reinvented. Beck recognizes the weight of responsibility people have, in this context, to write their own biographies and negotiate new forms of social commitment and security.

Beck is concerned with how individuals negotiate alternative ways of living and relating, and with the changing dynamics of relational life in reflexive modernity, as men and women are faced with decisions about how to be, and with the dilemma of being together. While he agrees with Giddens that this opens up some potential for more open and democratic couple and family relationships, for Beck, it also sets the scene for 'intimate battles'. The catalyst is the new individual female biography that has emerged since the 1960s. In contrast to Giddens' narrative of the impulse to negotiation, Beck and Beck-Gernsheim describe a messier picture, and suggest a long and bitter battle, since the more equal the sexes become, the more aware women become of persistent inequalities.

The possibility for conflict in heterosexual love and marriage arises in the changing dynamic between individual biography, the negotiation of new forms of relating and changes in working life. In a globalizing economy, the labour market demands changing work patterns and mobility from its workforce. Flexible working time, short-term contracts, under- and over-employment and the decentralization of work sites add another level of uncertainty to people's lives, so that work, for Beck, becomes the great divider in contemporary relationships. In spite of these insecurities, the prevailing ethic in late modern societies is self-actualization and control – a life of one's own – and individuals are impelled to be the makers of their own identity and livelihood. Beck's emphasis on the tensions and contradictions that arise between relating and working distinguish his approach from that of Giddens.

Intimate battles arise due to the contradiction between these new demands and the realities of people's lives, still partially rooted in modern institutions. The equalization of men and women cannot be created in an institutionalized family structure which presupposes their inequality. So, lacking institutional solutions, people must learn to negotiate relationships on the basis of equality. Personal conflicts in relationships are initiated by the opening up of possibilities of choice, leading to tensions between individual career needs, the division of household labour and child care. In negotiating decisions about who does what, the differing conditions of men and women become more obvious. In this way, Beck argues, the battle between the sexes becomes the central drama of our time, the personalized version of the contradictory trends of late modernity.

The potential for conflict and for democracy in the intimate sphere lie in the ways that the contradictions between family demands and personal freedom are negotiated and justified. Individualization, detraditionalization and globalization are the preconditions for the democratization of everyday life and relationships – towards an internalized democracy and the belief in the equality of relationships and in dialogue as the means of reaching decisions in personal lives. Where there are no simply given models of what family, marriage, parenthood, sexuality and love should mean, alternative ways of living with others open up. Beyond the security of traditional family structures, Beck and Beck-

Gernsheim suggest, love becomes the centre around which our lives revolve. It becomes at once the primary, self-affirming, but equally impossible, goal. In an individualized culture, you must allow your beloved to be free, but in wanting them to love you, you restrict their freedom. Each partner wants his or her freedom, and at the same time to be chained to the hands of the beloved. Out of this, and between love and freedom, a new ethics might emerge about the importance of individuation and obligation to others. It is in the everyday experiments in living that we might discover a new ethics which combines personal freedom with engagements with others.

Is it possible, in late modernity, for equals to reflexively relate to and love each other? What kind of love can survive liberation? With less work security, less stability in family and community life and more fear of being alone, how much room can partners give to each other to write their own biographies? As standard gender roles in relationships decline, Beck and Beck-Gernsheim paint a picture of couples unsure of how to be with each other. The crux of the problem is the balance between being oneself *and* being together with someone who is also searching for themselves and creating their own identity. This, for Beck, is the double-faced nature of the liberation process: a dialectic between its advantages and drawbacks, where we encounter the cold world of independence where love is defined as a burden and missed as permanent support. Since we cannot return to old ways of being, a new kind of relationship might emerge from this dilemma, to cater for two separate biographies. In confronting the risk of loneliness, people might potentially find new ways of living with one another which are egalitarian.

Order and uncertainty

Two similar stories emerge of social change and reflexive intimate life; of the nature and implications of these developments; and of their relation to the broader processes of individualization and detraditionalization. Both Giddens and Beck highlight the degree to which established models for relationships are increasingly untenable, and argue that having relationships today means experimenting with new ways of being together. There are, however, significant differences between them. Giddens, for example, focuses on increasingly negotiated and democratic forms of relating (families, couples, parenting and so on), while Beck emphasizes the tensions and contradictions encountered in relationships, which are harder to resolve. In comparing these accounts of the transforming patterns of intimate life in reflexive modernity, we can see how the similarities between the two lie in shared concerns with the implications, for individual identity and intimate relationships, of the processes of reflexive modernization. The differences lie in Giddens' and Beck's distinct theoretical diagnoses of these implications in the dynamics of intimate and public life, the language they use to explore these transformations, and the degree of optimism each carries for the democratization of everyday life.

Giddens and Beck are concerned with new ways of being and relating in late modernity, recognizing how women's increasing equality has blurred gender roles and undermined the dynamics of traditional relationships. For Giddens, this implies the pure relationship, where reflexive individuals seek each other and stay together only for as long as their commitment survives. He describes the emotional equality and commitment between them as confluent love, which is contingent on the degree to which each is openly revealed to the other. The transformation of the personal sphere which Giddens describes, has implications for the democratization of everyday life. For Beck, relationships are battle sites, shaped by the contradictions between the needs of self-affirming individuals, the negotiation of equality between partners, and the contingencies of the labour market. Love, for Beck and Beck-Gernsheim, expresses the pivotal conflict between the desire to be oneself and part of a lasting relationship, which has the potential to generate new forms of relating.

In his analysis, Giddens assumes fairly coherent processes of future change and suggests that the tensions between individuals in late modern relationships can be negotiated through dialogue. There is a sense of inevitability in Giddens' account that the democratization of intimate life will follow. Beck, however, finds that the battles between men and women, as they work out new ways of being together in the contingent relationship between private and working lives, carry the potential rather than the inevitability for the democratization of personal life. A key difference in their work is the strength of the hetero-normative assumption in Beck's analysis. This is more than a mere lack of recognition of sexual diversity and difference. While Beck's analysis is concerned with the new, it is firmly embedded in the language and concepts of traditional relationships. Central to Giddens' argument is that, inherent in processes of institutional reflexivity, heterosexuality becomes more like homosexuality – having the potential to become but one form among others. Beck's account, on the other hand, conjures up a vision of future relationships where key elements of institutional heterosexuality are untouched by transforming gender and intimate relationships.

Giddens and Beck understand the changes in personal life, in the self and relationships, in the context of broader economic, social and cultural change. For the former especially, the working out of new ways of living and life-politics (see Chapter 5) are driven by democratizing impulses that are viewed as almost inherent in institutional reflexivity. This theme has been taken up by Jeffrey Weeks (1995) and Ken Plummer (1995, 2003), key authors on sexual and intimate citizenship, who draw on Giddens' understanding of late modernity. They have developed detailed analyses of sexual, or intimate citizenship, where claims to democracy in a diversity of intimate relationships and their public recognition are mapped. There is a distinct parallel to be drawn between Giddens' (1992) concept of intimacy – the transactional negotiation of personal ties by equals – and Plummer's (1995) notion of intimate citizenship in which he talks about rights and responsibilities being enacted in decisions about: 'control (or not) over one's body, feelings, relationships; access (or not) to representations, relationships, public spaces etc.; and socially grounded choices (or not) about identities, gender experiences, erotic experiences' (Plummer 1995: 151, original emphasis).

Critics of intimacy

Lynn Jamieson (1998, 1999) presents a detailed critical engagement with the themes addressed by Giddens, and by implication some of those addressed by Beck. Jamieson is critical of the assumption of gender equality that is central to Giddens' and Beck's theories of late modern relational life, and especially Giddens' notion of intimacy as shared self-disclosure amongst economic equals. Notable aspects of her critique include the degree to which these analyses are new or particularly late modern; the role of expert knowledge in reflexive transformation; and the durability of the structures of gender inequalities.

First, Jamieson questions if these analyses are significantly new. The idea that personal life is becoming more intensely intimate or individualized, she suggests, is a longstanding theme in social thought. Intimacy, privacy and equality have also been part of the orthodox account, in sociological writing at least since the 1940s, of how the modern family developed. Further, she notes that in the 1960s theorists had already claimed that intense dialogue in couple/marriage relationships function to create ontological security. This prefigures a key element of Giddens' theory where the pure relationship is a crucial focus of the late modern project of the self (see Chapter 6). On the one hand, Jamieson notes, Giddens is suggesting that the pure relationship is important for shoring up a sense of ontological security and trust that is essential for a stable sense of self (see Chapter 6). On the other hand, the contingency inherent in relationships nowadays contains an internal tension between mutual trust and the knowledge that it may not last (Jamieson 1999: 479). While Giddens views this tension in a primarily optimistic way, as facilitating greater dialogical openness, Jamieson argues that it could be viewed as a sign of general malaise. In this respect, she suggests that Giddens sidesteps theories which: 'emphasize the inevitability of inner conflict, self-discontent and disappointment in relationships' (1999: 479). Importantly, she suggests that old problems in the sociological literature on the demise of the family between 1950s and 1970s re-emerge in Giddens' account, particularly in underplaying how continuing structural inequalities shape personal life.

Second, Jamieson is critical of how Giddens' account draws relatively uncritically on therapeutic discourse and self-help literature as documents about and symptoms of social change. This locates his analysis within the therapeutic discourse in contrast to academic arguments that are critical of the ideological nature of such discourse. She notes, for example, that David Morgan highlights the twentieth-century narrative in family and marriage – 'from institution to relationship' – as an ideological simplification of social change, and argues that the fit between ideological story and everyday relationships is not so clear-cut. It is possible, Jamieson argues, for expert knowledge on relationships to infuse everyday talk on relationships – while other factors concurrently work to mould and constrain everyday practice (1999: 480). In Jamieson's view, at the core of Giddens' thesis of late modernity lies a set of psychological assumptions that ignore the insights of, for example, theories that emphasize the problematic implications of reliance on experts, and particularly Foucault's analysis of the disciplinary working of therapeutic discourse (see Chapter 6 and discussion below). In Giddens' account, dialogical openness in relationships, as recommended by therapeutic and self-help experts, is uncritically viewed as a route to self-realization.

Third, Jamieson argues that Giddens' and Beck's accounts of the transformation of intimacy underplay continuing gender inequality. They do not provide any sustained discussion, she points out, of feminist scholarship that has theorized the interrelationships between the private, public, personal and political. She suggests that Giddens undermines the resilience of gender inequalities, and argues that it is unclear that a change in the quality of heterosexual relationships (which, she argues, is unlikely in itself) would dismantle the interconnection of gendered labour markets, gendered distributions of economic resources, and gendered division of domestic labour (1999: 482). In this regard, Jamieson notes that many theorists of gender and power would be unconvinced by Giddens' analysis. Many of these theorists, she argues, could 'envisage gender equality within heterosexual personal life within and despite patriarchal arrangements' (1999: 482). Jamieson argues that Giddens' analysis of intimacy overplays agency and undermines structure, a problem that in part stems from its failure to engage with feminist work on personal life. In her own review of the research, she argues that intimacy has several dimensions (such as couples, friendships, mother–child relationships), and that there is diversity in the make-up of intimacy within any one category of relationship. As opposed to democratizing personal life, she contends, relationships tend to be structured according to (and can reinforce) gender, class and ethnic divisions. She argues: 'Personal relationships are not typically shaped in whatever way gives pleasure without the taint of practical, economic and other material circumstances. Few relationships, even friendships, are mainly simply about mutual appreciation, knowing and understanding' (Jamieson 1999: 482).

Some of Jamieson's criticisms will be returned to later on in this chapter. The following sections, however, turn our attention to key theories of sexuality and gender relations that are crucial to understanding the differences and inequalities that Giddens and Beck argue are being overcome in contemporary social contexts. These theories place the question of how power works at the centre of their analyses. Foucault and his followers, on the one hand, are interested in sexuality as a technology of government in modernity, and as the focus of regulation and resistance. Feminist theorists, on the other hand, are interested in the relationship between sexuality and gender in the context of patriarchal operations of power. While there are a number of notable differences in how the relationship between sexuality, gender and power is conceptualized – both between and within these broad frameworks – there is broad agreement that modern sexualities and intimate relationships cannot be viewed as power-free (or only empowering) zones.

Power, sexuality and gender

Sexuality and power

Foucault has paid significant attention to sexuality in theorizing opera-tions of power in modernity (see also Weeks 1989; McNay 1992). As outlined in Chapters 3 and 6, Foucault's argument is that disciplinary mechanisms of power are central to the operation of modern societies. To recap, Foucault was concerned with a variety of expert knowledges and practices (or discourses) that emerged in the eighteenth and nine-teenth centuries which allowed for the subtle regulation of individuals and social life. Expert knowledge on bodies, subjectivities and relation-ships became established as the truth about how human beings are and should be, and individuals were incited to act, and live their lives, in accordance with established norms. This allowed for effective control by strategic powers over bodies, behaviours and ultimately over whole populations. For Foucault (1979b), the formation of expert discourses on sexuality has been one of the key ways in which power is exercised by ordering intimate relationships. This is in turn central to producing and maintaining the social order. In contrast to the notion that sexuality was repressed or forbidden in early modern societies, Foucault analysed how sexualities – sexual desires, identities and practices – were shaped, regu-lated and produced. Sexuality, he argued, emerged historically as a tech-nology of government and the focus of 'biopower' (or power over life). Biopower has two modes of operation in relation to sexuality. On the one hand, the focus is on regulating the population through techniques such as sex education, the control and management of sexually trans-mitted diseases, and defining and monitoring 'normal' relational and family life. On the other hand, individuals are incited to recognize them-selves as sexual subjects who possess sexual desires and identities that require expression and management. Throughout the twentieth century a host of experts (such sexologists, psychologists, clinicians, self-help gurus and so on) have produced knowledge about sex that guides indi-viduals in their self-monitoring. The result is the production of bodies that are usefully sexualized in specific ways.

Sexual desires and identities feel inherently natural and given and are nowadays viewed as the legitimate focus of pleasure, self-expression and self-development. Yet the notion of 'possessing' a sexuality is one that has its roots in nineteenth-century expert constructions of sexual norms and categories. Foucault argued that four broad areas were relevant to the modern construction of sexuality. First, there was the 'hysterization' of women's bodies, where the female body was viewed wholly in terms of its reproductive function, and was seen to require expert intervention for the sake of the healthy social body. Second, there was the problematization of children's sexuality, and expert and family intervention was encouraged to ensure the child's normal development to protect the future of the population. Third was an expert concern with normal reproductive sexuality within the heterosexual married couple, a primary site for controlling the population. Fourth was the construction of categories of sexual deviance, and the identification of the causes of (and cures for) perversion. Hence, four legitimate objects of knowledge about sexuality were constructed, with corresponding techniques for surveillance and intervention by experts. This governmental concern (see Chapter 3), Foucault argued, is the basis of modern sexuality.

Sexuality, according to Foucault, is intrinsically bound up with strategies of power. On the one hand, certain forms of sexuality are produced and regulated through discourse and institutionalized practice. On the other hand, sexualities are also the focus of resistance. In resisting the received norms and categories of sexual identities and behaviours there is the possibility of producing a reverse discourse. The sexual liberation movements of the 1960s and 1970s, for example, challenged the dominant notions that homosexuality was an illness or pathology. Similarly, the feminist movement challenged the notion that women's sexuality should be defined solely in terms of reproduction or male pleasure. In doing so, these movements produced alternative understandings of sexual pleasure, sexual identity and legitimate sexualities. Yet, for Foucault, the notion of sexual freedom or emancipation is itself problematic, as it fails to recognize that there is no true or authentic sexuality to be freed. Rather, the task of resistance is to create and experiment with forms of bodily pleasure and relationships that cannot so easily be categorized or normalized. This could, for example, include resisting or refusing sexual identity, and the normative privileging of the heterosexual monogamous couple.

A Foucauldian analysis can provide an alternative perspective to Giddens' on contemporary intimate relationships, and alerts us to the issues of power in relation to these. Three examples of this can be considered. First, as Jamieson (1999) implies, what Giddens views as the ideals of the pure relationships – where couples are engaged in ongoing open communication – Foucauldians might view as the cultural hegemony of therapeutic discourse that emphasizes the value of talk and confessional disclosure. In the pure relationships, Jamieson points out, couple life is no longer supposed to involve secrets and differences. Rather, members must commit to disclosure and, it could be argued, to more effective and thorough self- and mutual regulation. Second, as Gail Hawkes (1999: 48) suggests, expert knowledge on women's sexuality does not appear to have developed in the way that Giddens suggests. Rather, popular discourse on women's sexuality continues to be influenced by the expert constructions of 'problematic' sexuality in a way that is consistent with Foucault's theory.

In reviewing leading women's magazines sold in Britain, Hawkes argues that sexuality is consistently presented as in need of constant attention. To be 'good' at sex is presented as the individual's responsi-bility (the woman's responsibility in this case), and she is incited to think and speak about it in the 'right' way. Hawkes argues that the encourage-ment to see oneself as a primarily sexual being involves the production of anxieties about how good the individual is at sex, and further incite-ments to become a sexual consumer as a means of dealing with these anxieties:

> The endless advice, guidance, warnings and enthusiastic encour-agement for new and different sex consciously seek to entice us out from behind the disenabling screens of embarrassment, boredom or just downright ignorance ... 'Sex as a lifestyle' presents sex as a consumer product. Additionally, the sex as life-style discourses seek to *create* a desire for ... commodities ... [the] manipulation of consumption patterns depends ... [on] engendering anxiety about the effectiveness and success of the sexual self we choose to be.
>
> (Hawkes 1999: 51)

Hawkes is unconvinced by analyses, like Giddens', that equate the contemporary emphases on 'sexuality as lifestyle' with the liberalization of (hetero)sexuality. Contemporary discourses on sex may emphasize choice, she maintains, but they retain an emphasis on sexuality as '*the* principle marker for the individualized self' (1999: 53). Also, sexuality as a consumer product is of crucial value to marketing and advertising industries who sell us sex, and who aim 'to fix a sexual agenda through mobilization of anxieties about physical performance' (1999: 53). Contemporary consumer cultures, Hawkes' analysis implies, remain preoccupied with sex, and in late modernity there remains a cultural compulsion to see sex as the route to self-realization. While this is sold as sexual freedom, in Foucauldian terms it can be interpreted as an ever more effective incitement to produce and monitor ourselves as sexual subjects *through* consumption.

Third, the increasing (but still highly uneven) social acceptance of lesbian and gay sexualities, that Giddens views as evidence of an inherent democratizing impulse in modernity, could be viewed from a Foucauldian perspective as a process of the normalization of homosexuality. Indeed, the issue of normalization has been a feature in debates about the extent to which same-sex marriage should be viewed as a challenge to hetero-normativity or as the triumph of heterosexual norms. On the one hand, same-sex marriage can be viewed as the legitimate aim of lesbian and gay politics, and as the most appropriate strategy for non-heterosexual citizenship (see, for example, Sullivan 1996, 1997). This position understands the marriage contact as symbolizing an emotional and financial bond and suggests that the legalizing of same-sex unions can reshape and modernize the institution of marriage in keeping with the kind of gender and sexual equality that Giddens envisages. On the other hand, Foucauldian critics might be more inclined towards the argument that same-sex marriage represents the dominance of hetero-sexual values and undermines the distinctiveness of lesbian and gay cultures. This argument views the extension of marriage to same-sex couples as a form of social regulation, with profound normalizing implications for same-sex relationships and queer identities (see, for example, Warner 2000). The political desire for same sex marriage, this perspective suggests, is based on the hegemony of hetero-normative notions of commitment, which could lead to normative constructions of socially responsible and irresponsible homosexuals, and to the imposition of rules which may stifle the political radicalism and creativity of same-sex partnerships. While the issue of same-sex marriage could be indicative of the emancipatory possibilities existing in late modernity as suggested by Giddens, it could equally be indicative of the regulatory incitements that Foucault argued prompt people to politically invest in sexuality as a source of emancipation, and to personally invest in it as a source of self-realization.

Despite the insights that Foucault's work can provide into sexuality and power, his work has been subject to a number of criticisms (see Chapter 3). While his work has appealed to some feminist theorists, others have been critical of the gender-blindness of his arguments and the extent to which his conceptualization of power fails to address structural issues of gender inequality (Jackson 1996: 18). In discussing Foucauldian feminism, Jackson (1996: 18) argues that while there is some value in making gender more central in analyses of the historical construction of sexuality, and in exploring the construction of female sexuality as the object of disciplinary discourses and practices, there is too much emphasis placed on historical disjunctures and especially the explosion of discourses that emerged in the nineteenth century. Such analyses, for Jackson, underplay historical continuities and 'the resilience and flexibility of patriarchal domination under changing historical conditions' (1996: 18). She argues that in Foucauldian approaches not enough attention is paid to the persistence of gender hierarchy that profoundly shapes men's and women's sexualities and intimate relationships.

Jackson notes that in applying Foucault's insights to contemporary sexualities and relationships, theorists are often concerned with exploring the radical implications of diverse sexualities and alternative possibilities for sexual and intimate relationships. In exploring these alternatives, queer theorists, for example, aim to reveal that the norms that shape our sexual and relational practices are far from inevitable. Diverse sexualities (homosexuality, bisexuality, sado-masochism and so on), it is sometimes argued, can reveal the potential instability of heterosexual norms. For Jackson, however, this emphasis on the pluralization of sexuality is in danger of ignoring the structural bases of power and denying the importance of gender. There is, she argues, a risk of undermining the regularities that underpin diverse sexualities, and no way of relating them to 'dominant modes of heterosexual practice or of locating them within power hierarchies' (1996: 18).

Jackson is also wary of the value of Foucauldian notions of resistance and transgression. Given that power is always involved from the beginning in constituting sexual desires, and that the body is thoroughly inscribed with power, she argues, resistance and transgression are futile. Further, in understanding the place of sexuality in structuring gender relations, Jackson contends, there is a need to conceive discourses as ideological. In this sense, hegemonic discourses of sexuality must be understood to be bound up with the domination and subordination of women in patriarchal contexts. Discursive constructions of sexuality produce truths 'which have defined hierarchically ordered heterosexual relations as natural and inevitable' (Jackson 1996: 19).

Sexuality, gender and power

In contrast to Foucauldian approaches that highlight the centrality of sexuality to modern operations of disciplinary power, some feminist critiques have highlighted the role of sexuality in perpetuating women's oppression. In doing so they provide an alternative view of the depth of the challenges faced in attempting to construct egalitarian and reflexive relationships. They argue that the institutionalization of sexual relations through heterosexuality has historically worked to oppress all women, since the social relations that accompany heterosexuality are crucial to persistent male dominance and the operation of patriarchal societies. The feminist philosopher Adrienne Rich (1983), for example, has argued that heterosexuality, as a system imposed on women throughout history, regulates women's experience, history, culture and values which are distinct from the dominant patriarchal heterosexual culture. Through the devices of violence and romance women are subordinated. Ideologies of romantic love, this analysis suggests, lead women into unequal relationships with men, naturalize gender roles and unequal labour in the home, and privilege men's pleasure above that of women.

Sexuality, in this view, is a site of patriarchal power that is constructed from masculine definitions, and heterosexuality is a social organization of power that is crucial for maintaining gender inequalities. In this sense, heterosexuality is viewed as something that is historically imposed on women as compulsory (Rich 1983), as a means of maintaining patriarchal domination. Compulsory heterosexuality implies that women do not fully consent to it. Rather they are in some ways coerced or ideologically coaxed into heterosexuality by social and cultural practices that make heterosexuality seem inevitable and punish those who do not conform (for example, through economic sanctions and homophobic violence). Heterosexuality is not something that is programmed into individuals from birth, or a freely chosen sexual practice, but is a social institution. Dunne (1997: 13) describes this view of heterosexuality thus:

> Sexuality and emotions can take many forms, but ideological and material processes limit their expression, and provide justification for drawing women into relations of inequality with men. Institutionalized heterosexuality as a 'given' is constituted through the embedded processes of legitimation, reification and prohibition. These processes involve a range of ideologies (often

gender specific) bound by and binding each to another to form a belief system.

(Dunne 1997: 13)

Gender ideologies, it is argued by Dunne and others, construct men and women as unfulfilled opposites that can only be complete through a heterosexual union. Institutional heterosexuality therefore provides 'the logic underpinning marriage ... as a commonsense "normal adult goal"' (Dunne 1997: 16). Yet, for many feminist theorists, institutional heterosexuality, and the notion of a reciprocal state of dependency between men and women that underpins it, also 'shapes and is shaped by relations of production' (Dunne 1997: 16). In this sense, institutional heterosexuality naturalizes, and is reinforced by, gendered differences in relation to domestic and paid work. Ideologies of sexual difference, especially as they relate to heterosexual romance and family life, are seen to construct men's and women's interrelated social and economic roles as distinct, and to reinforce social inequalities between men and women. They constitute men and women as different economic actors, and reinforce men's dominant economic position over women. This leads us to the issue of the new economic equalities that both Giddens and Beck argue to be influencing the intimate transformations they discuss.

Demanding reflexivity: gender, work and intimacy

Rationalization and gendered reflexivity

In commenting on Giddens' analysis, Mary Evans (2003: 43) points out that the focus on the democratization of gender relations has both an analytic and a normative element. Giddens, she notes, is arguing that gender relations *should* be equalized. On the one hand, Evans views Giddens' analysis as important in that it combines themes in feminist work and more mainstream sociological arguments about the relationship between the personal, the individual and the social. On the other hand, she is unconvinced by Giddens' argument that the democratization of intimate relations 'underpins and informs the greater democratization of society as a whole' (2003: 43). If this were the case, she notes, it would be possible to demonstrate a clear link between a form of cultural change (the decline of patriarchal domestic authority) and broader social change. Evans argues that there is another way to interpret what Giddens views as the democratization of intimate relation-

138

ships, as: 'the *erosion* of distinctions between private and personal, and, above all else, the centrality of the expectations and aspirations of the market economy in the lives of both men and women' (2003: 43). Instead of seeing transforming patterns of intimacy as part of a move to greater democracy, she argues, it could be viewed as 'greater integration between social and personal worlds' (2003: 45). Marx, she suggests, would have seen the homogenization of male and female experience as part of the process of commodification where all forms of social relationships are transformed into relationships 'dictated by the cash nexus' (2003: 45). Evans argues that it is important to be sceptical about the idea that an increase in women's participation in paid employment, together with increasing choices in relation to sexuality and reproduction, imply emancipation. Via Weber, she argues that what Giddens describes as democratization might more appropriately be seen as rationalization. Indeed, the kind of couple and marriage relationships that Giddens envisages are highly rationalized arrangements – contracts that are entered into to suit the needs of each individual. Processes of rationalization, Evans argues, are as much part of today's social world as they were previously, and the relationships that Giddens describes could be evidence of the accuracy of Weber's proposition about bureaucracy becoming the predominant form of social organization; and that its 'iron grip would extend beyond the world of paid world' (2003: 53). Whether we view the issue as one of democratization or rationalization, Evans points out that it is important to acknowledge social continuities:

> before we move too rapidly to the assumption that modern men and women are choosing their partners for material reasons, and reasons of social convenience, we need to recall that this was *always* a possibility . . . the revolution in sexual attitudes and behaviour in the West in the past 30 years has changed the way in which relationships are conducted, but this is not to suggest that we have become any less (or more) circumspect and predictable than we were in the past about who we marry.
>
> (Evans 2003: 46, original emphasis)

For Giddens' argument about intimate democratization to be convincing, Evans argues, men and women must be economic actors who participate fully as members of the public world. This position is dependent on women's full participation in the workplace and the demise of traditional distinctions between gendered ways of being. She notes, however, that the research evidence suggests limited change in traditionally gendered patterns of participation in domestic tasks and childcare. Further, she argues, while women increasingly participate in professional and managerial employment, they have not generally gained high positions of authority and power (2003: 44). The reality, she suggests, is that women have yet to achieve real social power. Further, what were traditionally assumed to be natural differences between women and men have not been wholly erased (2003: 54). While some women may be integrated in public life as equals with men, those women most disadvantaged by the class system are unlikely to be. Such women form, she argues, a class of people set apart form the dominant order – an underclass – and are tied to traditional conceptions of femininity:

> The segmentation of the working class into the underclass and those who are gainfully employed and equipped with socially confirmed 'skills' is . . . associated with the disappearance of highly distinct forms of gendered behaviour, except among those who are most socially and economically disadvantaged. For working class women, unlikely to be able to afford either higher education or child care, it is socially effective to attempt to maintain the feminine or femininity since it may offer access to male support.
>
> (Evans 2003: 54)

The notion of emancipation, Evans implies, is not applicable to all women. Even when referring to those women who fully participate in paid work, the notion of freedom from assigned gender differences and inequalities should be viewed with scepticism. The needs of capitalism, Evans argues, have facilitated the employment of women as much as the commitments to sexual equality. Via Lovell she further argues that it is the characteristics identified with 'natural' femininity – such as caring, flexibility and relative passivity – that make women the ideal employees of the current form of service- and consumer-orientated capitalism (2003: 55). Many working women remain tied to imposed femininity that has historically formed the basis for women's exploitation. Also, there can be demands made on women to reflexively perform and *produce* certain kinds of femininity for the benefit of their employers and others. The following sections of the chapter consider a number of studies that further develop this point. The findings of these empirical studies cannot directly or simply be employed to counter the theories considered so far, as they are of specifically contextualized experience. They do, however, underscore the need to *critically* engage with the ideas of reflexive gender and relationships, and they alert our attention to the idea that reflexivity is not neutral.

Reflexive working, sexuality and emotion

Despite women's increasing participation in paid work – the basis of the gender 'equality' that Giddens and Beck refer to in their theories – empirical studies generally suggest a more complex picture of women's paid and unpaid working lives. This section considers arguments based on two studies that have explored the subtleties of continuing inequalities and exploitation that exist in relation to gendered working lives. In studying women's paid work, Lisa Adkins (1995) developed the link between institutional heterosexuality and relations of production that has been the concern of many feminist theorists, and explored how family, work and heterosexuality remain fundamental to structuring women's experience of the contemporary labour market. In a study of aspects of the leisure industry in Britain she examined how marriage and heterosexuality structure gender relations in the workplace, how women's labour was appropriated by men, and how women must reflexively perform as heterosexual workers. Her analysis suggested that in thinking about gendered patterns of work we should consider the extent to which women sell their labour under different conditions to men, and are subject to subtle forms of exploitation in the contemporary workplace – not least the requirement for reflexive production of gender.

Adkins' (1995) study focused on recruitment, management and the forms of gendered work that take place in the leisure industry in Britain. The study explored how women's conditions of employment within the leisure industry demands that they engage in a form of gendered and sexual servicing. To be employed, the women (unlike the men) had to meet both formal and informal requirements that included being caring, attractive and looking 'right'. To remain in employment the women she studied had to maintain their looks and attractiveness. Looking good, Adkins argued, was part of the informal contract, and male managers policed the correct appearance of women. Work clothing and the rules about how it was worn also sexualized these women as workers, who were expected to perform as objects for men's attention – as sexual workers. Sexual looks, Adkins argued, were an intrinsic part of the job, and the women she studied were under pressure (and often harassed) to engage in sexualized interaction with customers, male co-workers and managers.

For Adkins, there is a distinct relationship between sexual power and gender power. Men, she argues, subject women through sexual power. The women she studied were economically productive, but also sexually productive. In this context heterosexuality was compulsory and a condition of employment and performance at work. While the women she studied were not wholly without agency, they were in many ways powerless to change the relations of production that governed their working lives. Sexuality, Adkins argued, is a constitutive part of economic gendered relations. While sexuality structures service production, the gendering of work and production creates particular kinds of sexual relations in the workplace. In the kinds of service industries that Adkins studied, women often had no choice but to participate *as* sexual workers, and had little choice but to be heterosexualized. As such, they were exploited *as* women and did not participate with men as 'equals' in the workplace.

Elsewhere, Arlie Hochschild (as discussed in Cranny-Francis *et al.* 2003) focused on women's conditions of labour – and exploitation – as they concern emotional labour. While emotional labour is something that is required of women in certain kinds of paid work, it is also relevant to the gendered doing of intimate relationships, as will be illustrated in the following section. Hochschild developed the notion of emotional labour to refer to the contemporary requirement for workers to control and manage their feelings as part of their implicit working contracts. Feeling management, she argued, requires ongoing self-regulation and surveillance, and as such is a form of labour in itself. In the service industries especially, which are predominantly populated by women, emotional labour is increasingly demanded of workers in exploitative ways.

Hochschild is concerned with the increasing commercialization of human feeling, and through a study of the work and training practices of an airline company illustrated how women's association with caring and nurturing practices can become a requirement of paid work. To gain and maintain employment, women had to perform the capacity to care and nurture, which was unacknowledged and unrewarded. While the women studied had to take responsibility for their own feelings in order to perform the emotion work that was required of them, they were also required to take responsibility for the feelings of clients for the sake of the financial gain of the company they worked for. In fact, the women studied were actively trained in this commercialization of feeling by the companies they work for, and were subject to both internal and external regulation. Hochschild argued that there is a relationship between emotional and economic organization, and gender is crucial to understanding this relationship as emotional labour is a form of unrecognized work that is mostly undertaken by women. For her, the commodification of emotions is a key factor in shaping women's conditions of employment, and exploitation, in a global economy that is increasingly driven by service work.

Both Adkins' and Hochschild's studies, and the arguments they make on the basis of these, point to some of the subtle ways in which the growing service industries are making new demands on their workers to *reflexively* produce themselves as particular kinds of workers (caring, heterosexualized, subservient and so on). In these contexts women workers are often expected to reflexively produce themselves as feminine workers and, as Adkins suggests, often as sexual workers. Women, as Giddens and Beck suggest, are increasingly subject to the expectation that they will be full-time workers. On the one hand, this affords many women with historically new opportunities for financial and economic independence from men. On the other hand, gender and labour market experiences interact in complex ways, and Adkins' and Hochschild's work alerts us to the ways in which a certain kind of reflexive self-production is more likely to be demanded of women than men. This complexity of reflexivity is glossed over in Giddens' assumption that women and men are, or will become, equal workers, and Beck and Beck-Gernsheim's assertion that men and women share the *same* burden of an individual biography that is increasingly work-based. The reflexive biography is not neutral. While the globalizing economy and the labour market demands changing working patterns from its workforce, male and female workers are not always (or even mostly, some would argue) employed – or exploited – in gender-neutral ways. Rather, in the traditionally lower paid sectors of service work women continue to be employed *as* women, and are also expected to reflexively perform and work as certain kinds of women. In doing work, many of these women must also reflexively 'do' femininity, and must self-consciously perform as sexual, emotional and caring workers. As service industries form a central component of the globalizing economy, this is likely to continue to be the case. However, the reflexive practising of gender is not only relevant to the expectations and demands of paid work, but also links to women's and men's different expectations and experiences of intimate relationships.

Reflexive gender in intimate relationships

While expectations about practising gender can be important in structuring women's experiences of paid work, the notion of 'doing' gender has also been taken up in feminist theory and research on sexuality, family and intimate life. Contrary to Giddens' and Beck's theoretical analyses, which suggest the widespread undoing of traditional gendered ways of being in these contexts, empirical research instead tends to highlight the resilience of gender differences. In reviewing research on sexual behaviour and meanings, for example, Jamieson (1999) argues that while there is some modest evidence of an increasingly varied 'sexual repertoire' as implied by Giddens' notion of plastic sexuality, there is practically no evidence of gender convergence in sexual behaviour. Rather, she suggests, the research points to 'a rediscovery of patterns of gender difference' that have only changed marginally since research in the mid-twentieth century. Also, while there is some evidence of gendered convergence in ideas about sex (most notably in relation to couple relationships) she notes that in-depth studies reveal 'a persistent, tenacious and phallocentric view of heterosexual sex as something thing that men do to women' (1999: 484). Via the research of Holland *et al.* (1998) and others she notes that, contrary to Giddens' emphasis on the negotiated nature of contemporary relationships, young people's early experiences of sexuality rarely seem to involve the negotiation of mutual pleasure, or combine sex and intimacy.

The resilience of gendered differences is also evident in research on heterosexual domestic arrangements. In reviewing the British research on gender in this context over the previous 20 years, Dunne (1997) notes that in the majority of heterosexual partnerships women take responsibility for, and perform the bulk of, domestic tasks. She notes that this is the case where both partners are full-time waged; are without children; where women have higher occupational status; the man is unemployed; and even where couples see themselves as sharing the housework. Van Every (1995) has also noted the difficulties that arise in challenging gendered expectations in self-consciously anti-sexist living arrangements. Research also suggests that the practising of gender is also relevant to men's and women's different emotional lives within heterosexual couple relationships, in a way that profoundly challenges Giddens' emphasis on intimacy. To recap, Giddens' emphasis is on intimacy as a kind of dialogical ideal. As Jamieson puts it:

What is meant by intimacy is often a very specific sort of knowing, loving and 'being close' to another person . . . The emphasis
is on mutual disclosure, constantly revealing your inner thoughts
and feelings to each other. It is an intimacy of the self rather than
an intimacy of the body.

(Jamieson 1998: 1)

In contrast to the dialogical intimacy proposed by Giddens, a study by
Duncombe and Marsden (1999) suggested the importance of acknowledging the continuing existence – and sociological significance – of
gender divisions in emotional behaviour in relation to love and intimacy.
The authors note that the research evidence suggests that *conflict* arises
in heterosexual couples due to the ways in which women's and men's
differing management of emotion are socially shaped. In reviewing the
existing theory and research they note that women and men demonstrate
different abilities or willingness to think and talk in terms of love and
intimacy and to make the emotional efforts Giddens argues are necessary for egalitarian relationships.

Duncombe and Marsden argue that a key aspect of intimacy is gender
difference or an asymmetry in intimate emotional behaviour. In doing
so, they refer to Mansfield and Collard's (1988) earlier work that
suggested that in heterosexual married relationships men and women
tend to meet as 'intimate strangers'. This suggested that following the
demise of the initial romantic feelings about falling in love, men and
women seek 'incompatible' emotional goals in marriage. While men tend
to seek a *life in common* with their partners, women sought *a common
life*. For men, a life in common entailed a home life and stable base
'somewhere to set out from and return' (Mansfield and Collard, cited in
Duncombe and Marsden 1999: 93). For women a common life entailed
'an empathetic partner . . . a close exchange of intimacy which would
make them feel valued as a person not just a wife' (1999: 93). While
most women accepted inequalities in domestic work due to their partners paid work demands, they expressed disappointment with the
emotional asymmetry of their relationships. Men did not appear to
reciprocate women's understanding and caring by being open about, or
disclosing, their emotions (Duncombe and Marsden 1999: 93).

In reporting their own research, Duncombe and Marsden suggested
that the dominant pattern of their own female research participants'
experience was also an asymmetry of emotional response (1999: 95).
Most of their female participants pointed to a lack of men's active

emotional participation in their relationships. Most women reported that they did the emotional 'running' at the beginning of the relationships, and 'overwhelmingly women reported that their male partners had seemed to "physically desert" them by giving priority to work, becoming "workaholics" and working long hours or bring work home' (1999: 95). Women also reported that they did the running in persuading their partners to become parents, 'but with the unforeseen result that some men had abrogated physical and emotional responsibility, treating their children as belonging to their wives alone' (1999: 95). Couples' emotional commitments to one another became less intense, with much of their explicit communication being about their children. This could lead to disputes and challenges. Women sought validation, including emotional validation, but without explicitly demanding this. Despite women's criticisms of men's emotional distance, men argued that they did have emotions, but that they were theirs and not to be disclosed. Men sometimes felt pulled apart by the contradictory demands of family life and work (1999: 98).

There are obvious tensions between this research account and the theory of reflexive relationships, with its emphasis on the ideals of dialogue and communication, that Giddens outlines. Duncombe and Marsden outline a number of possible reasons why women appear to invest more work in managing their own emotions and men's. On the one hand, they suggest, it could be argued that women seek emotional validation from men because they are excluded from work-based status. On the other hand, it could be argued that while men value personal relationships, they express less as a consequence of the gendered division of emotion. They also suggest the issue might be viewed as one of power. In doing so they refer to Hochschild's point that emotional life is socially regulated by ideologies of feeling. As women are culturally assigned roles is recognizing, meeting and managing the emotional needs of others (see Chodorow, Chapter 5), it is they who carry out the emotion work. This involves a certain degree of reflexivity as it involves working on and performing the appropriate emotion or influencing how others feel. Ultimately, Dumcombe and Marsden reject any one answer to the question of *why* men and women 'do' emotion differently. They cite their own work and survey evidence to underscore the resilience of gender differences in the 'here and now'. In contrast to Giddens' optimistic analysis of the democratizing implications of dialogical intimacy they suggest: 'gender differences in emotional behaviour seem likely to become greater sources of friction and unhappiness among heterosexual couples as the "institution" of marriage is transformed by ideologies of the personal "relationship" which call for greater emotional communication' (Duncombe and Marsden 1999: 103).

Conclusion

This chapter has explored the insights that reconstructivist theories of modernity claim to generate for social change with respect to intimate and personal relationships. The theory of late or reflexive modernity argues that there are profound changes afoot in relational life. According to Giddens, these changes include a new emphasis on intimacy that has profound implications in terms of the democratization of personal life, and that could have a subversive influence on modern institutions as a whole. Giddens and Beck agree that there is a new shift towards equality in intimate and personal relationships that stems from demands for reflexive experimentation. The dynamics underpinning demands and experiments, they argue, come partly from new gender equalities in the labour market. Again, these analyses emphasize emergent universalities and the radical social, political and personal implications of these. Personal life is becoming more individualized for everybody, and because of this individual agency has no choice but to be mobilized. Everybody nowadays – men and women alike – must learn to get along as equals, and because of this it is possible that an ethos of equality will eventually predominate in all aspects of life.

In Giddens' analysis especially, there is the sense given that reflexive modernity has a democratizing impulse. Despite his explicit rejection of a teleological understanding of history and modernity, the normative thrust of theory again produces an optimistic interpretation of social change that many disagree with. This chapter has highlighted how different interpretations of intimate and gender relations derived from various modernist and postmodernist frames point to several bases on which the thesis of reflexive relating and intimacy – and arguments about reflexive gender underpinning it – is unconvincing. Modernist arguments suggest that the idea of intimate life becoming more individualized is problematic, and modernist and poststructuralist arguments illuminate how the thesis of reflexive intimacy and gender inadequately comprehends power. These analyses suggest there is much more to power than Giddens or Beck acknowledge, and that the discourse of dialogical or negotiated intimacy that the former promotes is itself bound up with the working of power. There is a long tradition of theorizing and sociology that both Giddens and Beck must ignore to mobilize their arguments, which include feminist, Foucauldian, Marxian and Weberian theories amongst others, and arguments based on empirical research. Combined, these suggest various ways in which reflexivity, intimacy and gender could be argued to work *against* equality and emancipation as much as they work for them. The issues of gendered relating, intimacy and work point to some of the ways in which reflexivity is not neutral.

8

DEATH, DESKILLING AND LIFE-POLITICS

Introduction

This chapter considers how death is viewed as a key example of the loss of shared meanings, or deskilling, in modernity, and as a core life-political issue in the theory of late or reflexive modernity. Death is one of the few certainties that we face in living, and it has been argued that we can judge a culture by the ways in which it deals with death. How we view death, several theorists argue, has a crucial influence on the social life we make together (Seale 2001: 98), and modern culture itself has been viewed as an attempt to deny death (Bauman 1992b). The loss of shared meanings and rituals around death in modern societies, and modern discomfort with it are, some theorists argue, indicative of modernity's collective deskilling in relation to core life issues (Bauman 1992b). The heightened risks that encounters with human mortality produce for a sense of personal instability in late modernity have also been a theme of theoretical discussions. Such discussions conjure up images of atomized and lonely modern individuals who are left without meaning and are thrown back on their own resources when faced with their own mortality. They suggest a modern world where people are disconnected from each other and where there is a loss of shared values. In the reconstructive theory of reflexive modernity, however, death and the personal challenges and insecurities it gives rise to become the focus of 'life-political' endeavours aimed at remoralizing social life. While dying in modernity is something to be managed and controlled away from the day-to-day business of life, in reflexive modernity, Giddens' argument implies, there are life-political pressures to incorporate it into day-to-day living through the remoralizing of social life.

The first section of the chapter introduces the modernist death and deskilling thesis by considering two influential accounts of how in modernity death becomes an invisible and private matter. In one of these accounts, by Philippe Aries, the invisibility of modern death is indicative of the loss of community solidarity, and the increasing control of experts over social and personal life. In the other account, by Norbert Elias, the privatization of death is a consequence of civilizing processes inherent to modernity where affective and emotional life is subject to high levels of self-control and regulation. Despite the differences that exist between these analyses, both suggest that modern societies and individuals have difficulties in dealing with death and hence endeavour to sequester or put it aside. The second section of the chapter considers the argument that death presents a particular problem for individuals in late modernity, as developments with respect to reflexive self-identity and personal life imply that human mortality threatens to come to the fore as a personal and collective moral issue. This suggests that ever increasing secularization has had profound implications for the lack of shared purpose and understandings in life and death. In short, it is argued that individuals are increasingly left alone to construct their own values in their lives, and there is a void that individuals attempt to address through the constant endeavour to maintain or create a coherent and stable sense of who they are. Lacking a more stable focal point, this project increasingly centres on a concern with our own bodies. However, the fragility of the human body and the inevitability of its demise imply that the sense of stability or rootedness it provides is inherently contingent, and threats to ontological security become more pronounced. While this is often viewed in a pessimistic way, the theory of reflexive modernity argues that death and deskilling has implications for emergent life-politics in late modernity, which points to the possibilities of reflexive 'reskilling' with respect to moral questions. In the final sections of the chapter, a number of questions are considered about the assumptions that underpin the death and deskilling thesis and arguments about life-politics, and whose experiences these address.

Modernity, death and deskilling

For a number of modern and postmodern theorists, including Berger and Luckman (1967/1990) and Bauman (1992b), death itself is unknowable. Dollimore (2001) and others argue that to fully contemplate and understand our own mortality is an impossibility – as living beings our own death is incomprehensible. It is dying, therefore, that preoccupies most theorists and writers: 'the manner of our death rather that death itself'

(Bury 1997: 145). Two writers have been highly influential on the modern 'death and deskilling' thesis, and their ideas have been subsequently incorporated (though not uncritically) into theories of late or reflexive modernity. The first of these, the historian Philippe Aries, authored the field-defining historical overview of the subject from the medieval to the modern period, *The Hour of our Death* (1991). The second, the social theorist Norbert Elias, authored the more concise volume *The Loneliness of Dying* (1985), which built on his general thesis of the modern 'civilizing process'. On the surface, both authors are concerned with the degree to which, in modernity, death becomes invisible and privatized.

Aries (as discussed in Bury 1997) draws from a study of cultural representations of death in different historical periods to explore changing perceptions of death that occur at different points of modernization. He identifies five major forms of death as modern societies developed: 'tame death', 'death of the self', 'remote or imminent death', 'death of the other' and 'invisible death' (Bury 1997). In short, he argues that until the beginnings of modern society death was visibly present in everyday life and dealt with publicly. Death was tame in that the collective dealt with it, talked about it and managed it openly. In contrast, the invisible death that characterizes the modern period is more controlled, but death is wild in that it is feared and outside our realm of day-to-day experience. As Bury points out, at the heart of Aries' understanding of the problem of invisible death is an understanding of modern society that has diminished community solidarity, and where death is dominated by medicine: 'For Aries . . . there is no real community today for "it has been replaced by an enormous mass of atomised individuals". Death has become sequestered from everyday life, and dying has, instead, become the site for professional guidance and expertise' (Bury 1997: 147–8).

Aries' account suggests that death in modernity is thoroughly medicalized. It has, he contends, become separated out (and hidden) from the mundane aspects of day-to-day living, and is now in the hands of medical professionals and experts (a position that is echoed by Bauman 1992b). Death in modernity is invisible, as it is located in hospitals. At the heart of the problem for Aries is an ever-extending individualism and increasing absence of collective norms and values. This view, as Bury (1997: 148) points out, continues to underpin contemporary theoretical discussions of the sociological significance of death.

On the surface at least, *The Loneliness of Dying* shares the pessimistic view of death as silenced and invisible in modern societies. Like Aries, Elias is concerned with the problems modern individuals have in dealing with death and the dying, and the degree to which there has been a shift from death as a public to a private matter. Elias argues that past societies were more likely to be comfortable with death and the dying, and more accepting of their presence. In present-day societies, he suggests, people do not know how to act in the face of death. One consequence of this is that contact with the dying (and the very old) is avoided – they are left in loneliness to their own very limited resources. This is bound up with (both as a cause and consequence of) the tendency in modern societies to keep the old and dying 'behind the scenes' of day-to-day life through institutional and informal means. For Elias, modern death and dying are distinguished from previous forms by their association with old age. In modern societies people generally live longer than they did in previous times. Medical interventions and increasingly pacified societies mean that death and the dying are not encountered routinely. Nowadays, normal death occurs in old age, and is removed from the everyday experience.

Despite the similarities in their analyses, Elias is critical of Aries' overly romanticized view of death in the past. He takes particular issue with the notion that in the past death was a serene event, and points out that most of the population would have experienced dying as painful and agonizing. While Elias is concerned with the consequences of the hospitalization of dying and death for undermining people's abilities to deal with death and the dying when they encounter them, he is highly critical of Aries' anti-medicine stance (and the anti-modernity stance it implies). Medicine, he points out, has meant that many will have a painless death, and that the decreasing emotional involvement with the dying may make loss more bearable. More broadly, Elias argues the necessity to acknowledge and appreciate the benefits of technological developments and modernization in terms of social improvements (Bury 1997: 150), which often go unrecognized in the anti-modern stance. In this respect Elias' deskilling thesis is a significantly different one to those that are underpinned by hostility towards modernization. Aries' and Elias' accounts of how societies deal with death and dying present two very different analyses of modernity. Aries' emphasis on medicalization is in keeping with an anti-medicine stance that is informed by a broader anti-modernization stance. Osborne characterizes the principles of the anti-medicine stance thus:

that mode of thought . . . which regards the history of medical
reason as a slow descent away from enlightenment towards
disenchantment and despotism. What unifies this ethos is the
claim that the medicine of the past two centuries or so has been
conducted increasingly . . . 'without regard for the person' –
hence the frequent critiques of hospital[s].

(Osborne 1994: 29)

Aries' deskilling thesis can thus be viewed as part of wider (modernist)
sociological criticisms of medicalization that implied that medico-
technological dominance has increasingly characterized modernity.
He draws on Illich's (1977) modernist critical approach, which was
informed by a concern with the extent to which the institutionalization
of healthcare had 'grown beyond tolerable bounds' (1977: 11). For Illich
the development of medical monopolies and the institutionalization of
healthcare were bound up with the misuse of scientific achievements to
strengthen industrial growth. This undermined subjective and personal
culture and community solidarity. In contrast, Elias' deskilling thesis
should be viewed in terms of his broader theory of the modern civilizing
process (Elias 2000, 2002).

For Elias the civilizing process is one whereby human conduct and
sentiment are shaped and moulded towards the restraint of threatening
and emotional behaviour. Self-restraint is central to 'civilized' behaviour
in modernity, where the most 'animalistic' traits in human behaviour
are increasingly hidden in the background of social life and invested
with a sense of shame (Elias 2002: 420). Instinctual and affective life are
regulated by self-control in modern societies, where the nation state's
monopoly of violence and force produces pacified social spheres that
are usually free of violent acts (Elias 2002: 421). As Bury notes, while
the pacification of society comes about through the nation state's
centralization of the means of violence, restraint comes about through
increased control in interpersonal relationships (Bury 1997). In Elias'
words:

What is established with the monopolization of violence in the
pacified social spaces is . . . a more dispassionate self-control . . .
[There is] a constant, even pressure to inhibit effective outbursts
. . . [and] damp down extreme behaviour and emotions . . . the
constant self-control to which the individual is now increasingly

accustomed seeks to reduce the contrasts and sudden switches in conduct, the affective charge of all self-expression.

(Elias 2002: 424)

For Elias, part of the civilizing process includes the screening off of core life issues (including violence, death and sexuality) and promoting self-restraint with respect to emotionally charged interactions. Self-restraint, the control of emotions and shame also explain the reluctance, as described by Elias (1985), of people in modern society to come into contact with dying and very old bodies (1985: 68–91). In their interactions with each other, both the living and the dying have difficulty in knowing how to behave towards each other. Both are consumed with shame and have few resources for managing this encounter – they do not know how to feel or what to say, and the search for the appropriate way of being in this situation 'falls back on the individual' (Elias 1985: 26). Death and the dying are therefore managed in modernity through sequestration.

The sequestration of death does not mean that death is not talked about or represented in modernity (see Armstrong 1987; Shilling 1993: 188–92). As Armstrong (1987: 651) notes, from a Foucauldian perspective, the modern silencing of death involves constantly speaking it. What are at stake are the places deemed appropriate for the dying to exist in, and the question of *who* is the appropriate speaker on modern death. The sequestration of death refers to the processes through which the dying themselves are removed from everyday life and silenced. In everyday life individuals do not expect (or desire) to have normal interaction with those perceived to be on the path to death (Elias 1985). The sequestration of death also refers to the processes through which the dying are allocated appropriate places to speak (the clinic, hospital and therapists' consultation rooms), and how experts are given the authority to represent – or tell the story of – the dying, and to speak on their behalf. As Bauman (1992b) suggests: '[Modernity] banished death and the dying out of sight, and thus out of mind . . . it has been allocated its own location in social space, a segregated location; it has been put in custody of selected specialists boasting scientific credentials' (Bauman 1992b: 152).

Both the inappropriate visibility and voices of the dying are experienced as highly problematic by the living in modernity: through audibly and visibly existing they bring home the (always hovering) existence of death to others. In modernity, this facilitates a return of 'the trained emotion of shame, that makes us numb when we meet death face to face' (Bauman 1992b: 129). This deskilling with respect to death is symptomatic of broader deskilling with respect to core life issues.

Late modernity, death and the self

Berger (1967), in *The Sacred Canopy*, provided an analysis of the social significance of death that has been highly influential on sociological understandings of the particular problem that death represents in modern societies. He argues that death is a central issue in the social construction of reality in all societies, and his work has been identified as an important attempt 'to place the consideration of death at the heart of the sociological enterprise' (Mellor 1993: 13). Turner summarizes Berger's argument in the following way: 'all reality is socially constructed . . . but human beings require stable meanings and cannot live in permanent awareness of the socially constructed and precarious nature of everyday reality, and they are forced to clothe these certainties with permanent significance' (Turner quoted in Shilling 1993: 177).

As Shilling (1993) suggests, shared meaning systems are seen by Berger as essential for putting aside the contingency of humans' world- and self-building activities. However, socialization is never wholly complete, and there is always the possibility for awareness of this contingency. Such moments are referred to by Berger (1990) as marginal situations. As Shilling summarizes it:

> Marginal situations push us to the borders of our existence; they force into our consciousness knowledge that the human world is open-ended and unstable, and that the meanings we attribute to our bodies and our world are based on nothing more solid than human activity. The major marginal situation is the individual confrontation with death, because this can radically undermine and call into question the 'cognitive and normative operating procedures' of day-to-day life.
>
> (Shilling 1993: 178)

Death, Berger argues, is a core element of what it is to be human. It is something that is unavoidable, and something all societies have to deal with. Shared meaning systems, such as those provided by religion and other community-based beliefs, have a role to play in legitimating what societies have constructed as reality – which is fundamentally precarious.

The efficacy of these shared meaning systems is dependent on the degree to which they enable societies and individuals to explain death in a way that is consistent with reality as it has been socially produced. Marginal situations – the major one being the confrontation with death – threaten to expose the socially constructed nature of reality, and in doing so threaten to undermine 'the social shield against *anomie* (the terror of personal meaninglessness)' (Mellor 1993: 14). Mellor describes the implications as Berger sees them:

> If particular societies fail to deal with death adequately, then not only will individuals have to face extreme terrors of personal meaninglessness, but the social order as a whole becomes vulnerable to a collapse into chaos with a more widespread attendant loss of meaning and order.
>
> (Mellor 1993: 14)

At this point we can return to Giddens' analysis of self-identity in late modernity (Chapter 6), and note that some aspects of Berger's and Giddens' work share striking similarities. To recap, Giddens argues that in late modern and detraditionalized settings self-identity has to be routinely created and sustained in the reflexive activities of the individual. However, in these contexts personal meaninglessness is also a fundamental psychic problem that potentially threatens our personal sense of stability and security. In this regard, Giddens emphasizes the role that the institutional exclusion of existentially and morally troubling issues has played in modernity for a sense of psychic (and social) order and control (see Chapter 6). Giddens argues that because death is particularly threatening for a sense of psychic security and order in modernity, it is institutionally sequestered (see Chapter 6). The exclusion of death is part of the broader exclusion of issues and modes of behaviour that are potentially disturbing for our sense of social reality from the core areas of life. It is not just that death has been routinely hidden from view, but death in modernity is a technical matter (see also Armstrong 1987; Bauman 1992b; Shilling 1993; Mellor and Shilling 1993):

> what death is becomes a matter of deciding at what point a person should be treated as having died, in respect to the cessation of various types of bodily function. Death remains the great extrinsic factor of human existence; it cannot as such be brought

within the internally referential system of modernity. However, all types of events leading up to and involved with the process of dying can be so incorporated. Death becomes a point zero: it is nothing more or less than the moment at which human control over human existence finds an outer limit.

(Giddens 1991: 162)

The impulse within modern societies is to make the reality of dying as silent and invisible a process as possible (Giddens 191: 162). This is a part of the putting aside of existentially troubling issues that enables modern individuals (and societies) to establish a sense of continuity and order in daily life. It implies that those who are dying must be removed from everyday life and day-to-day existence, to protect the realities of the living. However, death cannot be fully put aside, as it is 'something which is ultimately resistant to social containment and control, making any social acceptance of it problematic' (Mellor 1993: 13). As such, death becomes a *life-political* issue as it raises the lack of moral resources that we have for dealing with it; it becomes one of a number of issues that 'place a question mark against the internally referential systems of modernity' (Giddens 1991: 223), and thus calls for a remoralizing of social life.

The most obvious similarities between Berger's and Giddens' analyses relate to the emphasis that both place on the contingent nature of everyday life and reality; the requirement for societies and individuals to explain, manage or put aside existential issues (particularly death) that threaten individuals with the terror of personal meaninglessness; the concern with the mechanisms available for this task; and the threat of 'marginal situations' (or in Giddens' terms 'fateful moments', see Chapter 6) to the maintenance of a sense of social reality or 'ontological security'. However, despite these similarities, there are also some notable differences. Identifying some of these, Mellor (1993: 16) notes that, unlike Berger, Giddens is primarily interested in the distinctiveness of modern societies and with the historically *new* threats to personal meaninglessness that late modernity poses. These are largely due to the 'wholly unprecedented mechanisms which remove problems of meaning from public space, relocating them in the privatized realm of individual life and experience' (Mellor 1993: 16). Mellor points out that by placing the problem of death within the specific contexts of late or reflexive modernity, Giddens' ideas offer the possibility of understanding the particular problem that it represents for contemporary cultures and individuals. But Giddens also links these particular problems to new possibilities for remoralizing social life. The next section considers how Phillip Mellor and Chris Shilling extend Giddens' argument.

Death as a problem in late modernity

Mellor and Shilling (1993) draw from the various theories considered so far to outline the dynamics that make death the particular problem it is in late modernity. They frame their argument in terms of self-identity and the sequestration of death, and suggest that the organization and experience of death in late modernity is becoming increasingly privatized. They argue that death has acquired particular significance as a result of three core characteristics of late modernity: the increasingly important role of reflexively ordered biographical narratives in the constitution of self-identity; the increased identification of the self with the body; and the 'shrinkage of the scope of the scared'. They argue via Bauman that while people do have survival strategies when dealing with death, these strategies are becoming increasingly inadequate and problematic in the current conditions of late modernity.

Giddens' analysis of the role of reflexive biography in the formation and maintenance of self-identity, as outlined in Chapter 6, is mostly accepted by Mellor and Shilling. For the purposes of the present chapter the focus is on the aspects of their argument that relate to the body and the scared. They argue that in keeping with general tendencies relating to the 'privatization of experience', the experience of death has become increasingly individualized in the late modern world. Mellor and Shilling (1993) contend that in today's world there is a privatization of meaning, and a reduction in 'the scope of the sacred', that 'leaves increasing numbers alone with the task of establishing and maintaining values to guide and make sense of daily lives' (Mellor and Shilling 1993: 413). While science has replaced religion in explaining the world, and can facilitate a sense of control in modern life, it does not provide resources in the form of values that guide living. This has consequences in the form of an intense concern with the project of self-identity that individuals are required to undertake in reflexive societies (Giddens 1991; Mellor and Shilling 1993). This project has at its centre a concern with the body:

> With the decline of the religious frameworks which constructed and sustained existential and ontological certainties residing outside the individual, and a massive rise of the body in consumer

158

culture as a bearer of symbolic value . . . there has been a tendency for people to place more importance on the body as constitutive of the self . . . it is the exterior territories of the body that have most come to symbolise the self at a time when unprecedented value is placed on the youthful, sexual and trim body.

(Mellor and Shilling 1993: 413)

If the reality of death is disturbing for reflexively constructed narratives of the self, this is particularly so when they are centred on a concern with the body (Giddens 1991; Mellor and Shilling 1993; Shilling 1993). Indeed, the more that the individual's body becomes the focus for self-identity, the more disturbing the reality of its demise. This is compounded by the extent to which public legitimations of the reality of the social world in the face of death have become increasingly absent (Mellor and Shilling 1993: 413). Together these dynamics can have consequences in the form of an 'intense confusion, anxiety and terror which are frequently experienced by individuals before signs of their own mortality' (Mellor and Shilling 1993: 414). As Shilling (1993) notes in a discussion of the dynamics at stake:

Their cumulative effect is to leave many people uncertain, socially unsupported and vulnerable when it comes to dealing with death . . . Unable to confront the reality of the demise and death of their own bodies, the self-identities of individuals are often made insecure by the presence of death in other people's bodies. This can result in an increase in the boundaries surrounding the bodies of the living and the dying, and a consequent tendency to shun the dying.

(Shilling 1993: 190, original emphasis)

Mellor and Shilling use the example of AIDS as a critical phenomenon that has the potential to be deeply disturbing for societies and individuals in late modernity. If the body becomes increasingly central to the project of the self in late modern worlds, sexuality has also become the 'focus for considerable personal emotional investment' (Mellor and Shilling 1993: 422). The tie between sex and death is potentially deeply disturbing. As Mellor and Shilling note:

AIDS tells people not only that the meaning they have invested in their sexual relationships cannot protect them from the reality of death, but that the very focus of their investment can be the channel through which death now enters their life ... When death is associated with old age, young people can put off thinking about it: when they become aware that it may already be lurking in their bodies, and those of their sexual partners, its reality becomes more pressing.

(Mellor and Shilling 1993: 423)

In light of the increasingly interlinked relationship between the body and self-identity, and the demise of the sacred, death is particularly threatening to a sense of psychic security in late modernity – as evidenced in the panics that surrounded AIDS in the 1980s and early 1990s. AIDS also demonstrates the way in which survival strategies (Bauman 1992b) developed for dealing with death in modernity, which included keeping death at bay by hiding it from view, and denying death by engrossing ourselves in life projects, are not wholly effective. The threat of death is an ever-hovering one, as Bauman suggests, and as Mellor and Shilling argue life projects that are geared towards ensuring survival and healthy bodies cannot be wholly effective, as the demise of the body (and the self-identities constructed around it) are inevitable:

> The reflexivity of modernity, which systematically undermines the religious traditions ... is also the reflexivity of the self: self becomes a project to be worked on ... Since the reflexivity is 'chronic', its completion is never envisaged. This means that when individuals inevitably die their self-projects will be incomplete, their fragile attempts at personal meaning left shattered by the brute fact of death. The implications of this for those who outlive them are also alarming: the fragility of all they hold dear, all they invest in socially, psychologically and emotionally, will also be signalled.
>
> (Mellor and Shilling 1993: 427)

Resources for living

The various arguments made about death and dying in the previous sections point to a broad social theoretical agreement that death is problematic in modern and late modern societies. As modernity develops, most of these arguments agree, the greater the problem of death becomes and the more limited are the resources for dealing with it. Death and dying, these arguments suggest, have gone from once being publicly engaged with and acknowledged to being deemed personal or private issues in late modernity. From the modernist perspective of Aries, the problem of death is partly the problem of how industrial modernity diminishes personal culture, and how experts control life and death. For Elias, the issue is one of modern civilized control and its implications for self-restraint and shame. The civilizing process, from this perspective, involves the subjective internalizing of modernity's preoccupation with control. This allows for an ordered personal and private realm that matches the pacified social realms that result from state control of violence. Each of these analyses, in various ways, highlights how modernity's concern with control and order has implied a loss: a loss of shared values and meanings with respect to life and death. Put another way, viewed through the lens of mortality, modernity fails to fully provide resources for a meaningful life and death.

Combining these ideas with Giddens', Mellor and Shilling argue that the decline of the sacred, increasing individualization and the growing significance of body to self-identity imply that death is more problematic in late modernity than it ever was before. This implies that the risk of death is profoundly threatening for a sense of personal security in late modernity. Death and dying are nowadays individual problems and there are few collective resources that can be drawn upon to make sense of them. Following Berger, Giddens places the issue of death at the heart of the sociological enterprise in a significant way. He does this by placing existential threats – of which encounters with death and dying are often the most profound – at the heart of his analysis of subjective and personal life in reflexive modernity. Giddens broadly agrees with the argument that modernity fails to provide resources for comprehending death and dying, and with the argument that their sequestering is indicative of modernity's preoccupation with control or mastery. Indeed, Giddens (1991: 202) argues, in modernity mastery substitutes for morality. There are profound implications for individuals that become evident when they encounter 'fateful moments' (what Berger terms marginal situations). At such moments, which include serious illness, bereavement and other life crises, the reality of death that is usually held at bay can disturb a sense of personal order and life routines in a radical way. These moments cannot easily be dealt with 'without reference to moral/existential criteria' (1991: 203). However, unlike the other theorists considered so far, Giddens sees this as the return of the 'institutionally repressed', that has potentially radical and empowering political implications in late modernity. One expression of such potentials is the renewed interest in death. This is evident in:

> the resurgence of literature concerned with making the pheno-
> menon of death a subject for wider public debate. There are
> various institutional manifestations of such a trend: one of
> which is the development of hospices as environments in which
> death can be discussed and confronted rather than shunted away
> from general view.
>
> (Giddens 1991: 203)

The radical potential of movements such as that described in this quotation lies, for Giddens, in their relationship to life-politics. Death and
dying are life-political issues because, like other core life issues sequestered in modernity, they raise moral and ethical questions about how
life and death should be approached and the basis on which this should
be justified. Life-politics is the politics of ethical and moral resources –
a post-emancipatory politics. It is the politics of how we choose to live
post-emancipation, and concerns the political issues 'which flow from
processes of self-actualization in post-traditional contexts' (Giddens
1991: 214). Life-political questions stem from personal life because they
concern the politics of life decisions. They mark the return of those
moral and existential issues that were institutionally sequestered in
modernity such as madness, illness, sexuality, mortality, criminality and
the like. For Giddens, Foucault mistook the sequestration of core life
issues as discipline (see Chapters 4 and 6), and this gets to the heart of
the limitations of poststructuralist-influenced theories of postmodernity:

> According to such views, moral questions become completely
> denuded of meaning or relevance in current social circum-
> stances. But while this perspective accurately reflects aspects
> of the internally referential systems of modernity, it cannot
> explain why moral issues return to the centre of the agenda of
> life politics.
>
> (Giddens 1991: 224)

While life-political questions stem from personal life and life choices,
Giddens argues that it is not simply a politics of personal life. On the
contrary, globalizing influences penetrate deep into personal life and
prompt life-political questions. These life-political concerns, in turn,

influence global concerns. But a number of interrelated questions arise from this. Globally and otherwise, we can ask, whose personal lives influence, or matter to, life-politics? Whose experience is post-emancipatory and whose is not? How do economic, social and cultural resources limit or facilitate the capacity to engage in life politics? To what extent does the sociological concern with life-politics risk blinding us to the persistence of non-emancipated experience?

Life-politics and non-emancipated experience

Giddens' distinction between life-politics and emancipatory politics is worthy of some further consideration and criticism which, in this section, I undertake by focusing on the issue of AIDS. AIDS is in some ways a life-political issue par excellence, and as the earlier quotation from Mellor and Shilling indicates, the syndrome is often drawn on in discussions of mortality in late modernity to illuminate the new risks and contingencies that threaten the reflexive self. From the mid-1980s to the late 1990s AIDS was the cause of millions of deaths globally. It has been argued that AIDS is a post- or late modern disease because of the speed of its global spread, but also because of the challenges it has presented for modern medical science, which has been unable to fully understand or cure it. Two developments with respect to AIDS cast light on the problems associated with Giddens' conception of life-politics. The first relates to early developments where the syndrome was associated with particular risk groups. The second relates to recent medical developments in managing HIV infection that delay the onset of AIDS. Both developments illuminate how AIDS, like other life-political issues, is an issue of differential access to resources and fundamentally concerns power. AIDS raises life-political issues that are, in many ways, overshadowed by the emancipatory political issues it also raises.

AIDS was initially termed GRID – gay-related immune deficiency. Critics argued that this early term, combined with the early formulation of risk groups (including homosexuals, sex workers and Africans), signified how medical science perceived the syndrome to have a moral dimension (Patton 1988: 24–5). As there was no easily identifiable cause, medical scientists adopted a kind of medico-moral framework for understanding AIDS of the sort that Foucault and others had argued were historically implicated in the regulation of deviant sexualities in modernity (Foucault 1979b; Mort 1987; Weeks 1989). The early connections made by epidemiologists, government health officials and the media

between AIDS and sexual and moral deviance led to the sustained demon-
ization of those deemed culpable in spreading the virus (in the West,
mostly gay men, sex workers and African 'outsiders'). AIDS highlighted
the threat of death, and early social and political responses associated
this threat with deviant 'others'. While people infected by HIV (the virus
associated with AIDS) faced life-political questions about how to live
with the threat of death, they did so in everyday, expert and political
environments that were deeply hostile to their predicament. The life-
political dimension of AIDS, as it concerned living with an acute sense of
mortality, did not in its early days (and still does not today) achieve the
significance that AIDS panic and hostility to people living with AIDS
did. Instead of a sense of global connectedness with respect to a global
threat to health and life, it led to efforts to limit encounters with infected
'others' – evident in immigration restrictions placed on people living
with HIV, and in the Western identification of non-Western nations or
continents as 'risk'-ridden.

Since the late 1990s the availability of anti-retroviral drugs, which
stall the onset of AIDS, has changed the medical situation. For those who
can access them, anti-retroviral therapies imply that HIV infection is no
longer a 'death sentence', and more like a chronic illness. HIV infection
now, for many, implies a prolonged life with the heightened awareness
of the risk of death hovering in the background. In this sense HIV infection has become a life-political issue in a marked way, as it raises
profound issues about how people can and should live with an acute
sense of contingency, and raises a host of ethical and moral issues with
respect to sexual and intimate relationships, parenting choices and so
on. Viewed from this perspective, AIDS and HIV are indeed life-political
issues par excellence. But this is a perspective that privileges the experience of those relatively few (on a global scale) who can access medical
anti-retroviral intervention. Globally, those regions with the highest
incidences of HIV infection can least afford anti-retroviral therapies. In
those regions, AIDS radically shortens human lives, and threatens whole
families, communities and nations. This is the predicament of those who
cannot afford or access medical intervention – where there is no emancipation from poverty and global inequality.

The issue of AIDS reveals how life-politics, as conceived by Giddens,
is the politics of the relatively well-resourced and powerful within a
global context. Life-politics is a concern that is mostly afforded to those
who are far removed from the kind of day-to-day grappling with life and
death issues that poverty and inequality imply. While AIDS has always

had the potential to be a life-political issue (because of its global reach and its intimate connections with sex and death), for the global majority who live with AIDS, and who struggle in non-emancipated contexts, it is above all an issue of radically diminished chances of survival. The primary question in such contexts is not 'How should I live?', but rather 'Will I live?'

Death and reconstructivist sociology

The death and deskilling thesis conjures up images of atomized and lonely individuals, caught up in circumstances over which they have no control. At the time that matters most, they are alone and powerless in the face of their inevitable fates. Faced with the prospect of their own deaths, individuals encounter in a profound way the consequences that modernity has for alienation, and they can be faced with psychic terror. It is the question of values – and the loss of shared meanings and values – that is ultimately at stake in the various forms of the deskilling thesis – be it the modern form as outlined by Aries and Elias, or the more specifically late modern form as outlined by Giddens and Mellor and Shilling. In this respect, various versions of the thesis employ the problem of the dying to highlight what is lost and lacking: the security offered by the sacred, the security offered by meta-narratives; the ability to maintain and construct stable (and often narrowly defined) communities. The problem of dying is the example par excellence of the problem of living with this loss in modernity – and the ensuing contingencies and insecurities. The deskilling thesis is not, however, merely an account of how things are. In itself it is indicative of the particular anxieties that social theorists and sociologists associate with radical social change: anxieties about loss of control. The solutions offered and implied are varied, but often invoke mythical pasts and utopian futures where stability, security and order are the defining features. It is in this context that we should understand the image of atomized, lonely and isolated individuals that is often conjured up. There are a number of issues that can be taken into account in evaluating the late modern version of the deskilling thesis, which links to the reconstructivist sociological project that it is related to.

In discussing the modern death-as-taboo thesis, Walter (1991) argues the need to be sensitive to *who* it is that produces it. This is also a relevant question to ask of the producers of the deskilling thesis. Put briefly, Walter (1991: 302) outlines a 'limited taboo' thesis that argues that it is not modern society per se, but particular occupational groups within it that find death especially difficult to cope with. He identifies these as the two professions to which our society has 'entrusted the interpretation and ritualisation of death' – medicine and the media. He draws on the example of Kubler-Ross, one of the figures most closely identified with the position that modern societies are death-denying, and points out that as a hospital psychiatrist she may have 'mistaken her world for society as a whole' (Walter 1991: 302). He further draws on Kellehear's research where patients colluded with doctors in avoiding talk of death because of the embarrassment of medical practitioners around the subject. He points out that both Kellehear and Kubler-Ross themselves found individuals more willing to talk about dying and death than the death-denying thesis would suggest. Like doctors, Walter suggests, 'those who work in the visual and news media find themselves in an occupation in which death is an embarrassment, even as they deal with it daily' (1991: 303). It is not so much society as a whole, then, but these two key institutions for which death is taboo: 'One can now begin to understand the welter of TV programmes and books by psychiatrists propagating the taboo thesis' (1991: 303).

We can ask how applicable this argument is to those interpreters of death considered in this chapter – social theorists and sociologists. In the case of Aries and Elias we can note the close fit between their interpretations of death and dying and modern discourse about 'death as taboo'. In the case of late modern theories of deskilling there are also salient questions to be asked, not least the degree to which the concern with the invisibility and silence of death is a more accurate account of *modernist sociology*'s ignoring of death and dying as an appropriate area of study (Mellor and Shilling, 1993) than it is of broader society's and individuals' inability to deal with the matter. We might also ask if reconstructivist theory's current concern with the loss of meaning around death is, in part at least, a reflection of the challenges that sociologists face in reconstructing their own meanings and understandings as a result of the 'deconstructive' turn. As Mellor (1993: 22) indicates, the issue of death is one of the important ways in which the relationship between modernity and sociology is being examined by theorists who are concerned with reconstructing sociology:

> The sequestration of death in modernity mirrors the absence of serious attention to death within the discipline of sociology. The increasing awareness of the need to construct sociology in the

aftermath of the collapse of modernist meta-narratives, which gave form to political programmes and nation states as well as to academic disciplines such as sociology, is itself a product of the pervasive reflexivity of high modernity, although it is often articulated as a response to 'postmodernity' (Bauman 1992). This reconstruction of sociology offers a promising opportunity for the sociology of death to become of central significance to the discipline as a whole.

(Mellor 1993:22)

It might be argued that reconstructivist theorists and sociologists are interested in death as one of the few remaining human experiences that can easily be talked about in universal terms. This does not imply that late modern sociology has no insights to offer into the problems and opportunities that societies and individuals encounter in giving meaning to and managing death. Following Walter's analysis, however, it does highlight that sociologists' views of these issues are shaped and influenced by the contexts, approaches and problems of their disciplines (as much as the perspective of psychiatrists and those who work in the media are shaped by their location within the traditions and contexts of their professions). This is also a salient issue when considering late modern theory's concern with contingency – one of the issues that the topic of death is drawn upon to illuminate and illustrate. While there may be an increased prevalence of risk in contemporary society, and this may promote an unprecedented sense of contingency for many, the radical doubt that reconstructivist theorists are concerned with is also an expression of the preoccupation with the loss of sociological authority. The undermining of modernist meta-narratives has had a profound impact on various aspects of the modernist enterprise and modern life, including the questioning of key underlying assumptions in sociology. The reconstructivist theoretical concern with the anxieties associated with death is partly an expression of an anxiousness to reconstruct sociology.

Conclusion

This chapter has considered how mortality has been taken up in the theory of reflexive modernity (and the sociology it promotes) to talk about the remoralizing of social life and an emergent form of life-politics. While the issue of death is often used in modernist social theory

167

to illustrate the loss of shared meaning in modernity, in the theory of reflexive modernity it is used to talk about the return of institutionally repressed moral and ethical questions. Death is important to the reconstructive theory of reflexive modernity because it is one of the few incontestable universalities in human life. Modernity, the theory of reflexive modernity argues, puts aside or hides death because of the existential issues it raises, which are fundamentally troubling for the modern individual. Having demystified traditional frames for understanding death, modernity provides no answer to it. In late modernity, increasing individualization means that death is an existentially troubling issue that people must increasingly face alone. This appears a damning indictment of modernity, but the theory of reflexive modernity draws on existential issues related to death to articulate a movement towards remoralizing social life. The return of the institutionally 'repressed' issues in late modernity provides the basis for movements to reincorporate moral and ethical issues into life. Unlike other modernist arguments considered in this chapter, the theory of reflexive modernity argues that personal life and subjective culture is not only diminished; it is making claims for renewal and is influencing changes beyond personal life itself. Despite the attraction of these ideas, the degree to which reflexive life-politics is not neutral emerges as a crucial issue, that the reconstructive theory of modernity does not recognize, and one that is powerfully illuminated by the issue of AIDS. While AIDS is often viewed as the life-political issue par excellence, it raises the issue of whose lives and experiences are imagined or featured in the theory of reflexive modernity, and which lives matter. This question of whose experience informs the reconstructed theory of modernity, and the reconstructed sociology it promotes, is further considered in the next and concluding chapter.

9

THE SOCIOLOGY
OF REFLEXIVITY OR
REFLEXIVE SOCIOLOGY?

Introduction

The theory of reflexive modernity and criticisms of it raise important questions about the kind of sociology we want to participate in and (re)construct. Reconstructivist theories of modernity are appealing for a number of reasons, not least because of the project for sociological renewal they imply. However, we should be cautious about the kind of renewal they envision. We should also be cautious about the argument that deconstructive approaches to modernity and modernist sociology are spent forces, or that they have gone too far. The deconstructive movements in theory and sociology considered in this book offer diverse approaches to conceptualizing the modern and the postmodern. They also offer diverse ways of envisioning the sociological project. Ironically, it is the deconstructive sub-movement that is least regarded in theoretical responses to the deconstructive turn that provides one of the most convincing arguments against the kind of reconstructed sociology that theories of reflexive modernity promote. This is the movement associated with interrogating sociological practice and constructing radically reflexive sociology. This approach advocates recognizing how difference and power shape the sociological narratives that we tell. It is, in this respect, distinct from the kind of sociology that reconstructivist theories propose. This points to a crucial difference that is focused on in this concluding chapter: between reflexive sociology and the sociology of reflexivity. Whereas the former advocates the critical acknowledgement of difference and power in constructing the sociological narrative, the latter constructs a powerful narrative that puts aside difference for the sake of narrative coherence. These are not necessarily mutually exclusive approaches. It is fair to say, however, that sociology of reflexivity as articulated in the reconstructive theory of reflexive modernity is far removed for the ideals of reflexive sociology. Before discussing this, however, it is necessary to recap the central arguments of the preceding chapters.

Situating reconstructivist theories of modernity

Modernity and the social: constructions, deconstructions and reconstructions

Contemporary theories of modernity, like Giddens' and Beck's, are only fully understood when they are situated within a history of social thinking about the modern. From this perspective, they can be viewed as radical modernist and reconstructivist theories. They have powerful implications for reconstructed understandings of modernity, and for reconstructing sociology. Theses theories, and the sociology they promote, are indebted to and break away from the ideas that were central to founding sociological constructions of the modern (see Chapter 2). They develop new understandings of modernity as an advancing force, and in doing so focus on changes at an institutional level and their relationship to developments in personal life. They maintain founding social thinkers' concerns with how the social, cultural, political and personal are (re)configured in modernity. However, they reorientate these concerns away from national-territorial contexts and towards a global one. Modernity now, they argue, has profound implications for globalizing, but also individualizing, tendencies. They reject founding ideas that modernity has a definite end goal, and acknowledge the problems with Enlightenment-influenced theories of knowledge that underpinned this view. Reconstructivist theories of modernity recognize that uncertainty and contingency are here to stay, and that the legitimacy of sociological knowledge is no straightforward matter.

The dynamism of modernity, the theory of reflexive modernity argues, implies that uncertainty and contingency must be reflexively incorporated into social life and into sociology itself. In contrast to founding social thought, this theory acknowledges that there are no certainties with respect to modern progress and social change. It shares Bauman's position that sociological knowledge should now be conceived in interpretative rather than legislative terms. In this spirit, Giddens' and Beck's theories offer powerful interpretations of modern renewal and of new universalities and commonalities in human experience. By focusing on the interconnections between the global and the local, and the institutional and the personal, they generate an interpretation of social change that, for some, fits better with contemporary empirical realities than postmodernist interpretations do. In doing so, they reconceive the possibilities for human agency and politics in post-emancipatory settings. These settings differ substantially from those that concerned founding social thinkers. This implies the need for new ways of viewing institutional, social and personal life, and new ways of conceptualizing sociology. The sociology of late modernity, they argue, should seek to synthesize and retain the insights of founding sociological frames, but also move beyond them.

The radical modernist theories of Giddens and Beck are reconstructive in seeking to rethink inherited frames for conceptualizing modernity and the social. They are also reconstructivist in how they seek to counter the deconstructive turn associated with poststructuralist, radical difference and postmodern thinking (see Chapters 3, 4 and 5). They reject poststructuralist deconstructive analytical strategies, and refute arguments that radical difference should be placed at the centre of the analytical frame to comprehend power. They reject postmodern ideas that suggest modernity and its associated projects (social, cultural and political) are exhausted or finished, and counter postmodernist arguments that ours is a post-social world. They agree with the postmodernist position that modernity is changed in ways that strictly modernist approaches fail to grasp. They also agree that contingency and uncertainty stem from doubt with respect to meta-discourses or meta-narratives. They refute, however, postmodern theories that suggest contemporary culture reveals that the social is broken up and fragmented. They also contest deconstructivist positions that advocate the foregrounding of radical difference and the deconstruction of universalities. They focus instead on new unities and universalizing tendencies. Such tendencies, reconstructivist theories argue, come about as a consequence of globalization. They are shaped by global flows and developments in the economy, media and communications, cultural networks, and heightened risks and insecurities.

Reconstructive theories of reflexive modernity dismiss deconstructive approaches that emphasize the fragmentation of self and identity. Contrary to deconstructive conceptions of the self and identity as inherently split, and as bound up with discursive strategies of power, they argue that self-identities are reflexive constructions that indicate how empowerment is routinely available to individuals in late modernity. They reject the idea that self and identity are forms of discursive subjection, as argued by poststructuralist and radical difference theorists, and argue instead that expert discourse is a resource for self-making. Self-identity, they argue, is a reflexive project. It takes place in a global context where the significance of otherness is being counterbalanced by new commonalities in experience. New universalities are becoming as important as old differences, if not more so. At a global and local level, the recognition of commonalities with respect to the contingencies associated with core life experiences (for example, in relational life and with respect to the frailty of the human body) leads to a new kind of politics – life-politics. In contrast to the political and moral pessimism associated with postmodernist thinking, life-politics is deemed radical because it concerns remoralizing social life.

The reconstructivist theories of modernity considered in this book derive their analytical innovation from their conceptions of reflexivity, and the centrality they afford it in understanding the processes that shape late modern life (see Chapter 5). Combined, Giddens' and Beck's analyses talk powerfully about new challenges and possibilities that emerge in reflexive modernity. Despite their different conceptions of reflexivity, both analyses employ the concept to talk about modernity's self-awareness or consciousness. Institutional reflexivity stems from and promotes institutionalized doubt. But there is also reflexivity in day-to-day life that implies both chronic monitoring and creative potential in personal life. Reflexivity, in this latter sense, implies enhanced agency – this is more a demand than a choice in late modernity. The possibilities opened up by institutional and day-to-day awareness and monitoring stem from their interconnectedness through a kind of reflexive loop.

The reconstructive theory of modernity argues that the heightened reflexivity of late modernity has many expressions. One of these is the deconstructive turn in sociology itself. This can be viewed as modernist sociology's critical reflection on itself, but it is also symptomatic of modernity's broader confrontation with itself. Viewed in this way, the postmodern paradigm discussed by some theorists (that deconstructs the bases of modernist knowledge, and cuts across a range of academic and scientific disciplines) expresses modernity's confrontation with reason as the foundation of legitimacy and progress. In contrast to deconstructivist movements in sociology, that see deconstruction as an end in itself, the reconstructivist approach views it as the starting point for a process of reflexive reconstruction – of the concept of modernity and sociology itself.

Reconstructing sociology: the sociology of reflexivity

Deconstructive movements with respect to modernity have profound implications for modernist sociology. They challenge the philosophical, epistemological and theoretical bases on which modernist social knowledge is legitimated, and question the modernist preoccupation with the social. The analytical strategies they promote tend to privilege the cultural instead. In the most radical cases, deconstructivist approaches argue the case for thoroughly post-social analytical strategies. In doing so, they problematize the contemporary relevance of modernist sociological concerns, and suggest that sociology itself might be redundant. What, they ask, can sociology be without the modernist emphasis on the social? Diverse modernist critics challenge deconstructivist arguments on the basis of their radical posturing and their failure to recognize modern continuities. Reconstructivist critics echo these criticisms but go further by emphasizing the reconfiguration of the modern and the possibilities for reconfiguring sociology. They refute arguments about the redundancy of sociology, and instead propose a reconstructed sociology that grapples with the reflexivity of social, institutional, political and personal change. They argue that the recognition of sociology's interpretative (as opposed to legislative) role implies the necessity of re-envisioning the sociological project and how it conceives social change. Their work suggests that such re-envisioning should begin by recognizing the influences on, and the implications of, globalization, detraditionalization and individualization, and how these link to developments in economic, social, political and personal life. The task for sociology, they imply, is to engage with the new challenges and possibilities that emerge as a consequence of these developments for (re)configuring the central institutions of modernity; (re)organizing social life; (re)shaping personal lives; and (re)imagining the political. Reconstructing sociology, they argue, necessitates a shift away from the dualisms and dichotomies that dominated in modernist analytical frames, and entails recognizing that adequate accounts of social life cannot be generated through them. Giddens, for example, argues that social life is a product of the mutual constitution of structure and agency. Moving beyond dichotomies implies a new focus on human creativity in (re)fashioning the social world. Reconstructing sociology implies reshaping and reimagining it to inform and facilitate late modernity's reflexivity.

This vision of a reconstructed sociology is appealing for a number of reasons. First, instead of relying on grand philosophical or epistemological claims, this sociology would develop an interpretative approach to theory and research that aimed for close empirical correspondence. Second, it would concern itself with radical social changes, and not marginalize the social. Third, in recognizing globalizing *and* individual-izing tendencies, it would concern itself with sources and expressions of new unities and universalities. Fourth, it would re-envision agency and explore the creativity of social life, and not adopt a reductive approach to structure. Fifth, it would incorporate the 'macro' and the 'micro' into the analysis, and in doing so would consider global economic, organiza-tional and technological developments but also speak to a broad range of contemporary life concerns (including self and identity, relating and intimacy, environmental issues, lived ethics and the like). By placing personal life at the centre of the frame, this sociology would acknowl-edge how the reflexivity of modernity's core institutions and day-to-day life are interlinked. It would explore personal life as a potentially radical political source for global change. The attraction of such sociology for sociologists themselves appears obvious when compared to what a wholly deconstructive (or deconstructed) sociology would look like. Despite this, we should be cautious about embracing it. The following discussion indicates why this is so, by recapping the problems of the soci-ology of reflexive personal life as considered in the previous chapters.

Reflexivity, social change and personal life

The arguments about personal life that were considered and critiqued in the second part of this book provide a grounded way of exploring the reconstructed sociology that theories of reflexive modernity propose. From this perspective, the sociology of self and identity would focus on the reconfiguration of trust and risk, and their implications for indi-vidual agency. This sociology would move beyond modernist and post-modernist concerns with how different conceptions of self and identity are bound up with power and are a matter of material, social and cultural positioning. It would focus instead on the general possibilities for empowerment that exist for reflexive self-making through engaging with expert resources. Similarly, the reconstructed sociology of intimate and personal life would focus of the consequences of reconfiguring patterns of gender relations, and the links between new patterns of equality in personal life and in the world of work. It would examine the implications for new relational forms, and for dialogically based emotional democracy. It would explore the possibilities this holds out for the broader democratizing of modern institutions. This sociology would move beyond modernist and postmodernist arguments about sexuality and personal relationships being bound up with power and the (re)production of social order. It would focus less on relational, gender, work and economic inequalities, and consider instead the possibilities that reflexive relationships present for an egalitarian order. Finally, the reconstructed sociology of death and dying would examine the new possibilities emerging for life-politics, and how personal life raises ethical and moral issues of global significance. It would explore death and dying as part of the broader examination of how institutionally repressed moral and existential problems come to the forefront as personal and public concerns to form the basis for life-politics. This sociology would focus on the possibility of generating shared values and meanings, and would put post-emancipatory concerns on an equal footing with emancipatory ones.

Overall, the reconstructed sociology of personal life that is promoted by the theory of reflexive modernity would emphasize agency, creativity and opportunities. It would be as concerned with these as much as modernist critical sociology is concerned with difference, inequality and power, and as much as deconstructive analytical approaches are concerned with radical difference and power. Under the influence of Giddens' work, this sociology would share founding social thinkers' concerns with order and would seek to articulate the possibilities of new social and personal order. Under the influence of Beck's work, this sociology would share more of the concerns of critically deconstructivist sociology. It would be less preoccupied with envisioning the conditions of new order and more with open possibilities. From both perspectives, however, this new sociology of personal life would be one that foregrounded reflexivity in social and personal life.

There are many questions to ask of this sociology, and many potential criticisms to make of it (see Chapters 6 to 8). The questions and criticisms that stand out are related to two interconnected issues: difference and power. What significance are questions of difference and power to be afforded in this sociology? On the basis of the discussions in Chapters 5 to 8, it is clear that reconstructivist theories put aside difference and in doing so make power invisible. This is one basis on which theories of reflexivity are contestable (and contested) from modernist and deconstructivist perspectives. For example, a broad range of modernist and deconstructivist arguments suggest that difference should be central to the sociology of self and identity. These include arguments about the significance of differences *between* identities (class, gender, sexuality, 'race' and ethnicity and so on) for the reproduction of social inequalities; arguments about 'differences *within* difference' that aim to recognize the most marginalized experiences; and arguments that suggest concepts of coherent identity to be discursive constructions that are bound up with power. These arguments suggest that difference should be central to sociological concerns with self and identity. The absence of difference in the sociology of reflexive identities raises questions about *whose* self-identities are being theorized and explored, whose are made invisible, and the operations of power that the sociological erasure of difference support.

Modernist and deconstructivist approaches to relational life would similarly contest the sociology of reflexive intimacies and relating. A broad range of perspectives argue that intimate, sexual and relational life is intrinsically bound up with power and the (re)production of modern social order. Foucauldian (and feminist–Foucauldian) arguments suggest that reflexive intimate life could be viewed as effectively governed or monitored relational forms. They suggest the erasure of differences between heterosexual and queer relationships indicates less the possibilities of sexual and relational freedom, and more how powerful the illusion of such freedom is. Instead of seeing dialogical reflexivity as potentially revolutionary in relational life and beyond, they suggest it to be indicative of the dominance of psychotherapeutic and self-help discourse that is related to productive power. Modernist feminist arguments suggest that the idea of reflexive intimacies, sexualities and relationships is powerful in its ideological effects. They contest the notion that gender equality has been achieved, or is easily achievable. They point out that while some women may have achieved equality with men in their working and relational lives, the global majority have not. The differences between men and women are important, but so are the differences between women themselves. This position suggests that the reflexive production of femininity that is demanded of different women in different contexts, and its relationship to gendered power, is worthy of sociological exploration. The questions about reflexive intimacy and relating that arise from these critical perspectives are similar to those that arose with respect to self-identity: whose sexualities and relationships are being theorized, envisioned and imagined in the theory of reflexive personal life? What operations of power does the sociological discourse of dialogically reflexive relationships and personal lives – and reflexive gender – support?

Finally, in terms of death and dying, a number of perspectives contest the understandings and possibilities associated with life-politics on the basis of the differences it ignores, the operations of power it reflects and the political interests it supports. While death and dying might promote a concern amongst some people with the absence of moral and ethical frames to give meaning to life, some commentators suggest that such preoccupations are specific to certain classes and professional groups. These include the classes and groups that dominate in professional sociology. The implication is that this preoccupation overplays the extent to which life-political issues are of universal concern. It concurrently undermines life *survival* issues related to economic and social inequalities on a global scale. The emphasis on life-politics potentially orientates sociological interests towards emancipated experiences and away from non-emancipated ones. The focus on life-politics risks universalizing what, in global terms, is relatively *exclusive* experience.

Reconstructing sociology in the manner suggested by the theory of reflexive modernity would, despite its attractions, lead to an impoverished sociological project. This reconstructed sociology of reflexive life could only ever be a *partial* one– in the sense of being incomplete, but also in the sense of promoting the exclusive interests of those who are, on a global scale, relatively advantaged and powerful. This is principally because the concern with new universalizing tendencies and commonalties, and with envisioning late modern social order, leaves unaddressed the significance of difference and power to social life. This sociology would leave unexplored a vast array of different human experiences, and leave untouched key questions about the relationships between difference, inequality and power. The issue is not (only) that the sociology of reflexivity would not be inclusive, but rather that operations of power as they work and are expressed through and involve difference would be unacknowledged. A reconstructed sociology of reflexivity would fail to grasp operations of power with respect to the global, local and personal to the extent that it failed to acknowledge difference and incorporate it into the analytical frame.

Reflexive sociology: where difference and power matter

Despite its attractions, the reconstructed sociology that the theory of reflexive modernity promotes is problematic. It would fail to generate convincing analyses of social life and social change to the extent that it failed to incorporate difference and power – to the extent that it failed to be *reflexive*. The distinction between the *sociology of reflexivity* promoted by the theory of late modernity and *reflexive sociology* is an important one. Reflexivity has a wide variety of meanings, as Alvesson and Skoldberg point out in their discussion of the different kinds of reflexivity noted by Bourdieu and Wacquant (1992):

> These include ethnomethodological ethnography as text, social scientific studies of the (natural) sciences, postmodern sociology, critical phenomenology and the writings of authors such as . . . Giddens (double hermeneutics). Bourdieu's own variety – where the researcher is seen as being inserted into a social field, with specific relationships of competition and power conditions generating a particular 'habitus', that is a pattern of action dispositions, among the participants – also belongs here.
>
> (Alvesson and Skoldberg 2000: 5)

The theories of reflexivity considered in the latter part of this book (Giddens' and Beck's) are distinct from the ideas about reflexive sociology that were discussed in Chapter 3. The latter have more in common with the postmodern sociology that Alvesson and Skoldberg mention, and are influenced by poststructuralist and radical difference deconstructive theories, as well as by ideas about ethnography as text. While reconstructivist arguments about modernity talk about social and personal reflexivity, they are not reflexive in the sense of critical reflection on the dynamics of difference and power involved in the production of the sociological narrative. They do not explicitly explore the limits of the analysis in terms of whose realities are represented or made invisible and what interests of power are promoted (explicitly and inadvertently). They do not promote reflexive sociology because they seek, above all, theoretical and narrative coherence. They achieve this by putting aside questions of difference and power. They put forward coherent narratives of reflexive modernity and social change, but not in a reflexive way. Indeed, the coherence of these narratives is, from the perspective of the arguments (poststructuralist, radical difference and reflexive methodology) considered in Chapter 3, also an expression of their limited reflexivity with respect to the complexities of social life and social change. To acknowledge complexities of difference and complex flows of power, these arguments suggest, is to complicate coherence.

In contrast to the sociology of reflexivity that Giddens' and Beck's ideas promote, Pierre Bourdieu (1977; Bourdieu and Wacquant 1992) proposes a vision of reflexive sociology that places difference and power at the centre of the conceptual frame. As the quotation from Alvesson and Skoldberg suggests, this centres on his conceptions of social fields and habitus, but also on the issue of resources. Put briefly and simply, Bourdieu argues that we can view the social as made up of overlapping fields (education, academia, leisure, occupations, the arts, popular culture and so on) that operate according to their own 'rules of the game'. The positions that people occupy in these social fields, and the advantages or disadvantages that accrue from this, are dependent on the their access to interrelated economic, social and cultural resources. What appears as an intuitive knowledge of the rules of the game is dependent on the embodiment of the 'right' kind of resources. For example, those people who have been socialized through middle-class families, have attended middle-class schools, have the professional qualifications for middle-class occupations, present and express themselves in a middle-class way, and 'intuitively' have middle-class tastes, will embody middle-class habitus (or way of being) and benefit from the advantages that accrue from this. They will possess, have access to, and embody the resources (economic, social and cultural) that give them advantages in social fields (such as university, the employment market and the like) that favour middle-class habitus over others. Reflexive sociology, from this perspective, requires that the sociologist is sensitive to how particular social fields work, the rules of the game that apply to them, and the distinctions and resources that matter in giving some groups advantages over others. It entails recognizing that such advantages are the consequences of how access to combined resources promote the empowerment of some groups at the expense of others. While Bourdieu emphasizes class distinctions and class relations in theorizing habitus, his analysis is applicable to other kinds of distinctions and relations (such as gender, 'race' and ethnicity and the like), and his theory has been employed by sociologists to generate nuanced analysis of the play of difference, resources and power in diverse social settings. Bourdieu's vision of reflexive sociology provides an important corrective to analyses such as Giddens' that overstate the possibilities that reflexivity affords for agency and empowerment. For Bourdieu, the habitus cannot be made fully conscious, and sets limits on the extent to which social action and interaction can be reflexively managed. His vision of reflexive sociology is, therefore, an altogether different one from the reconstructive theory of reflexive social and personal life. However, more radical arguments for reflexive sociology aim to push beyond the limits Bourdieu's modernist frame.

As considered in Chapter 3, deconstructive approaches to reflexive methodologies have argued the case for radically reflexive sociology. These arguments are sometimes developed under the combined influence of poststructuralist and radical difference theories (feminist, queer and postcolonial). The most radical of these approaches argues the case for viewing sociology as a form of narrative production that involves power. The production of sociological narratives, they argue, involves the negotiation of diverse and contested versions of reality that are impossible to include or represent in any one narrative. Sociological narratives, therefore, involve the privileging of some versions of reality over others. The versions of reality that are represented tend to be those that fit most closely with the sociological narrator's own experience and resonate with their own values and habitus. Even where sociologists interrogate how their own values shape the narratives they tell, they cannot simply neutralize their values, or control how these narratives will be received and interpreted. Further, language is not a neutral medium through which sociological theories, ideas and narratives are simply or straightforwardly expressed. Rather, as poststructuralist, radical difference and postmodern theorists argue, language is itself a relay route for power. These arguments are deconstructive to the extent that they challenge modernist sociological assumptions. But they are also reconstructive to the extent that they propose ideas for re-envisioning sociological practice. These include an ethic of critical reflection, and an openness and willingness to subject disciplinary assumptions, procedures and narratives to intense scrutiny. In advocating these, the intention is to acknowledge and make visible – as far as it is possible – the dynamics, assumptions and experiences that shape sociological knowledge. While some modernist proponents of reflexive sociology suggest strategies to produce 'better' or 'purer' knowledge, radical proponents of reflexivity aim for something more modest, but nonetheless complex: to acknowledge how sociology is involved with strategies of power. In doing this they suggest a number of reflexive principles. First, reflexivity acknowledges that there can be no neutral sociological project or knowledge that is untainted by power and political interest. Second, reflexivity does not aim to correct bias as such, but to investigate, make visible and problematize the procedures and assumptions that underpin sociological claims and interpretations. Third, reflexivity is a political strategy that recognizes sociology's part in the politics of knowledge. Fourth, reflexivity is an endeavour to produce situated knowledge that explicitly alerts its audience to the interests that inform it to the extent that they are known and knowable.

Can the sociology of reflexivity be reflexive sociology?

The kind of reflexivity discussed in the previous section could only ever provide the basis for a modestly reconstructed sociology: one that is attentive to the potential political effects of its interpretative claims and explicitly recognizes its own limits. It has its roots in the kind of analytical strategies that take difference seriously as an expression and medium of power (for example, those strategies associated with feminist, queer and postcolonial analyses; see Chapter 3). Such analytical strategies tread carefully where grand theories and ideas are concerned, as they are attuned to the risks they present for erasing difference and the political effects of this. These strategies tend not to be discussed in, or engaged with by, reconstructive theoretical responses to the deconstructive turn. However, the radical sociological reflexivity they promote provides a strong counter-argument against reconstructivist ideas about reflexive modernity, and the sociology of reflexivity they promote. In summary, reflexive sociology emphasizes the need for explicit critical reflection on the dynamics of difference and power that are central to the construction of sociological narratives. The sociology of reflexivity is more concerned with constructing a powerful narrative that, for the sake of coherence, puts aside difference. These are not necessarily mutually exclusive approaches to envisioning modernity or sociology. But it is fair to say that the theory and sociology of reflexivity has so far failed to consider seriously the arguments for reflexive sociology. The reconstructive theory of reflexivity fails to generate a convincing account of the dynamics of modernity ('grand' and 'local', institutional, personal), and a convincing basis for a reconstructed sociology. It does this to the extent that it fails to engage seriously with arguments for reflexive sociology.

REFERENCES

Adkins, L. (1995) *Gendered Work: Sexuality, Family and Labour Market*, Buckingham: Open University Press.
—— (2002) *Revisions: Gender and Sexuality in Late Modernity*, Buckingham: Open University Press.
Alvesson, M. and Skoldberg, K. (2000) *Reflexive Methodology*, London: Sage.
Aries, P. (1991) *The Hour of our Death*, Oxford: Oxford University Press.
Armstrong, D. (1987) 'Silence and Truth in Death and Dying', *Social Science and Medicine* 24(8): 651–7.
Baudrillard, J. (1998) 'The Ecstasy of Communication', in H. Foster (ed.), *The Anti-aesthetic: Essay on Postmodern Culture*, New York: The New Press.
—— (1999) *The Revenge of the Crystal*, London: Pluto Classics.
Bauman, Z. (1992a) *Intimations of Postmodernity*, London: Routledge.
—— (1992b) *Mortality, Immortality and Other Life Strategies*, Cambridge: Polity.
—— (1993) *Postmodern Ethics*, Oxford: Blackwell.
—— (2000a) *Liquid Modernity*, Cambridge: Polity.
—— (2000b) 'Shopping Around for a Place to Stay', in J. Rutherford (ed.), *The Art of Life*, London: Lawrence and Wishart.
—— (2003) *Liquid Love*, Cambridge: Polity.
—— (2006) *Liquid Fear*, Cambridge: Polity.
Bauman, Z. and Tester, K. (2001) *Conversations with Zygmunt Bauman*, Cambridge: Polity.
Beasley, C. (2005) *Gender and Sexuality: Critical Theories, Critical Thinkers*, London: Sage.
Beck, U. (1992) *Risk Society: Towards a New Modernity*, London: Sage.
—— (1994) 'The Reinvention of Politics: Towards a Theory of Reflexive Modernization', in U. Beck, A. Giddens and S. Lash, *Reflexive Modernization: Politics, Tradition and Aesthetics in the Modern Social Order*, Cambridge: Polity.
—— (1999a) *What is Globalization?*, Cambridge: Polity.

—— (1999b) *World Risk Society*, Cambridge: Polity.

—— (2000) 'Zombie Categories', in J. Rutherford (ed.), *The Art of Life*, London: Lawrence and Wishart.

Beck, U. and Beck-Gernsheim, E. (1995) *The Normal Chaos of Love*, Cambridge: Polity.

—— (2002) *Individualization: Institutionalized Individualism and its Social and Political Consequences*, London: Sage.

Beck, U., Giddens, A. and Lash, S. (1994) *Reflexive Modernization: Politics, Tradition and Aesthetics in the Modern Social Order*, Cambridge: Polity.

Berger, P. (1967/1990) *The Sacred Canopy: Elements of a Sociological Theory of Religion*, New York: Anchor Books.

Berger, P. and Luckman, T. (1967/1990) *The Social Construction of Reality*, New York: Anchor Books.

Best, S. and Kellner, D. (1997) *The Postmodern Turn*, New York: The Guilford Press.

Bottero, W. (2005) *Stratification: Social Division and Inequality*, London: Routledge.

Bottomore, T. (2002) *The Frankfurt School and its Critics*, London: Routledge.

Bourdieu, P. (1977) *Outline of a Theory of Practice*, Cambridge: Cambridge University Press.

Bourdieu, P. and Wacquant, L. (1992) *An Invitation to Reflexive Sociology*, Cambridge: Polity.

Bury, M. (1997) *Health and Illness in a Changing Society*, London: Routledge.

Butler, J. (1990) *Gender Trouble: Feminism and the Subversion of Identity*, London: Routledge.

—— (1993) *Bodies that Matter: On the Discursive Limits of Sex*, London: Routledge.

Calhoun, C., Gerteis, J., Moody, J., Pfaff, S. and Virk, I. (2002a) *Contemporary Sociological Theory*, Oxford: Blackwell.

Calhoun, C., Gerteis, J., Moody, J., Pfaff, S., Schmidt, K. and Virk, I. (2002b) *Classical Sociological Theory*, Oxford: Blackwell.

Callinicos, A. (1989) *Marxist Theory*, Oxford: Oxford University Press.

Chodorow, N. (1978/1999) *The Reproduction of Mothering: Psychoanalysis and the Sociology of Gender*, Berkeley, CA: University of California Press.

Craib, I. (2001) *Psychoanalysis: A Critical Introduction*, Cambridge: Polity.

—— (2004) *Classical Social Theory: An Introduction to the Thought of Marx, Weber, Durkheim and Simmel*, Oxford: Oxford University Press.

Cranny-Francis, A., Waring, W., Stravropoulas, P. and Kirkby, J. (2003) *Gender Studies: Terms and Debates*, London: Palgrave.

Delanty, G. (1999) *Social Theory in a Changing World*, Cambridge: Polity.

Dews, P. (1987) *Logics of Disintegration: Post-structuralist Thought and the Claims of Critical Theory*, London: Verso.

Dodd, N. (1999) *Social Theory and Modernity*, Cambridge: Polity.

Dollimore, J. (2001) *Death, Desire and Loss in Western Culture*, London: Routledge.

Duncombe, J. and Marsden D. (1999) 'Love and Intimacy: The Gender Division of Emotion and "Emotion Work"', in G. Allan (ed.), *The Sociology of Family Life*, Oxford: Blackwell.

Dunne, G. (1997) *Lesbian Lifestyles: Women's Work and the Politics of Sexuality*, London: Macmillan.

Durkheim, E. and Hall, W.D. (1984) *The Division of Labour in Society*, London: Palgrave Macmillan.

Elias, N. (1985) *The Loneliness of Dying*, Oxford: Blackwell.

—— (2000) *The Civilizing Process*, Oxford: Blackwell.

—— (2002) 'The Social Constraint towards Self-Constraint', in C. Calhoun, J. Gerteis, J. Moody, S. Pfaff and I. Virk (eds), *Contemporary Sociological Theory*, Oxford: Blackwell.

Elliot, A. (2001) *Concepts of the Self*, Cambridge: Polity.

Evans, M. (2003) *Gender and Social Theory*, Buckingham: Open University Press.

Featherstone, M. and Lash, S. (1995) 'Globalization, Modernity and the Spatialization of Social Theory: An Introduction', in M. Featherstone, S. Lash and R. Robertson (eds), *Global Modernities*, London: Sage.

Foucault, M. (1979a) *Discipline and Punish*, Harmondsworth: Penguin.

—— (1979b) *The History of Sexuality*, vol. 1: *An Introduction*, Harmondsworth: Penguin.

—— (1989) *The Birth of the Clinic*, London: Routledge.

Freud, S. and Bersani, L. (2002) *Civilization and its Discontents*, Harmondsworth: Penguin.

Frisby, D. (2002) *Georg Simmel*, London: Routledge.

Fuss, D. (1989) *Essentially Speaking: Feminism, Nature and Difference*, London: Routledge.

Giddens, A. (1990) *The Consequences of Modernity*, Cambridge: Polity.

—— (1991) *Modernity and Self-identity*, Cambridge: Polity.

—— (1992) *The Transformation of Intimacy: Sexuality, Love and Eroticism in Modern Societies*, Cambridge: Polity.

—— (1997) *Durkheim*, London: Fontana.

—— (1999) *Runaway World: How Globalisation is Reshaping Our Lives*, Cambridge: Polity.

Habermas, J. (1986) *The Theory of Communicative Action*, vol. 1: *Reason, Rationalization and Society*, Cambridge: Polity.

—— (1989) *The Theory of Communicative Action*, vol. 2: *Critique of Functionalist Reason*, Cambridge: Polity.

—— (1998) 'Modernity – An Incomplete Project', in H. Foster (ed.), *The Anti-aesthetic: Essays on Postmodern Culture*, New York: The New Press.

Hall, S. (1996) 'Introduction: Who Needs "Identity"', in S. Hall and P. du Gay (eds), *Questions of Cultural Identity*, London: Sage.

Hawkes, G. (1999) 'Liberalizing Heterosexuality?' in G. Allan (ed.), *The Sociology of Family Life*, Oxford: Blackwell.

Heaphy, B. (1996) 'Medicalisation and Identity Formation in the Context of AIDS/HIV', in J. Weeks and J. Holland (eds), *Sexual Cultures: Communities, Values and Intimacy*, London: Macmillan.

Holland, J., Ramazanoglu, C., Sharpe, S. and Thomson, R. (1998) *The Male in the Head: Young People, Heterosexuality and Power*, London: Tufnell Press.

Illich, I. (1977) *Medical Nemesis*, London: Calder and Boyers.

Jackson, S. (1996) 'Heterosexuality as a Problem for Feminist Theory', in L. Adkins and V. Merchant (eds), *Sexualising the Social: Power and the Organization of Sexuality*, London: Macmillan.

Jamieson, L. (1998) *Intimacy: Personal Relationships in Modern Society*, Cambridge: Polity.

—— (1999) 'Intimacy Transformed: A Critical Look at the "Pure Relationship"', *Sociology* 33(3): 477–94.

Lasch, C. (1991) *The Culture of Narcissism: American Life in An Age of Diminishing Expectations*, London: Norton.

Lash, S. (1993) 'Reflexive Modernization: The Aesthetic Dimension', *Theory, Culture and Society* 10: 1–23.

Latour, B. (2005) *Reassembling the Social: An Introduction to Actor-Network-Theory*, Oxford: Oxford University Press.

Lemert, C. (1997) *Postmodernism is Not What You Think*, Oxford: Blackwell.

Lepenies, W. (1988) *Between Literature and Science: The Rise of Sociology*, Cambridge: Cambridge University Press.

Lyon, D. (1999) *Postmodernity*, Buckingham: Open University Press.

Lyotard, J. (1984) *The Postmodern Condition: A Report on Knowledge*, Manchester: Manchester University Press.

McNay, L. (1992) *Foucault and Feminism*, Cambridge: Polity.

—— (1994) *Foucault: A Critical Introduction*, Cambridge: Polity.

Mansfield, P. and Collard, J. (1988) *The Beginning of the Rest of Your Life*, London: Palgrave Macmillan.

Marx, K. and Engels, F. (2003) *The Communist Manifesto*, London: Bookmarks.

May, C. (1997) 'Degrees of Freedom: Reflexivity, Self-identity and Self-help', *Self, Agency and Society* 1(1): 42–54.

May, T. (1996) *Situating Social Theory*, Buckingham: Open University Press.

Mellor, P.A. (1993) 'Death in High Modernity', in D. Clark (ed.), *The Sociology of Death: Theory, Culture and Practice*, Oxford: Blackwell.

Mellor, P. and Shilling, C. (1993) 'Modernity, Self-identity and the Sequestration of Death', *Sociology* 27(3): 411–31.

Mishler, E. (1986) *Research Interviewing: Context and Narrative*, Cambridge, MA: Harvard University Press.

Morrison, K. (1995) *Marx, Durkheim and Weber: Formations of Modern Social Thought*, London: Sage.

Mort, F. (1987) *Dangerous Sexualities*, London: Routledge and Kegan Paul.

Nicholson, L. and Seidman, S. (1995) *Social Postmodernism: Beyond Identity Politics*, Cambridge: Cambridge University Press.

Osborne, T. (1994) 'On Anti-Medicine and Clinical Reason', in C. Jones and R. Porter (eds), *Reassessing Foucault: Power, Medicine and the Body*, London: Routledge.

Patton, C. (1988) *Sex and Germs: The Politics of AIDS*, Boston, MA: South End Press.

Penna, S., O'Brien, M. and Hay, C. (1999) 'Introduction', in M. O'Brien, S. Penna and C. Hay (eds), *Theorising Modernity Reflexivity, Environment and Identity in Giddens' Social Theory*, London: Longman.

Plummer, K. (1993) *Telling Sexual Stories: Power, Change and Social Worlds*, London: Routledge.

—— (2005) *Intimate Citizenship: Private Decisions and Public Dialogues*, Toronto: McGill-Queens University Press.

Ramazanoglu, C. (1992) 'On Feminist Methodology: Male Reason versus Female Empowerment', *Sociology*, 26(2): 207–12.

Rich, A. (1983) 'Compulsory Heterosexuality and Lesbian Existence', in A. Snitow, C. Stansell and S. Thompson (eds), *Desire: Politics of Sexuality*, London: Virago.

Rigby, S. (1998) *Marxist History: A Critical Introduction*, Manchester: Manchester University Press.

Rose, N. (1996) 'Identity, Genealogy, History', in S. Hall and P. du Gay (eds), *Questions of Cultural Identity*, London: Sage.

—— (1999) *Powers of Freedom: Reframing Political Thought*, Cambridge: Cambridge University Press.

Schrijvers, J. (1991) 'Dialectics of a Dialogical Ideal', in L. Nencel and P. Pels (eds), *Constructing Knowledge: Authority and Critique in Social Sciences*, London: Sage.

Seale, C.F. (2001) 'The Body and Death', in S. Cunningham-Burley *et al.* (eds), *Exploring the Body*, London: Macmillan.

Segal, L. (1999) *Why Feminism? Gender, Psychology, Politics*, Cambridge: Polity.

Seidman, S. (1996) *Queer Theory/Sociology*, Oxford: Blackwell.

Shilling, C. (1993) *The Body and Social Theory*. London: Sage.

Simmel, G. and Levine, D.N. (1973) *On Individuality and Social Forms*, Chicago, IL: University of Chicago Press.

Sitton, J.F. (2003) *Habermas and Contemporary Society*, London: Palgrave Macmillan.

Skeggs, B. (2003) *Class, Self and Culture*, London: Routledge.

Smart, B. (1998) *Facing Modernity: Ambivalence, Reflexivity and Morality*, London: Sage.

Steier, F. (ed.) (1991) *Research and Reflexivity*, London: Sage.

Sullivan, A. (1996) *Virtually Normal*, New York: Vintage Books.

—— (ed.) (1997) *Same Sex Marriage: Pro and Con – A Reader*, New York: Vintage Books.

Turner, B.S. (1995) *Medical Power and the Social Construction of Knowledge*, London: Sage.

—— (1999) *Classical Sociology*, London: Sage.

Van Every, J. (1995) *Heterosexual Women Changing the Family*, London: Taylor & Francis.

Walter, T. (1991) 'Modern Death: Taboo or Not Taboo?', *Sociology* 25(2): 293–310.

Warner, M. (2000) *The Trouble with Normal: Sex, Politics and the Ethics of Queer Life*, Cambridge, MA: Harvard University Press.

Webb, S. (1997) 'Editorial: Discourses of Self and Agency', *Self, Agency and Society* 1(1): 3–8.

Weber, M. (1978) *Economy and Society*, Berkeley, CA: University of California Press.

—— (2003) *The Protestant Ethic and the Spirit of Capitalism*, New York: Dover Publications.

Weeks, J. (1989) *Sex, Politics and Society: The Regulation of Sexuality Since 1800*, London: Longman.

—— (1995) *Invented Moralities: Sexual Values in an Age of Uncertainty*, Cambridge: Polity.

Young, J.C. (2003) *Postcolonialism: A Very Short Introduction*, Oxford: Oxford University Press.

INDEX